COVID Catholic

COVID Catholic

The Crooked Path That Led to God

JESSE ROSE

RESOURCE *Publications* • Eugene, Oregon

COVID CATHOLIC
The Crooked Path That Led to God

Resource Publications
An Imprint of Wipf and Stock Publishers
199 W. 8th Ave., Suite 3
Eugene, OR 97401

www.wipfandstock.com

PAPERBACK ISBN: 979-8-3852-7297-6
HARDCOVER ISBN: 979-8-3852-7298-3
EBOOK ISBN: 979-8-3852-7299-0

VERSION NUMBER 02/05/26

For my husband,
who walked beside me on the crooked path,
steady in love, laughter, and faith.

Contents

Author's Note

This is a true story. Mostly. It's crooked, messy, and full of grace. It's a confession, a love letter, a spiritual scavenger hunt, and a mildly chaotic walk with God. If you're looking for polished theology or perfect behavior, you may want to close the book now and find something holier.

I'm still a sinner. I say bad words. I fail to remember to pray. But I believe in grace, and this book is full of it.

COVID Catholic traces my real-life journey through the pandemic when the world got quiet and God got loud. I didn't set out to become Catholic. I set out to survive. What happened instead was a crooked, beautiful, occasionally ridiculous path toward faith paved by three companions: God, my husband, and a man named Jeffrey, whose silence shaped me as much as his presence.

Some names have been changed. Some scenes have been stitched together. A few moments may be slightly exaggerated (but only the ones that beg for dramatic flair). The emotional truth, though, is all mine. I lived it. I wept through it. I laughed at it. And now I'm writing it down.

This book isn't about sainthood. It's about stumbling toward God with coffee in one hand and doubt in the other. If you've ever felt spiritually lost, relationally tangled, or just plain tired of pretending to have it all figured out, welcome. You're in good company.

Keep reading. It gets messier. It gets holier. Somehow, it's both at once.

Preface

"Whether you turn to the right or to the left, your ears will hear a voice behind you, saying, 'This is the way; walk in it.'"

—Isaiah 30:21

I didn't set out to write a book. I set out to survive. This story began as fragments, journal entries, prayers, whispered questions in the dark. I was unraveling. The pandemic cracked open my faith, my relationships, and my sense of belonging. What remained was longing. What appeared was grace.

COVID Catholic is not a polished testimony. It's a crooked path paved with grief, doubt, and unexpected holiness. It's the story of a woman haunted by memory, held together by Scripture, and slowly stitched back into belief. It's Gabrielle's story. It might be yours, too.

I wrote this for the wanderers; for those who've been blocked, ghosted, silenced, or told to wait. For those who've stood at the edge of faith and whispered, "God, are you still there?" For those who've found healing in dreams, in Mass, in messy conversations with strangers who felt like angels.

Each section begins with a verse. Each verse is a thread. Each thread is a prayer. Together, they form a devotional journey through ache and arrival.

This is not a straight line. It's a sacred spiral. And if you're reading this, you're already part of it.

Acknowledgments

To "Jeffrey":

You were never just a character in my story. You were a turning point.

From the moment our paths crossed, I felt something shift, like God had nudged me and whispered, "Pay attention." I wanted to bring peace into your life, to listen without judgment, to make you laugh when you forgot how. I dreamed of hugging you so tightly that your broken pieces might knit back together. (Yes, dramatic but sincere.)

Of the seven billion smiles in this world, it was yours that melted mine.

But I misjudged. I became someone you saw as toxic, and you chose distance. So, I loved you quietly from afar, with prayers instead of presence. I still believe you were sent to me by God, a divine messenger disguised as a complicated human. And I still believe we were meant to connect, even if only for a season.

There are things I never said. Things I still carry. I hope that one day, guided by grace and maybe a little divine mischief, our paths will cross again. If they do, I'll be ready with an open heart and a whole lot of words.

Until then, I pray you've found peace, joy, and someone who sees the light in you.

I'm forever grateful for how you helped me find God and rediscover the beauty in this messy, miraculous world.

You'll always be my 11:11 wish, even if you only visit me in dreams.

With love, always,

J

Introduction: The Crooked Beginning

"I will go before you and make the crooked places straight."

—Isaiah 45:2

Imagine unraveling, life a blur of grief and regret. You can't breathe. You can't pray. You barely recognize the face in the mirror. Stitched together with broken dreams and thin threads of hope, you whisper a plea, not polished, just raw and aching. In the shadows, a whisper of peace brushes your soul, like Elijah's still small voice.

Imagine standing in a Catholic church for a funeral. You don't belong. You don't know the prayers. You're just a broken heart looking for a safe place to land. Then the funeral director speaks: "You're exactly where your fate has brought you." His words feel like prophecy. His presence feels holy. For a moment, you believe you're not alone.

Then the messenger disappears, you are blocked, deleted, erased. You beg God to bring him back. You beg the church to let you in. They say wait. Nine months. So, you wait. You pray. You show up every Sunday, haunted by a ghost and held together by grace.

The pandemic hits. RCIA postponed. Mass suspended. Your fragile faith cracks again. You feel abandoned by the Church, by the messenger, maybe even by God. Regret, echoes. Shame lingers. You wander through pain of your own making.

Imagine waking from a dream. The funeral director appears. His eyes hold a heavenly truth. "God wants to communicate with you," he says. "Embrace the Church." You step into the sanctuary. You wait. You ache. You pray. Still, the messenger is gone. The memory of a mistake echoes in your soul. You push God away. You feel unworthy. You feel ashamed. You feel alone.

Imagine this was your life for five years. Gabrielle's life, a crooked path paved with longing, loss, and unexpected grace.

Imagine God showing up anyway. In dreams. In photographs. In quiet moments of surrender. He whispers through memory. He nudges you toward healing. And slowly, crookedly, you begin to believe again, not in perfection, but in grace. This is Gabrielle's story. It's a reminder that even in the wilderness, even in the ache, even in the silence, God writes straight with crooked lines.

The Gentle Unraveling

"You hem me in behind and before, and
you lay your hand upon me."

—PSALM 139:5

IN 2018, GABRIELLE VOWED to create. Inspired by her father's woodworking and her mother's quilting, she launched a crafting business. Her home brimmed with creativity; love measured in stitches and sawdust. But sales lagged, and two months later she quit, promising she'd return.

Then came May. Her mother-in-law passed suddenly. Hours earlier, she'd said, "Have a good evening, make lots of money, and I'll see you tomorrow." Tomorrow never came. Grief settled. And that's when Gabrielle saw him again: Jeffrey. Not just a funeral director but warmth wrapped in professionalism. He hugged instead of shaking hands. He remembered them. In the Catholic Church, he spoke to Gabrielle about addiction, mortality, and forgiveness. His words soothed Gabrielle's spirit. "You're exactly where you need to be," he said. Then: "Don't put a period where God only meant a comma." That sentence stayed with her.

Gabrielle couldn't stop thinking about him. His eyes held sadness, his smile quiet melancholy. A friend revealed he was recently divorced. Curious, Gabrielle searched social media, and she found his profile, hovered over "Add Friend," clicked. He accepted. Through his posts, she glimpsed fragments of his life, children, work, and thoughts. Beneath the intelligence, she sensed ache. Hope flickered. Boundaries blurred. Jeffrey felt like a divine punctuation, more than a fleeting encounter at a Catholic Church.

Then came California. Gabrielle and her husband had dreamed of San Francisco's charm, Sonoma's racetrack, Giants and Athletics games. But grief lingered. Torn between guilt and longing, they questioned the trip. Yet they could almost hear her mother-in-law whisper: Go. Breathe. Heal.

At the departure gate, Gabrielle noticed a shift in her husband. His bravado wavered. "What if one of us dies?" he whispered. Death haunted him since his mother slipped away. Gabrielle laughed. "Then one of us would be dead." Not comforting but true. He loved Gabrielle fiercely. "You must see a doctor," he insisted. Diet, exercise, long lives. Gabrielle soothed him but felt the pull of something else: Jeffrey.

California unfolded in snapshots: Sonoma Raceway, Golden Gate Bridge, Oracle Park, Fisherman's Wharf, Monterey's coastal curves. Lombard Street's twists mirrored her emotional state. "This street is like my life," she muttered. He laughed. She didn't. Her husband's joy was palpable, but Gabrielle felt hollow. Jeffrey haunted her. His comments on her posts, *I love In-N-Out too*, felt like breadcrumbs.

Back home, routine resumed, but Gabrielle was changed. She scheduled the doctor's appointment her husband insisted on. Results were fine, but unease lingered. Jeffrey lingered. His comments. His likes. Digital breadcrumbs. Coincidence or divine choreography? She opened her messages. Typed. Deleted. Typed again. *Hi Jeffrey*. Her fingers hovered. Her heart raced. She didn't hit send.

Gabrielle devised a plan: funeral preplanning paperwork would be her excuse. She called the funeral home. They agreed to meet. But fate intervened. Jeffrey canceled. Miscommunication masked truth. She called him. He apologized; he had an emergency with his kids. They'd reschedule. Connection hung suspended.

Days passed. Jeffrey's absence gnawed. Was he avoiding her? She scrolled on his social media, a photo with his kids. Was that the emergency? Judgment wrestled with hope. On day four, she called again. His voice was warm, apologetic. Work had been a whirlwind. They made a silent pact: no judgment, no blame.

The next day, Gabrielle entered the funeral home. Jeffrey greeted her, sympathetic, professional. He asked about California; he'd seen her posts. She hesitated, sensing genuine interest. In the quiet room, she spoke of her husband's fears, doctor visits, mortality. Jeffrey nodded. Their conversation wandered. It felt refreshing. Before she left, he apologized again.

She forgave him. Back home, she discussed paperwork with her husband. But her thoughts lingered on Jeffrey.

A week later, she called again. Jeffrey agreed to meet, but his tone was colder. At the funeral home, he waited with a sentinel beside him, his eyes sharp, posture guarded. Creepy, but purposeful. They walked down a narrow corridor. Jeffrey reviewed the paperwork, offering cryptic reassurances. Was he communicating with the man outside? Their exchange felt coded. Something was off. This wasn't the Jeffrey she remembered. Finally, he said, "Everything looks fine." But his eyes betrayed uncertainty. "I'll review it again and email you." No hugs. No handshakes. Just a brisk walk to the door. "What a douchebag," Gabrielle muttered. Hero or villain? She didn't know. Had she imagined the connection?

In late August, Gabrielle posted a split photo: before and after. California, wild hair, snug jacket. Home, casual tee, twenty pounds lighter. Little pills had fueled her transformation. Jeffrey liked the post. Was it a silent apology? A cryptic invitation? He had become her muse, a twist defying logic.

In September, her friend organized a fundraiser. Custom shirts. Jeffrey joined. Gabrielle was tasked with delivering his. At the funeral home, the sentinel waited, muscles taut, eyes sharp. Then Jeffrey appeared. She handed him the shirt. "Ready for the event?" she asked. His reply: "I will spend the day with you. All day." No formalities. No farewells. Just audacity. "Douchebag," her inner voice muttered. But her heart fluttered.

On the event day, Jeffrey arrived late. Disheveled. Apologetic. Stress clung to him. Then his ex-wife and kids appeared. He left abruptly. No goodbye. Gabrielle messaged him: *Typical New Yorker*, she teased, attaching a photo. His reply: *Thanks*. The enigma remained.

October arrived. Gabrielle, thirty pounds lighter, stood at a crossroads. She and her husband traveled to Nashville for their anniversary, reveling in simple joys and the Grand Ole Opry. Barbecue smoke led them back to the restaurant where they'd shared their first meal as newlyweds. Time folded; they were young again. Social media lit up: likes, comments, Jeffrey's subtle thumbs-up.

A few days later, Gabrielle reached out. "Are you working tonight?" Jeffrey replied, "Yes." Then asked, "Will you and your husband attend the service?" She declined. "I have something to discuss, but I don't want to disturb your work." No response.

Three long days passed. Silence. Frustrated, she sent a message, equal parts sass and vulnerability: "Three days ago, I said I needed to talk but didn't want to bother you. Here we are, three days later, and I'm wondering why you're not the least bit curious. I have a few theories:

1. You don't give a shit.
2. You're scared of women.
3. You're a typical New Yorker douchebag.

So. . . which one is it?"

She kept checking her phone, hoping for a reply. An hour later, it came:

"Curiosity kills cats! First, smart-ass, I'm busy every day with fires burning. If it's not on the front burner, I don't have time. There are only a few things I'm scared of. And yes, being from New York, I'm a douchebag! LOL!"

They exchanged messages for a delightful fifteen minutes. Gabrielle concocted an excuse: her mother's paperwork needed transferring. Then, with courage, she asked, "Would you care to join my husband and me for dinner? We could discuss the paperwork over a warm meal." Jeffrey replied warmly, "I'd be delighted to help your mother. Just swing by with the paperwork, and I'll gladly take a look." Relief washed over her. Her message had cracked the surface. But the dinner invitation carried more than logistics.

She couldn't resist sharing a glimpse of their household: "Our abode has its quirks. The lady of the house wields a sharp tongue but has culinary magic. The man of the house spins yarns from yesteryears until the stars themselves nod off."

Jeffrey replied, "I can manage a smart-ass woman in the kitchen, but back-in-the-day stories might send me packing with a to-go plate." Gabrielle's excitement bubbled. "Whenever you're ready for that dinner, just name the date. I'll be waiting." But silence followed.

A few days later, Gabrielle stepped into the dimly lit funeral home, clutching her mother's paperwork. Jeffrey was precise. Formal. He outlined practical steps. Her heart yearned for more. She wanted to declare her truth. But her reflection mocked her. "Wait until you're below 200 lbs.," she told herself. As if weight loss would confirm her emotions.

She watched him scan the paperwork. The unspoken invitation hung in the air. When she finally asked, he apologized: "Busy, but I'll try." Disappointment etched lines on her face, but hope clung stubbornly.

On a crisp November morning, Gabrielle returned to the doctor's office. Weight loss had become her obsession, but the mirror still reflected a silhouette she longed to reshape. The doctor offered the ancient prescription: "Diet and exercise." Gabrielle nodded politely, but her mind whispered: Or pills. Or patches. Or prayer. Jeffrey had become a symbol of vulnerability, desire, something unspoken. Fueled by desperation, she embarked on a clandestine quest: weight loss pills, patches, stimulants, sedatives. She stood at a crossroads. 200 lbs. An uncharted summit.

In November, Gabrielle embraced a daily ritual of sharing blessings on social media. Each morning, she asked, "What am I thankful for today?" Sometimes coffee. Sometimes promotions. Sometimes grace.

Then came November 29th. A post honoring Jeffrey. Six months earlier, Gabrielle had stolen a memento, a simple ink pen from Jeffrey's funeral home. Its slender body whispered secrets of resilience. She traced its contours, inscribed her commitment to change. Jeffrey's legacy pulsed through that stolen pen, urging her forward.

This was Gabrielle's post:

"Six months ago, I may or may not have stolen this pen. Six months ago, we said goodbye to my mother-in-law. Watching a once-vibrant woman decline is never easy, and it took a very unhealthy toll on me mentally and physically. Six months ago, I had a conversation with a man about death, addiction, and dying. It was a conversation we'd had before three years ago, when my stepson died from a heroin overdose. I keep this pen in the console of my vehicle as a reminder of how far I've come. That conversation, along with a few other eye-opening experiences, made me decide it was time to change or I'd become a statistic. Jeffrey, whether you remember the conversation or not is irrelevant. I'll always be grateful, thankful, and blessed that you had it with me not once but twice. I'm a little stubborn and sometimes need to hear things more than once. You somehow knew. Thank you for being in my family's life when we needed you, and thanks for the pen."

She posted the pen story at midnight.

By 9:00 a.m., Jeffrey had shared it on his timeline.

His comment read:

"I noticed this post and as I read your truly kind words, I was overwhelmed and humbled. You see, I find myself more often than I like in a dark place. Just this morning, during the wee hours, I was questioning whether what I do makes a difference, whether I help the families who trust me. Your post and words were the answer to the prayers and conversation I had with God last night. Thank you for caring enough to share your thoughts."

Gabrielle responded with a heart emoji. Another woman, Jeffrey's friend and colleague, added, "Answers come right when we need them. Sometimes we question the way things are going and start to doubt. Then God sends an angel to show we're on the right path."

After that post, Gabrielle's world shifted. The digital veil lifted. Jeffrey became more than a profile picture. Their conversation in the Catholic Church had sparked something. Now, it burned. Days blurred into nights. Gabrielle hungered for substance, depth, connection. He had become her enigma. Their shared moments, virtual and fleeting, were breadcrumbs leading to something sacred.

A few days later, she reached out again. More paperwork. Jeffrey agreed to meet. Their messages were sporadic; sometimes warm, sometimes silent. Frustrated, she teased, "You need better salutations and valedictions. Something to soften the silence."

When she dropped off the paperwork, Jeffrey greeted her with a flourish: "Hello, Madame," he said, bowing slightly. His eyes sparkled with amusement. Gabrielle flushed. As he turned away, he glanced back: "How was that for a salutation?" She smiled, speechless. The moment etched itself in warmth and unspoken words.

But beneath the sparkle, obsession brewed. Little pills promised vitality. The scale mocked her, 200 lbs., both daunting and tantalizingly close. Jeffrey's presence hummed in her mind, drowning reason. Fueled by longing and stimulants, she broke. A late-night message. Raw. Reckless. A desperate plea echoing her inner chaos.

December 5th, 12:12 a.m. "I have a moment of truth, a confession, and a question. Truth, you've been on my mind nonstop. Confession, you are the sexiest man I've ever laid eyes on. I've felt this way since I first met you. Every time I see you, my urge and lust grow. I want to kiss you. Touch you. Own you. I want no-regrets, no-remorse sex with you. Question, are you interested?"

Then she waited. The night stretched. Doubt crept in. Morning arrived. Panic surged. *What if he showed the message to her husband? What if he said yes? What if he said no?*

9:34 a.m. His reply landed. Concise. Brutally honest: "Thank you. I do not know how to answer this other than being truthful, no, I am not interested."

Her heart performed an acrobatic routine. First, relief. Then the plunge. Rejection, even gentle, bruises. She stared into the mirror. Dissected every imperfection. "Is he better than me?" she wondered. "Or just better at boundaries?"

10:18 a.m. Gabrielle replied: "The one time where it would've been OKAY for no response, instead, you crushed my ego and my heart with one statement."

10:26 a.m. Jeffrey: "As I stated, I did not know how to respond to this, nor do I like sharing my personal afflictions or disabilities with anyone without going into detail and I will not. I am not able. Again, I apologize for hurting your feelings."

10:36 a.m. Gabrielle: "I didn't say anything about my feelings. I said my ego and my heart, both will heal. I was expecting your douchebag no response. I was trying to put you into my life. If you don't want to be there, that's your choice and I respect it."

No response.

10:50 a.m. Gabrielle: "However, you can continue to expect smart and sarcastic comments from time to time as you are still my favorite douchebag."

Jeffrey's immediate reply: "Same here."

Same here? Gabrielle blinked. What did that even mean? She cried more than she'd ever cried over a man. She had a husband. She didn't need Jeffrey. So why had she sent that message?

At 1:00 p.m., she rose. Headed to the gym. A refuge from life's currents. She reached into her SUV's console. Her fingers brushed something unexpected: the pen. The very pen she'd pilfered from Jeffrey. A relic from the days after her mother-in-law's passing. A witness to their exchanges. Jeffrey's wisdom echoed: "Don't put a period where God meant a comma." Each bead of sweat carried the weight of that advice. A comma. Not a period. The promise of continuation.

1:55 p.m. Gabrielle wrote: "I went to the gym to get my mind right. I reached into my console to grab my headphones and there it was. This damn pen staring at me in the face. I was reminded that it was you who told me not to put a period where God intended a comma. I'm not giving up on you. I don't care about your personal afflictions or whatever disability you may or may not have. I want to be part of your life, a friend, in whatever capacity that may be. And if I must ask 1,111 separate ways before I get a yes, then so be it. It may not be daily, weekly, or even monthly, but I'm going to keep asking. So, buckle up, buttercup."

As she pedaled, her thoughts spiraled: "I'm not good enough. I'm too fat. I'm ugly. I'm not classy enough. I'm not in his league. What is it about this man that makes me feel this way?"

2:38 p.m. "And if nothing else, it'll be a great self-help book. I'll call it *1,111 Ways to Be Turned Down by a Douchebag.*"

No response.

7:45 p.m. The sun dipped low. Gabrielle woke from a restless nap and reached for the pill bottle on her nightstand, a desperate attempt to coax sleep into her weary bones. As the medication took hold, memories flooded her mind. Jeffrey's face appeared, stubborn and unyielding. His laughter. The way his eyes crinkled when he smiled. Why did he persist, even in the hazy twilight of half-sleep?

Social media beckoned. She scrolled, hoping for a sign. Nothing. Then, there he was. Jeffrey, suave and enigmatic, staring back from her newsfeed. Tousled hair. Stubble. Black suit clinging to broad shoulders. A snapshot of allure and mystery. Her thumb hovered over the heart icon. She hesitated. Instead, she took a screenshot. Jealousy twisted in her chest. Why did he haunt her? Why did his rejection sting so sharply? Tears blurred the pixels. She traced his face with her fingertip, seeking answers. *Why had he said no? Why wasn't she good enough?* The room shrank. She wept for lost chances, unspoken words, and the ache within.

At 10:00 p.m. Gabrielle woke to her alarm's gentle chime. The mirror reflected a face marked by triumphs and heartaches. She stepped onto the scale: 205 lbs. Thirty-five pounds lost since May. Jeffrey haunted her thoughts. She imagined shedding five more pounds; maybe then he'd see her differently. Maybe then he'd want to share secrets and laughter. She dressed for work. Her reflection wavered between who she was and who she longed to be.

Days passed. She curled into her favorite chair by the fireplace. The chill outside seeped in. The flames danced. She cradled a beer, imagining Jeffrey across from her. He wasn't just a goal. He was the missing piece. The ember was waiting to ignite a blaze.

Two days later, she reached out again. A message trembling with vulnerability. The collateral damage was staggering. A shattered friendship. Tears flowed freely. The silence on the other end echoed louder than any reply.

9:40 a.m. She wrote: "Hi! I'll be at the gym near your work on Monday for my weigh-in and measurements. I usually go to Starbucks afterward, reward or punishment depending on results. Would you like to join me for coffee and conversation? I'd like to explain myself and my actions. You can pick the topic. I'm a plethora of useless knowledge and have theories about everything. I'd like a dose of douchebag in person. I know I haven't been fair to you or myself. I'm sorry I put you in this position. I just want a chance to explain. I just want us to be friends. Please don't delete me or block me out of your life. I'll be at Starbucks Monday at 9:00 a.m."

Jeffrey replied immediately: "Good luck with your weigh-in and keep up the good results. Thank you, no. I have a lot in my life, an ex, three children, a business, and health issues. I'd rather be left alone. Thank you for understanding."

She should have left it there. But she couldn't.

She replied: "I respect you, but don't put a period where God intended a comma. You gave me three excuses. Sometimes God puts people in our lives for a reason, to teach, to heal, to offer friendship. God put you in my life for a reason. Please don't shut me out."

His response came swiftly: "I do not have room in my heart or my life in any capacity for someone like you. I asked you to stop and leave me alone. Please respect my request."

In an instant, Gabrielle was erased. Blocked. A word carved into her psyche. Her existence severed. His timeline vanished. His smile disappeared. A pixelated void. Had he ever been real? Her heart screamed yes. Her mind whispered no.

Days blurred into a tear-stained haze. Coworkers offered tissues. They didn't know her tears weren't for physical pain but for a broken heart. She had fallen for a man who didn't love her back. Their connection was a mirage in her lonely desert.

Five days passed. Reality settled. Jeffrey was gone. She contemplated calling him. Showing up. But he had made his intentions clear. Still, the "what if" lingered. *What if he had said yes? Would she have risked her marriage?* Jeffrey had become her Pandora's box. A trigger. A temptation. A mirror. She wrestled with her demons. Questioned her sanity.

Then there was her husband. The rock. The promise-keeper. How could she betray him? Her tears blurred the lines between longing and guilt. Was she mourning what she lost or what she could have gained? Gabrielle was lost. Torn between desire and duty. Between the forbidden and the familiar. The confession loomed. She would have to tell her husband. Reveal her transgressions. But how do you bridge the gap between thought and action?

In the stillness of the night, Gabrielle lay ensnared by shadows. The medicine cabinet beckoned, tiny capsules offering escape. But Jeffrey's memory lingered. In that final act, she sought reunion: a glimpse of his face, even if only in the afterlife. Her husband sensed her unraveling. Loneliness wrapped her. She longed for someone to grasp her hand, to silence Jeffrey's ghost. On the edge of despair, she knelt beside the bed and whispered, "Grant me a miracle. Show me a way back to the light."

5:55 a.m. The veil between dreams and waking thinned. Gabrielle awoke trembling, sweating, and chilled. Her husband stirred. "What's wrong?" he asked. She spoke of her vision: Jeffrey, standing in a church's hallowed halls. His voice echoed, "Here you shall uncover answers. Now is the appointed hour." Her husband listened. A pilgrimage to church might offer solace. They made a pact: to seek answers in the pews that coming Sunday.

That Sunday, Gabrielle dressed with trembling fingers. Church clothes felt foreign, the same Catholic church where her mother-in-law's funeral had been held, the same place where she and Jeffrey once bared their souls. The doors creaked open. The congregation sat in reverent silence. Gabrielle felt exposed. Would they judge her?

She settled into a pew. The priest ascended the pulpit. "Sometimes," he said, "we must release what binds us. Only then can we move forward." His gaze pierced her defenses. Tears blurred her vision. In the quiet, Gabrielle prayed. Jeffrey's face materialized. She pleaded silently: "Please put him back in my life."

After the service, she and her husband stepped into morning light. Over brunch, he asked, "Do you want to keep attending church?" Redemption hung in the air. Gabrielle had long carried guilt. Her husband leaned in: "Becoming a member requires classes." They would learn and grow together.

Gabrielle glanced at him. The weight on her soul lifted. The rituals and grace of the church would be her compass. Jeffrey's forgiveness lay within its hallowed walls. That evening, tears traced her cheeks as twilight painted the sky. An unwritten chapter, guided by light.

After her husband's call to the church, a delicate dance began. Gabrielle stepped into the hallowed halls. Richard, the spiritual director, asked, "Why now?" Her guarded heart revealed fragments, stress, whispers from beyond. Richard explained the RCIA process, a transformative pilgrimage. The doors were closed for now; she would have to wait nine months for the next class to start. But hope lingered. He whispered, "Your husband can be your guiding light."

A few days later, her husband vanished early. Gabrielle wondered about his burden. Their marriage now held a new thread: confession. As church bells chimed, she stood in her workplace lobby. He appeared, eyes holding vulnerability. He reached for her hand. "I went to confession," he said. "To unburden my soul." He wanted them to be part of something greater. His whispered promise lingered: "It won't be easy, but it will be worth it." Gabrielle believed. Their path of forgiveness, redemption, and love had begun. And when the time came, she would confess her hidden fears.

On a serene Sunday morning, anticipation tugged at Gabrielle's heart. She tiptoed across the room; the cold floor met her feet. The scale blinked: 199 lbs. For the first time in over two decades, she slipped beneath the elusive 200-pound threshold. Pride and disbelief swirled within her, a journey marked by sweat-soaked workouts and questionable pills.

Before the mirror, Gabrielle studied her softened face. Her clothes clung differently. Her husband, capturing her raw vulnerability, whispered, "I'm proud of you. I love you." But Jeffrey's shadow lingered. Their connection frayed. Would her weight loss change his perception? Could she become someone he'd be proud to know?

That morning, Gabrielle stepped out feeling inexplicably transformed. Crossing into the church, anticipation thickened the air. Eyes followed her. The sacred service chipped away at her burdens. Redemption glimmered. She bowed her head and dared to utter Jeffrey's name, a plea for reunion. But how?

The answer arrived: a Christmas card. A vessel for unspoken truths. She scoured shelves, searching for something simple, a solitary snowflake, blank inside, inviting her pen to dance. She wrote remorse, gratitude, longing. The card sat on her desk. She prayed.

On a crisp morning, Gabrielle sat in the doctor's office. The scale blinked: under 200 lbs. Her doctor studied her, knowing her secret regimen, the pills, the shortcuts. "You've made remarkable progress," he said. "But at what cost?" His words hung heavy. Gabrielle shifted, guilt pooling in her chest. "You're hurting your body," he continued. "These pills are a double-edged sword. They've etched their imprint on your psyche. Therapy is your lifeline. We must unravel the tangled threads."

And so, Gabrielle entered detox. Three days. A sterile facility: white walls, thin blankets, group therapy, journals soaked in secrets. She felt déjà vu, college dorms, or maybe *One Flew Over the Cuckoo's Nest.* Sanity teetering. After three days, she emerged. Renewed. Back home, she wrote. The Christmas card became a fragile bridge.

She penned:

Dear Jeffrey,

I know you asked me to leave you alone, and I respect that. But I need to explain myself. I made mistakes, things I'm deeply ashamed of. Truth: *I struggled with addiction. I became unrecognizable. Truth: My visits weren't about paperwork. They were about you. Our conversation at my mother-in-law's service spoke to me. You made me want to be better. My husband is my rock. He deserves more than I've given. That conversation about addiction and the pen I stole kept me going. I turned to the church. I pray for forgiveness. I hope one day you can forgive me. I pray for a message with three simple words: "I forgive you." I also pray for the chance to be friends again. I promise, if that day comes, I won't take it for granted. Everybody needs a douchebag New Yorker in their life. You'll never know how bad I feel that I lost mine.*

Gabrielle.

Would she send it? Or tuck it away forever? In the quiet night, Gabrielle bared her soul. Each word etched in ink formed a fragile bridge. The paper absorbed her vulnerability, cradling hope and fear. Would her confession ignite a spark? Would he read it with the same intensity she had poured into it?

Morning arrived with purpose. The letter, folded neatly, nestled in the Christmas card. Gabrielle hesitated at the mailbox, sealing her vulnerability. She imagined him receiving it, the weight in his hands, the ink staining his fingertips. Would he decipher the cryptic language of longing? She left her heart at the mercy of time and distance.

Days passed. Gabrielle's life revolved around a single heartbeat: Jeffrey's response. Each beep from her phone sparked hope. Would his message arrive, carrying forgiveness?

At home, crimson roses adorned the table. A velvet box held emerald earrings. Her husband's tenderness wrapped around her. "I love you," he whispered. "No matter what storms rage outside, we are in this together."

And there it was, the biggest guilt trip of her life. Gabrielle's mind raced: Jeffrey. The card. The fragile bridge. *Is it possible to love two people at once?* she wondered. She placed the earrings in her ears; green hues mirrored the emerald depths of her heart.

Jeffrey's card remained unanswered. In those quiet days, he consumed her thoughts. Had he received it? Had he read it? Their past conversations lingered: forgiveness, vulnerability, redemption. But silence persisted.

January settled in. Reality crystallized: Jeffrey had chosen indifference. The silence screamed louder than anger. It etched itself into her bones. To be ignored felt like erasure, as if her existence had no consequence. She grappled with conflicting desires. Anger would be easier; anger acknowledged her. Silence erased her. She considered reaching out again maybe an email. But the digital barricade was impenetrable. Blocked. Erased. She replayed their last conversation, dissected every syllable, and found only emptiness.

Work became her refuge. Her journal, a confessional. His ghost lingered in every corner. Could he hear her silent prayers? Sundays found her in the pews, whispering into the ether. She clung to faith, believing that someday, he would step out of the shadows.

On January 20th, Gabrielle organized a surprise birthday party and fundraiser at work. She invited Jeffrey through a mutual friend, secretly hoping he'd attend. Word circulated: he had whisked his children away for a weekend getaway. His absence was expected. His disinterest in anything related to her was clear.

But that day, unbeknownst to her, marked the beginning of the end. After twenty-four years, Gabrielle's tenure was quietly unraveling. She waited for her colleague Erin, her partner who was helping her with the event. But Erin never came. A text arrived: "Call me later after it's all over." Something was wrong. Doris, their boss, had wielded her authority. She'd instructed Erin not to attend. A mysterious meeting loomed. A clash of wills. A disgruntled patron. An investigation.

The next day, Erin called. Her voice trembled. A customer complaint had triggered an internal review: suspension, demotion, transfer. Gabrielle listened, heart heavy. It wasn't fair.

Days later, Gabrielle confronted Doris. "What happened to Erin?" Doris's reply was sharp: "Mind your own business. It doesn't concern you." Gabrielle persisted, not fighting Erin's battle but to bear witness. "So noted," Doris said. Gabrielle retreated. She had learned when to engage and when to let the currents carry her. This time, she stood down. But the wound was real.

On a cold January day, Gabrielle stepped onto the scale at the doctor's office. Sixty pounds lost. But pride eluded her. Her body's silent rebellion.

The doctor's concern was clear: "Depression. Anxiety. They're closing in." Therapy. New medication. Gabrielle nodded, but her heart screamed. How could she be healthy when Jeffrey dismantled her world with a few callous words? He had vanished her. Blocked her. Erased her. Despair clung to her. Hopelessness whispered, "*Nothing matters anymore.*"

And yet, each Sunday, Gabrielle and her husband rose early. They went to church. The priest's voice wove tales of hope, forgiveness, redemption. After the service, they shared meals, talked, laughed, lay side-by-side, hearts tuned to a celestial rhythm. Those Sundays were elixirs, woven from love and faith, drawing them closer to each other and to God.

But in the corridors of her professional life, a storm brewed. Gabrielle asked for Sundays off, a simple, sacred respite. Doris saw rebellion. "Lazy," she muttered. "Irresponsible." She saw Gabrielle as a cog, not a soul. But Gabrielle had given everything: late nights, missed holidays, sacrifices etched into her bones. "Sundays," Gabrielle said, "just one day. A sanctuary for faith, family, and renewal." Doris nodded, frosty, begrudging. She didn't understand. Doris retaliated: whispers, extra work, phone calls on stolen Sundays. Gabrielle whispered to the winds, "*I won't give up.*"

In February, Gabrielle sought refuge in the gym. The treadmill's hum drowned out echoes of lost love. She sculpted resilience, but Jeffrey's indifference carved fault lines through her.

In March, memories returned, her father's death. Her mentor. Her hero. And Jeffrey. Still blocked. Still gone. She clung to remnants, a name heavy with longing. Against her better judgment, Gabrielle yearned for his presence. But Jeffrey had severed the fragile threads. He wielded the digital sword: deleting her from social media, blocking her number, leaving her heart in shards. His actions spoke louder than words: "*You are no longer a part of my life.*"

Yet Gabrielle clung to the remnants, unwilling to release the past. She composed an email and cast it into the abyss of his work address. Months ago, he had promised to manage her mother's funeral paperwork. But his promises crumbled. Anger surged. Had he deliberately neglected his duty? Jeffrey's presence, even in absence, haunted her. She hit send. Her heart raced.

Days passed. Then, his name appeared. Clinical words: "Mistake in the paperwork. Missing or incorrect information. Needs redoing."

Urgent. Important. No apology. No warmth. But Gabrielle didn't care. His email was a lifeline. He hadn't abandoned her. Not completely.

She replied: "Can I fill out the paperwork? Can I drop it off? Will you be there?" She held her breath. His response: "Yes." Three letters. Simple. Profound. Ecstasy surged. She danced around the room. This was it, a chance to mend, to bridge the gap.

She envisioned their meeting: the paperwork forgotten, laughter, forgiveness. She filled out the forms, printed them, folded them carefully, wrapped her hopes in a protective cocoon. She drove to the funeral home. The door swung open. A young man greeted her, warm, curious. "I have paperwork for Jeffrey," she said. He nodded. "Wait here."

Minutes passed. Then he returned. His expression had shifted. "Jeffrey is busy," he said gently. "He reviewed your paperwork. He'll refile it." Gabrielle's chest tightened. Jeffrey remained elusive. The pain surged. Anger and sadness collided. She blinked back tears. *Why does he keep pushing me away?*

She held the pen, the one she had stolen months ago. A relic. A bridge. She thrust it toward the young man. "Tell Jeffrey this belongs to him. I guess I won't need it anymore." He accepted it, sympathetic. But Jeffrey remained hidden.

Gabrielle stepped into the evening air. Her car awaited. Tears flowed freely as she slipped into the driver's seat. The engine hummed. Jeffrey's name echoed in her mind. *What had she done wrong?* She gripped the wheel, buried her face in her hands. For twenty minutes, she wept. His indifference cut deep.

She couldn't let it go. She poured her soul into another email, confessing everything: the pen, its meaning, her longing. "It doesn't matter anymore," she typed. "You're the man who didn't have room for me in his heart." Hope and desperation swirled. Would he reply? Would he care? His silence mocked her vulnerability.

Days blurred into weeks. Time became her tormentor. Sleep offered solace. In dreams, she relived their moments. Was this love or madness? Jeffrey had become her obsession. She clung to sleep, hoping dreams could mend what reality had shattered.

Work pulsed through her days: spreadsheets, reports, emails. Jeffrey's absence gnawed at her. *Why did he retreat? Why avoid her?* Depression and anxiety clung to her soul. She lay awake, staring at the ceiling, wondering if his silence held the key to her unraveling sanity. Work blurred into exhaustion. Tears flowed silently in the dim glow of her laptop. Something had to give.

Gabrielle and her husband craved spontaneity, a break from the grind, a breath of joy. They found it in St. Louis. At Busch Stadium, they joined the sea of Cardinals fans, immersed in the game's pulse, laughing, cheering, remembering how joy used to feel. They stood beneath the Gateway Arch, the Mississippi River stretching wide and quiet below. Their casino visit wasn't about winning; it was about rekindling connection, sharing tender moments that reminded them of who they were before life got heavy.

St. Louis was only the prologue. Next came the Indianapolis 500. The sun beat down. Engines roared. But it wasn't the race that left its mark; it was Gabrielle's quiet rebellion. She chose joy over obligation. Her husband watched her, admiring the fire in her eyes. "Quit," he said. "Your happiness is worth more than any job." When heat exhaustion overtook her, the universe pressed pause, a traumatic interlude. Her husband shielded her, sending a message to her boss.

Back home, Gabrielle clutched a doctor's note, her armor against corporate retaliation. She recounted months of stress: the fallout from defending her demoted colleague, the scrutiny Doris had unleashed. Doris, once a mentor, now a predator. She wanted Gabrielle to be broken. But Gabrielle stood tall. "You're back," Doris said, her smile brittle. "But not unscathed."

The inquisition began: three hours, emails, tasks, a list of sins to confess. Gabrielle typed each sentence like a brick in her fortress. She submitted her report, not beaten but bold. Her husband's support was her strength.

The next morning, Doris called. Her voice was sharp. "Teamwork," she said. But her tone betrayed command, not camaraderie. Gabrielle clenched her fists. Her colleagues watched, eyes filled with concern. She remembered her achievements: her office had flourished; her team had thrived. But Doris brought a chill that lingered long after she left the room. Gabrielle stood at a crossroads. Should she raise her shield or seek a new beginning?

Vacation approached. A melody of anticipation played softly in the background. But Doris loomed, an unwelcome specter. She dissected Gabrielle's unfinished tasks with predatory precision. Gabrielle completed each one with grace, her mind already wandering to the open roads ahead. That night, she packed. She was shedding the layers of burden.

The next morning, Gabrielle and her husband chose the road over the runway. Each mile unfurled the landscape and with it, her soul. The car became sanctuary. She voiced her frustrations; her husband listened. "Quit," he urged again. "Let this be your new beginning."

Yet even in freedom, Jeffrey lingered, the missing piece, the ache. Could she ever show him who she truly was? Maybe the answer lay in a letter. But would he read it? Would he understand?

They detoured to Kauffman Stadium: baseball, ballpark treats, digital memories shared online, breadcrumbs for Jeffrey to find. Then Denver: Pikes Peak, historic mines, bison farms, Rockies games, Coors factory tours. Each moment documented. On the return trip, Mount Rushmore stood silent. Her husband slept beside her. Gabrielle drove, wondering if Jeffrey had seen their joy.

Back home, she felt renewed. Jeffrey's memory lingered. He remained a silent companion, woven into the fabric of her thoughts. She returned to work with renewed energy.

But a terse message from Doris shifted the day's course: "Report to the local office first." Gabrielle's heart pounded. Why the summons? Why the secrecy?

She arrived, footsteps echoing down the hallway. The meeting room door beckoned. Inside, the air was heavy. Twenty minutes passed as Gabrielle waited, her mind racing through scenarios. She knew the company's tactics, experts in psychological warfare.

When Doris and Amanda entered, their synchronized stride betrayed no warmth. The room tightened like a noose. Their eyes dissected her. "You didn't manage the situation properly before your vacation." Gabrielle had documented everything. But they weren't there to listen; they were there to break her. Silence became her armor. She sat, a lone soldier facing a two-headed hydra.

When the storm subsided, she stumbled out, bruised but unbroken. Doris shadowed her, scrutinized every keystroke, nitpicked every decision. Colleagues exchanged knowing glances. Some urged her to fight. But Gabrielle knew this was her battle. She soldiered on. Her fingers danced across the keyboard; her mind remained a fortress.

That night, Gabrielle made a doctor's appointment. The next day, she sat in the waiting room, rehearsing her truth. The doctor listened, prescribed rest, and provided a written endorsement. Gabrielle clung to that note. She informed Doris via text, attached the proof.

The next morning, her sick leave was approved. Medication in hand, Gabrielle began her healing: ten days of quiet. No emails. No phone calls. Just silence and self-reflection. At the gym, each step was a march against stress. Returning home, her husband surprised her: a trip to Minneapolis. Twins game. Mall of America. And a reunion with college friends.

The clinic visit stirred anxiety. The scale read 209 lbs. Not ideal, but considering the storms she'd weathered, it was progress. The social worker prescribed a remedy: *write.* So, Gabrielle did. She journaled. She prayed.

Then Minneapolis. Dinner. Discovery. A rain-slicked Twins game, fireworks bursting through drizzle. She posted online, cryptic, hopeful. *Would Jeffrey see?* The Mall of America shimmered with nostalgia. Her husband marveled. They had lunch, browsed, laughed. Then the reunion: college friends, twenty-five years apart. Laughter. Stories. Sorrows. Joy. Her husband embraced their wildness.

On the outskirts of town, they found it: the world's largest six-pack. Six colossal beer tanks, seven million cans' worth. They snapped photos. Then, "No more pit stops," her husband said. "Let's drive straight home." Gabrielle took the wheel. Her mind wandered. Jeffrey surfaced. *Would he ever see her again?*

But another matter pressed closer: her workplace. The social worker's advice echoed, document *everything.* So she did: emails, texts, recordings, notes.

Back home, Gabrielle collapsed into bed exhausted but determined. She rose. Laundry hummed. She organized her case; each page bore witness. She envisioned an attorney and prayed for justice.

That evening, she and her husband attended a dine-and-donate event. Familiar faces surrounded them. Gabrielle's eyes scanned the room. *Was Jeffrey here?* They were all part of this intricate web of mutual friendships. Jeffrey remained elusive; his absence was a presence all its own.

Her friend's gratitude enveloped her. They hugged, hearts bridging the gap between words and unspoken understanding. Gabrielle yearned to confide in her, to share the weight of her own unraveling. But she and her husband had made a pact: silence. For now. Work had gnawed at Gabrielle's sanity. She took refuge at the gathering. Clinking glasses drowned out the office's cacophony. "Time off," she told her friend, her voice a fragile thread. Her friend nodded, eyes kind and knowing.

Days later, a cryptic text shattered Gabrielle's fragile peace. Doris and Amanda had descended onto her workplace, two hours of scrutiny, dissecting her absence, strategizing her return. A one-hour meeting loomed: a battlefield. But Gabrielle had her arsenal: notes, emails, texts, a paper trail of tyranny. She had become a reluctant detective, piecing together injustice.

And then, the attorney. Gabrielle's email floated into cyberspace, carrying her hopes and fears. Would they respond? Would time stretch and torment her? She waited.

The next day, Gabrielle napped while her husband mowed the lawn. Her thoughts ricocheted: Jeffrey. The attorney. The ache. The hope. 3:30 p.m. The call came. They had a case, contingency basis, no payment unless they win. Her husband's response was immediate: "Let's do this." Gabrielle called the attorney back. Their meeting was scheduled. But first, a doctor's visit, a shield against the corporate battlefield.

Two days later, Gabrielle sat in the exam room. "I need more time," she said. "I want to see the social worker again." The doctor nodded, filled out the paperwork, prescribed relief.

Back home, Gabrielle sent Doris a screenshot of the doctor's note. "Get better soon. Call me weekly," Doris replied. Gabrielle clenched her jaw. Twenty-four years unraveling. Twenty-five, once a milestone, now a mirage. Her exit would not be graceful; it would be quiet rebellion.

The next day, Gabrielle called Doris. No answer. She left a professional voicemail. Doris returned the call hours later. Gabrielle bit back her frustration. "No thank you. I'm fine." Her husband listened, proud of her restraint. "The attorney will take care of us," he said. "We'll win this." Gabrielle clung to that hope.

In the quiet days that followed, Gabrielle danced between anticipation and trepidation. She traced her steps back to January: emails, texts, recordings, a chronicle of harassment, bullying, rights trampled. Unfair reviews. Denied promotions. Threats of termination. Venomous voices. Humiliation. Gabrielle compiled her pain into neat, concise notes. *Would the attorney see what she saw? Could they weave these threads into a case?*

And then, Jeffrey. His absence gnawed at her soul. She missed the banter, the smart-ass comments, the lifeline. He had blocked her, deleted her, restricted her. It felt like betrayal. She mourned him. Grieved him. Wondered if he ever thought of her.

Sunday dawned. Church called. Gabrielle bowed her head, prayed for Jeffrey's health, for his return, for clarity. Work loomed. She prayed for strength, for courage, for the right path.

Before the altar, they stood. The priest beckoned. "RCIA classes," he said. "Are you ready?" Gabrielle nodded. Her heart fluttered. Becoming Catholic was a leap of faith. Her husband's presence steadied her. The priest's blessing lingered, a whispered promise.

Post-church, her home became her sanctuary. Documents sprawled across the table. Her husband scanned each page. "Impressive," he said. "You've marshaled your case well." Grammar tweaks. Final polish. The handbook. The appraisals. The violations.

Gabrielle retreated to the porch. Her egg chair cradled her. She thought of Jeffrey, the void he left, the story she wished she could rewrite. *Maybe in forgiveness, peace would find her.*

The next day, Gabrielle and her husband stepped into the attorney's office. The room was hushed; the air was thick. The attorney welcomed them, listened, her eyes full of empathy. Gabrielle felt seen, validated. She watched as the attorney sifted through the stack of documents; Gabrielle had meticulously prepared. The attorney nodded, her voice steady: "You've built a compelling case. We'll file a claim." Her words were a promise. Justice was no longer a distant dream; it was within reach. Gabrielle signed the retainer agreement. The weight of her truth shifted. She wasn't alone anymore. She had an advocate.

Outside, Gabrielle and her husband made a pact: silence. No leaks. No whispers. Only the attorney would know. They imagined the scene at work, Doris and Amanda reading the letter. *Would they squirm? Panic? Deny?* Gabrielle yearned to be a fly on the wall. She knew Doris would deflect, discredit, deny. But Gabrielle had armor now: the law. Her evidence. Her resolve. They couldn't retaliate. They couldn't break her.

The next day, the lawsuit loomed. Stress and anxiety gnawed at Gabrielle. She retreated to bed, but sleep offered no peace. Her fingers itched to type, to pour her heart onto social media, but caution held her back. The lawsuit was a labyrinth: secrets, consequences. She dared not risk exposure. She yearned for a confidante, someone who understood.

That evening, the Moose Lodge beckoned. A fundraiser for a friend, a noble cause, a needed distraction. Gabrielle arrived, hoping to see Jeffrey. But his absence hung in the air: heavy, intentional? *Had he heard she'd be there? Had he stayed away?*

Her mind raced: anger, blame, regret. Jeffrey, once their staunchest supporter, had vanished from every event that year. Was Gabrielle the reason? She tried to dismiss the thoughts, but they clung to her. Jeffrey's face haunted her. She longed to talk, to apologize, to mend the rift. But he remained elusive.

The Moose Lodge buzzed with life. Gabrielle joined in, masking her turmoil with practiced smiles. The fundraiser promised a good turnout, but her mind fixated on the missing piece, the one person who could make sense of it all. As the night wore on, Gabrielle promised her friend she'd return the next day. But deep down, she knew it wasn't her she was looking for. It was Jeffrey. The man who held answers. The man who could unravel the knots of guilt and longing.

Gabrielle left the Moose Lodge, her footsteps heavy with unspoken words.

The Voice in the Quiet

"Whether you turn to the right or to the left,
your ears shall hear a voice behind you."

—Isaiah 30:21

Gabrielle pushed herself at the gym, determined to meet her doctor's goal. That evening at the Moose Lodge, she found comfort in the crowd until she saw Jeffrey. He looked happier than she remembered, and though she tried not to stare, she couldn't help herself. Fear kept her from approaching him, but his presence unsettled her.

A friend hugged her. "Rumors," he said. "Work issues," she replied. Jeffrey walked by, waving and smiling, but not at her. She felt like a pawn in a silent game, unsure if she was being noticed or ignored.

Later, her friend whispered, "He loves you and your husband." Gabrielle wondered what he meant. Across the room, Jeffrey spoke with her husband, and jealousy gnawed at her. What words passed between them? She longed to know but didn't dare ask.

Gabrielle and her husband left the event, silent together about his conversation with Jeffrey. She didn't press. Sometimes, not knowing was easier. Church bells tolled. Gabrielle prayed for Jeffrey, each chime a note in her symphony of hope. That night, she posted a tribute to her husband, but Jeffrey lingered, a whisper in the quiet.

Monday brought a new doctor. "Let's extend your leave," she said. "Let's begin healing." Gabrielle left comforted. At home, solitude wrapped around her. Her husband was away. Thoughts of Jeffrey surfaced a tapestry of what-ifs. She honored his silence, sent prayers into the ether.

Later that week, her attorney's email chimed: the claim was ready. Gabrielle signed hope and doubt waltzing in her mind. That night, Jeffrey's memory returned. She prayed for peace, for closure.

Family gatherings offered distraction, but her heart wandered. She recommitted to her health: two pounds a week, eighty-nine pounds by June. Eric, her virtual fitness friend, became a steady voice of encouragement, his messages arriving like grace. Still, shadows lingered. The lawsuit tightened its grip. Sleep evaded her.

August marked her father's birthday, a day of memory and quiet strength. Sundays became sanctuary. "God," she whispered, "remove Jeffrey from my heart." Tears blurred her vision. Eight months had passed since their friendship ended. Why did she still hold on? The mirror reflected her doubts: too fat, too ugly, not smart enough. What had he seen or not seen? She didn't know. But she began to envision a future unbound by past ties. Her spirit was ready for forgiveness.

Then came Eric. A message buzzed: "Good morning sunshine!" A sticker followed, playful and affirming. Eric, her virtual fitness friend, had woven himself into her daily rhythm. His timing was uncanny. Gabrielle replied with heartfelt thanks; his encouragement arrived like grace.

Sunday mornings became her haven. Church wrapped her in sacred embrace. Jeffrey's name fluttered on her breath, a delicate hope. Eric's presence was steadfast, platonic, kind. Jeffrey's memory watched over her. Her lawyer waged wars of words. Gabrielle balanced her heart between hope and surrender.

Monday's sun nudged Gabrielle awake. Eric's sticker arrived: "I hope today is an awesome day for you." Curiosity led her to his social media, a girlfriend, a child, a reminder their exchanges were friendly jests.

Then came the twelve-page questionnaire from her insurance company: mental state, daily life, short-term disability on the line. *Bullshit*, she thought. Gabrielle laced her sneakers, walked five laps around the block. Her husband sensed her mood and gave her space.

Later, at her desk, the questionnaire loomed. She emailed her attorney. "Go ahead," came the reply, "but send it to me first." Gabrielle imagined her attorney parsing each line for pitfalls.

A call between legal teams loomed. Would it bring resolution? Time stretched. Then a message blinked on her screen. Eric, with words of positivity. *How did he always know when she needed encouragement?*

Another connection surfaced: a friend from work reached out. "I miss you," she said. "I hope you're well." Gabrielle replied: "Taking time for self-care. Silencing work notifications." The truth hung unspoken but understood. Rumors whispered. Would Gabrielle return? Would she reclaim her place? Her friend responded: "I have eighteen months left. Then retirement beckons." Gabrielle cheered her on. Two women, two paths, stitched with resilience.

At 4:00 p.m., Gabrielle gathered her hopes, good vibes, prayers, whispers. At 4:35 p.m., her inbox chimed: "Promising negotiations ahead." Her attorney's words glimmered. A settlement package. A path forward. "Let's discuss your financial expectations." Tomorrow at 1:00 p.m.

The next morning, friends arrived for the pilgrimage to Bristol Motor Speedway. Gabrielle listened as her attorney's call cut through the hum of conversation. Negotiations had begun, figures danced, promises dangled. "Expect no swift reply," her attorney warned. They arrived at the hotel, weary but eager for distraction.

Day two brought sweltering hours to the track. Engines roared, the crowd thundered, and Gabrielle endured the heat with aspirin and grit. Midnight return. At 3:00 a.m., she lay awake while her husband slept, her mind circling Jeffrey, imagined conversations, his smile. Truth was stark: he didn't want her. Eric's nightly message arrived: "Rest well." Gabrielle replied, grateful for his kindness.

Day three blurred, tailgating, racing, exhaustion. Her husband's eyes lingered. Gabrielle clung to her secrets. Love and guilt waged war. The race offered respite, but her thoughts wandered. Jeffrey's absence was a wound that refused to close.

The next day, friends beckoned them toward the casino. Plans shifted: slot machines, crab legs, cocktails. Gabrielle watched her husband dance on the edge of inebriation, half-amused, half-worried. By 9:00 p.m., she was the designated driver.

Back at the hotel, fatigue claimed them both. Eric's message pierced the quiet: "You are beautiful inside and out." His words warmed hollow spaces.

Homecoming was quiet, a shared collapse onto the couch. Gabrielle whispered, "We will weather this storm." She imagined reclaiming routines: shared breakfasts, laughter, stolen kisses. Yet uncertainty lingered.

Monday morning, Gabrielle sat by the phone. The call never came. Waiting unraveled her patience. Then clarity bloomed: her tenure had reached its closing chapter. Surprisingly, peace followed. *People don't quit companies; they quit people.* Doris and Amanda were thorns she would never miss. Eric's message arrived: *Good morning, beautiful one.* His words glowed, innocent yet comforting.

Tuesday, Gabrielle met with the social worker again. She decided to stop the sessions; her attorney had become her beacon. "If I need you again," she said, "I'll call." Eric's morning message arrived: *"I'm believing you'll have a wonderful day. If not, I'm praying it gets better."* It was as if he sensed her emotional coordinates, his words arriving just when she needed them most.

Later, a text from a friend delivered seismic news: the office was closing. Downsizing swept away long-term employees. Gabrielle shared the news with her attorney, hoping it might tip the scales. Behind the scenes, negotiations stirred. Her attorney responded with a graceful hint of behind-the-scenes movement.

As twilight painted the sky, another email arrived, a reminder to send in her short-term disability paperwork. But when Gabrielle logged in, her benefits had been terminated. The summary offered scant comfort, arbitrary and unjust. Her husband, fueled by righteous anger, vowed financial war. "We will make these assholes pay!" he declared. Gabrielle urged restraint. "Patience," she said. "We've entrusted this battle to her."

Friday evening brought a reprieve: friends, music, and a Reba concert. Escapism shimmered under casino lights. That night, Jeffrey appeared in her dreams. Gabrielle prayed for clarity, torn between wanting him back and yearning for release.

Monday brought two appointments: the nutritionist and the doctor. Her husband joined her. The nutritionist smiled in recognition. Gabrielle stepped onto the scale, six pounds shed. A small triumph. They discussed portion control and mindful snacking.

Next stop: the doctor. Gabrielle shared her progress, energy rising, and life manageable. The doctor nodded, scribbled notes, and handed her a return-to-work slip unshackled by restrictions.

Days later, a letter arrived: mediation was set. Gabrielle dialed her attorney, pulse quickening. They would navigate this together. She penned a concise, hopeful email. Closure hovered; the waiting game began. She reveled in the luxury of not working, but reality loomed, her paycheck dwindled, the clock ticked.

Meanwhile, Richard from Saint Michaels sent tidings of RCIA classes. A spiritual journey awaited.

Gabrielle and her husband embarked on a final hurrah to Chattanooga. Seven hours of winding roads, pit stops, shared meals. They arrived at a cozy hotel on the Tennessee River. Midday, Eric's message danced across her screen: *Hope you are having an awesome day.*

Evening descended. Their room rebelled, the air conditioning quit, sweat beaded, patience waned. At 8:30 p.m., her husband called the front desk. "The air is not working."

The associate sprang into action. "Allow me to upgrade you." His hair was a fiery cascade of red. Her husband, in playful exuberance, dubbed him "Ginger Snap." Gabrielle laughed. The nickname carried unintended warmth. Ginger Snap, indeed. If only he knew how perfectly his title fit into the sweetness of their story.

The sun rose over undulating hills. Gabrielle and her husband explored Lookout Mountain's enchantment. First stop: Ruby Falls, descending 1,120 feet into the earth, water thundering through ancient limestone.

Next, the incline railway, the world's steepest climb.

Then, Rock City: red and black barns, enchanted gardens, stone bridges, vistas that whispered wonder.

Evening brought Logan's Roadhouse: grilled steaks, warm bread, stories shared.

That night, in their hotel room, Gabrielle spoke to Jeffrey in her heart, across the veil: *Please God, put Jeffrey back in my life.*

Morning came. Atlanta awaited. Traffic was light. Eric's message chimed: *Did you survive the mountains?* Gabrielle replied: *I survived, but my calves feel like wobbly jelly.*

They arrived early; Gabrielle doubted check-in, but her husband insisted. The universe conspired, early check-in granted. They wandered to the Battery, enjoyed Wahlburgers, and secured tickets for a doubleheader.

From the outfield, Gabrielle watched the game unfold, but her heart tugged elsewhere. Jeffrey's absence echoed: his smart-ass banter, his presence, her silent wish. She treaded carefully, respecting boundaries, but the ache remained.

Under stadium lights, Gabrielle whispered to the breeze: *Jeffrey, if you only knew how much this silence weighs upon me.*

Morning arrived. Eric's message buzzed: *Good morning, my gorgeous, beautiful friend.* Was it friendship or something more? They had met on a fitness app.

Game two unfolded: the crack of the bat, the roar of the crowd, a welcome distraction. Her husband was a quiet anchor, but Gabrielle saw the cracks: the extra glass of wine, laughter tinged with sadness, his happy drunkenness, a coping mechanism. Gabrielle, the sober witness, prayed for them both.

The day after the game, fatigue tugged at their bones. They drove home. Her husband pushed forward, unyielding. Back home, the gym became sanctuary. Eric's message was a beacon: *Your day will be amazing, awesome, and wonderful.* Gabrielle clung to his prophecy. But the *what ifs* haunted her. What if she'd spoken differently? Jeffrey's friendship, a fragile thread. Had her silence severed it? The lawsuit: did it hold the key? She stood at a crossroads, heart and mind divided. Jeffrey or reason? Lawsuit or liberation?

During those days away from work, life settled into its own rhythm. Her husband orchestrated mini vacations, hoping to distract her from the relentless specters: Jeffrey and the lawsuit. But these escapes only skimmed the surface. Jeffrey's name echoed through her thoughts. Their friendship fractured, suspended between forgiveness and irreparable loss. The lawsuit consumed her mental reserves. She felt hollow. Gabrielle found solace in the mundane, but her weight loss journey stalled. The mirror reflected discouragement. She yearned for change.

In quiet hours, Gabrielle composed a letter, Jeffrey's name dancing across the page. Ink traced longing and memory. *Should she send it?* Her heart clung to hope, weaving threads of possibility. Maybe he'd read her words. Maybe he'd recognize the ache. Maybe he'd extend an olive branch. Tears blurred her vision as she wrestled with the emotional tug-of-war.

Then an email: her employer severed her pay. No warning. Just silence. Anger flared. She reached out to her attorney. A formal offer issued. Negotiations were ongoing. Gabrielle's soul recoiled. Twenty-four years poured into the job, now slipping through her fingers. The past couldn't be reclaimed. The future loomed uncertain.

Ironically, Jeffrey remained her sole distraction from the legal maelstrom. His absence gnawed at her sanity. But the thought of reconnecting sent tremors through her heart. *Would he forgive her? Would their friendship rekindle?*

Each day, Gabrielle grappled with the emotional teeter-totter: Jeffrey, the lawsuit, the job, all swirling, threatening to drown her resolve.

On a sun-kissed Saturday, Gabrielle and her husband embarked on their annual pilgrimage to the Brickyard. Not a single cloud marred the sky. Gabrielle stood on the asphalt, her "wife points" earned with a smile. Their Ohio friends materialized, merry souls, beer-fueled antics, raucous joy. Their laughter lifted heavy hearts.

The race unfolded. Kyle Busch claimed victory. Her cheers were half-hearted. Still, the race glided faster than years past. Life outside the track was a tempest. Work loomed. Jeffrey haunted her thoughts. She yearned to reach out, but fear clamped her tongue. So, she penned letters.

After the race, Subway beckoned. No dishes, just sandwiches, TV, and the lingering specter of Jeffrey. Her mind churned as she lay in bed, contemplating the future. Prayers whispered in the dark. Maybe the week ahead would bring answers.

Twenty-four years surrendered to the grind. Corporate Kool-Aid imbibed. *Never again*, Gabrielle vowed. Her heart craved balance, a Monday-through-Friday oasis where work bowed to life.

Sunday dawned. They returned to the track. Kevin Harvick, her favorite, claimed victory. The sun dipped low, shadows stretched. Surprisingly, Gabrielle found solace in the cacophony. Eric's motivational messages arrived; hope stitched into her weary heart. Work or life. Jeffrey or silence?

Monday morning, Eric's message chimed: *Cling to your resolve. Trace your footsteps. Remember why you started.* The gym beckoned. Guilt whispered. Gabrielle laced her sneakers.

Post-workout, exhaustion draped over her. Breakfast blurred. A mid-morning nap called. Her husband tiptoed. He, too, succumbed to rest, their shared fatigue a silent bond.

As the sun dipped low, Gabrielle's attorney's email pierced the quiet. A settlement offer: eight weeks of pay, three months of COBRA, and a feeble promise of job assistance. A slap so sharp it echoed through her thoughts. "Job placement?" Gabrielle scoffed. Her husband mirrored her indignation. "Let them shove it," he declared. But he knew when to temper her rage. "Trust your attorney," he advised.

Evening stretched. Her husband played emotional firefighter, dousing her fury with soothing words. Yet beneath it all, determination simmered. "Every last dollar," he vowed. "We'll bury those cocky bastards." His laughter echoed through their home. Gabrielle clung to his unwavering support, grateful for a partner who understood the stakes.

Morning arrived. Gabrielle dialed her attorney, unavailable. An email promised a late callback. Gabrielle's thoughts spilled onto the screen, dissecting the offer and her anger. When her voice finally cracked through the phone, she calmed the tempest within. A counteroffer emerged.

As the week unfolded, Gabrielle anticipated a breakfast date with her girls. The thought of their company warmed her heart. She hadn't shared the lawsuit but hoped they'd understand.

The morning arrived. Gabrielle slipped into a cozy café. Stories and laughter flowed. Guilt tugged at her insides. She resolved to unburden herself and spilled the beans. Their eyes widened, but instead of reproach, they offered understanding nods. "Life takes unexpected turns," one said, her hand resting on Gabrielle's. "We're here for you, no matter what." Relief washed over her.

As the day unfolded, Gabrielle took it easy. The weight of her truth had lifted, but adjustment still lingered. Too young to step away, too old to chase new dreams. Maybe her husband would grant her the luxury of staying home. They had shared twelve blissful weeks. Gabrielle mused on life's cosmic balance. Why not a lottery win? Or a prompt legal settlement? Stress gnawed at her. She yearned for closure, for a clean ending.

Then work, the looming return. Dread settled in. They would watch her like hawks, scrutinize every keystroke, every break. She'd have to muzzle her candid tongue lest it land her in hot water. But there was a silver lining: Gabrielle returned as a protected team member. Her claim was filed. Her voice was documented.

In autumn of that year, Gabrielle and her husband stepped into the sacred halls of St. Michael's. Excitement stirred, a spiritual voyage into Catholicism had begun. The chapel welcomed them into a community bound by faith's promise. Over thirty-four weeks, they would traverse RCIA, a tapestry of worship, care, and social justice. Mass became timeless communion. Prayer, study, and shared stumbles of faith wove a communal symphony seeking grace. In vulnerability, they found strength. In fellowship, they journeyed toward enlightenment.

The next morning, Richard's email arrived:

Dear Catholics in Training, join us for Sunday mass, a spiritual work that strengthens your soul. Immerse yourselves in tradition, feel the rhythm of prayers, and connect with the community. Hold onto moments of peace: they are glimpses of something greater. Blessings on your journey, Richard.

Later that day, a letter arrived from Gabrielle's employer. Her FMLA had run out. Her doctor's note had her returning post-FMLA, but they could not guarantee her position. Disconcerted, Gabrielle sent the letter to her attorney. Frustration echoed. Her husband, colorful in language, vowed to fight. They stood united.

Her attorney contacted the company's legal team, seeking clarity, urging fairness. Gabrielle reached out to Doris. The response was cryptic. More questions than answers. A friend shared a screenshot of her tentative schedule. Her attorney emphasized: *document everything.* Gabrielle would limit interactions to written exchanges.

Disillusionment grew. Regional leadership left a bitter taste. Gabrielle hoped for a swift, pointed response. Then a revised letter: she would return to her previous role, unaltered in capacity. A small victory. Gabrielle pictured Doris seething—it made her smile. But Doris's evasiveness persisted. Her schedule remained a mystery. Gabrielle reached out to another manager. Her week's schedule appeared, meetings dominated. Curious, for someone returning from leave. Her patience waned.

Dawn broke. Gabrielle's chest weighed heavy. The settlement remained elusive. She sought solace in the pews, clasped her hands, prayed for peace, prayed for Jeffrey. Back home, reality awaited. Work loomed. Gabrielle dreaded her return. Would Doris greet her with sympathy or indifference? Maybe a surprise phone call would grant her a reprieve. Wishful thinking. But hope clung to her heart.

Eric reached out, no agendas, just encouragement. His words lifted her when the weight threatened to crush her. Evening shadows lengthened. Gabrielle sat by the window, phone in hand. Jeffrey. Eric. The lawsuit. A complex tapestry of emotions.

The sun hung low. Gabrielle dressed for her first day back. The clock read 2:00 p.m. Armed with dread and determination, she waited for a divine reprieve, a phone call, a miracle. But the universe remained silent. Duty called.

Eric had sent her a message earlier, invoking blessings and calmness for her return. Gabrielle chuckled at the irony. Still, she appreciated the sentiment. Sitting in her car, staring at the office building, Gabrielle wondered what awaited her inside. Doris, sharp-tongued and unpredictable, loomed. Would she be all smiles, masking her true intentions? Or would her barbed comments pierce through Gabrielle's armor?

Summoning courage, Gabrielle pushed open the door. There was Doris, perched at her desk, eyes scanning the room like a hawk. Gabrielle hesitated, considered retreating, but her legs propelled her forward. A polite hello. She slipped past, heading straight to the breakroom.

Clocking in, Gabrielle greeted colleagues. The assistant had already spilled the gossip. Gabrielle smirked; Doris had no idea her secrets were already out. When Gabrielle casually mentioned the situation, Doris's face was contorted, shocked, and annoyed. Score one for the underdog.

Doris tried to make small talk. Gabrielle eyed her phone, recording it discreetly. Trust was rare. Doris droned on, filling Gabrielle in on the last twelve weeks. Gabrielle nodded, feigning interest, while her mind replayed the assistant's revelations.

By 3:00 p.m., Doris retreated. The assistant followed. Gabrielle was alone, almost. The cameras watched. She imagined Doris dissecting her every move. Gabrielle played it safe: bare minimum, just enough.

Her kids' smiling faces stared back from her phone. She snapped a selfie, proof of her triumphant return. Social media would see joy. Her kids didn't care about office politics; they just wanted hugs. As the clock ticked toward 5:00 p.m., Gabrielle reflected. Maybe Eric's prayers worked: drama-free, secrets spilled, surveillance survived.

Day two. Gabrielle reached out to her attorney about payment. The attorney said yes. Gabrielle composed and sent the email. Silence. The administrator remained elusive. Then, a counteroffer from the company lawyer, a slap to the face. Frustration. Determination. Doris flitted in and out.

Twilight embraced the sky. Gabrielle found herself in St. Michael's embrace. RCIA delved into the enigma of Jesus. A film reframed him as a norm-defying rebel. Her husband's keen interest was a heartwarming distraction.

They received a handout: *Gospel Portraits of Jesus.*

- Matthew: the new Moses.
- Luke: the compassionate healer.
- John: the divine Son.
- Mark: the teacher in motion.

Gabrielle went home and read Luke. Mercy. Forgiveness. There may be hope after all. She needed mercy. She needed forgiveness. She would carry her cross. She would pray.

Day three. Gabrielle had become a pawn in their corporate chess game. A reluctant acrobat, teetering on the tightrope of mediocrity. Her actions were calculated. She had mastered the art of treading water. The ghosts of former colleagues haunted her thoughts. Passion extinguished. Spirits broken. Gabrielle empathized with their silent rebellion, but she refused to fade.

Social media awaited. She yearned to expose the puppeteers, to reveal the strings. But invisible chains bound her. A professional veneer stifled her righteous fire. The Kool-Aid, once sweet, now bitter. Gabrielle should have spat it out long ago, questioned the flavor, sought the antidote. Her countdown to liberation ticked relentlessly. Eric's well wishes, innocent and well-meaning, collided with her reality. *If only he knew the labyrinth she navigated.* Gabrielle soldiered on. She would bide her time and wait for the opportune moment.

Day four. Gabrielle took a decisive step. Fingers poised over the keyboard, she composed an email to her attorney: *"Appeal of Denied Sick Benefits."* She laid out her plan to challenge the denial that had stripped her safety net. Her attorney responded promptly: *I have no objection. But my expertise in labor laws is limited. Keep me informed.*

Gabrielle embarked on a quest for knowledge. She dialed the office. Her heart pounded. The voice on the other end belonged to another worker. They discussed the enigma of sick leave for salaried employees. No written policy found.

Undeterred, Gabrielle dove into legal texts, statutes, precedents. She had a right to know. Late into the night, Gabrielle crafted a letter to the office administrator. She invoked her denial letter, demanded transparency. Anger simmered. A year of bullying and tactical maneuvers had forged her resolve.

Day five. Gabrielle's birthday. A mix of emotions. Laboring for a company that cared little weighed heavily. Her husband took her out for breakfast. A bouquet. A heartfelt card.

Later, Doris appeared. Her presence threatened Gabrielle's fragile mood. She handed her a vest, months overdue. Peace offering? Calculated move? Gabrielle couldn't tell. Snide remarks hung in the air. Gabrielle wondered if Doris documented every word. But Gabrielle refused to be her pawn.

After getting home past 1:00 a.m., Gabrielle rose and went to church. She prayed for strength, for a return to the woman she was before that fateful December day. Back then, she was shedding weight physically and emotionally. But one ill-fated decision shattered her equilibrium. Jeffrey. Her heart still ached. But she was piecing herself together, seeking a fresh start beyond a lawsuit-bound career.

Back home, she and her husband settled in. Gabrielle yearned for more days when work didn't consume her.

Day six. Gabrielle worked from 10:00 a.m. to 6:00 p.m. Camaraderie bloomed. They commemorated the day with a team photo. Social media's invisible police would dissect it, furrowed brows, scrutinized smiles. As the shift neared its end, Gabrielle felt the tug of anticipation. The longing to break free intensified.

At 5:00 p.m., she veered off course, snagged elusive products, made a beeline for home. *To hell with it.* Counting down the days became her silent mantra.

The evening unfolded in her husband's embrace. Three months had woven them together. Returning to work felt like a reluctant farewell. Then Jeffrey, his name, danced through her thoughts. Where was he? What occupied his hours? Whose company did he keep? Gabrielle missed his nonexistent birthday wish. A phantom echo of what could have been. Their friendship could have blossomed. Instead, her heart bore the ache of not being enough, of missing out on a place in his world.

Day seven. The universe conspired in Gabrielle's favor. A symphony of events peaked into one of the most gratifying days of her career. At 8:00 a.m., Gabrielle stepped into the office. Her manager's expectant gaze locked onto hers.

The catalyst: a counterfeit $20 slipped into the safe. Gabrielle became a detective. Security footage. Hours of scrutiny. Every shadow traced. There it was: the smoking gun. The assistant. Doris's favorite. Caught in the act. A twist of fate. Perfect karma.

Gabrielle smiled. The universe had dealt its hand. She was ready to play. The next day promised a showdown. The assistant, blissfully unaware. Gabrielle envisioned the moment Doris would see the unraveling of her pet.

That evening, Gabrielle shifted gears. Her husband's birthday. Red Lobster. Joy in his eyes. But beneath the surface, Gabrielle's mind churned. Justice awaited. The office would be her stage. The assistant, her unwitting co-star.

Day eight. Gabrielle composed a cryptic text: *I need to talk to you about something important.*

Doris replied: *I will swing by today.*

At 3:00 p.m., Doris arrived. Curiosity. Mild annoyance. Gabrielle gestured. The game began.

- First: crew manager debacles. Gabrielle veered from the script.
- Next: safety inspection. Falsified documents. Digital breadcrumbs.

- Then: cash irregularities. Photos. Counterfeit choreography.

Doris's eyes widened. Disbelief etched her face. "How do we manage this?" Gabrielle asked.

Doris deflected. "Follow protocol."

Gabrielle chronicled her struggle. Doris's refusal fueled her. The next day, Gabrielle would email Doris, Amanda, and HR her recommendations.

As the workday dimmed, Gabrielle traded her corporate guise for her church. RCIA. Session three. Sister Katherine. Denim. Pink Crocs. Warm welcome. "Your relationship with Him is uniquely yours." No rigid dogma. No prescribed path. Just hearts seeking solace. The Trinity unfolded: Father, Son, Holy Spirit. A divine dance.

Gabrielle left the church, her heart echoing with understanding. Faith and office politics intertwined. She vowed to navigate both with grace.

Day nine. Gabrielle filled out the investigation form. Submitted it. An email arrived: *Review tomorrow.* A shift in communication. A shift in power. Gabrielle reflected. Despite the chaos, she was still in charge, at least until mediation. Covering shifts. Frustration palpable. But Gabrielle soldiered on. She yearned for change. The twenty-four-hour schedule had taken its toll. She longed for banker's hours. 9:00 a.m. to 5:00 p.m. It was time to explore starting her own business. Her own hours. Her own rules.

On a brighter note, Gabrielle was thrilled: the next day off, a reprieve. A concert, Kid Rock and Hank Williams Jr. Before leaving the office, Gabrielle sent a final email. Heavy-hearted, clear-eyed, she documented the disheartening atmosphere she returned to after her leave. She didn't expect a reply, but she felt empowered.

The letter was a blend of reflection and resolve. She spoke of her dismantled "happy wall," the dwindling team, the absence of recognition. She questioned the fairness of disciplining a manager she hadn't seen in months. She called out the mysterious personal improvement plan that appeared in her mailbox.

Gabrielle's email was more than a complaint; it was a plea for understanding. She had once called this company home. Now, she was preparing to leave it behind.

Day ten. The universe dealt a cruel hand. At 5:00 a.m., bleary-eyed and aching from a midnight concert, Gabrielle dragged herself to work.

The office was understaffed; her comrades had abandoned ship. Gabrielle waded through chaos.

Around 1:30 p.m., she ventured into the freezer to retrieve a box. Pain shot up her spine, sharp, searing, unforgiving. Gabrielle crumpled, clutching the cursed box. Desperation drove her to dial another store. *Send reinforcements!*

Her husband whisked her to urgent care. No broken bones, just agony. A vial of painkillers.

The next day blurred. Meds turned her into a drowsy marionette. The recliner cradled her. Doris deserved an update. Gabrielle dialed. Silence. She texted. Her husband had already fired off a message. Doris replied: *Okay, keep us posted.*

Meanwhile, an investigation brewed. The assistant, Doris's pet, was accused of counterfeit chicanery.

Then at midnight, the phone rang. The office needed supplies. Gabrielle rubbed her temples. Her husband answered: "Call someone else." Calm. Firm. Unbothered.

The next day, Gabrielle shuffled into the doctor's office. "Too swollen," the doctor said. New meds. No imaging.

Back home, Gabrielle texted Doris again, and attached her doctor's note. Silence. The office administrator chimed in: "Forms."

"Come to the office." Gabrielle scoffed. "Send them to me. I can't drive."

They complied.

Then: "Your husband can drop them off." Gabrielle laughed. Seriously?

She filled out the forms, wobbly penmanship. No response.

Then: "Workers' comp claim?"

Gabrielle consulted her attorney. "Pursue it," she said. Gabrielle typed her reply, determined.

Then: "Bring your keys."

Gabrielle replied: "My husband will drop them off."

He delivered them to the assistant. "The thief." The store teetered. Doris stirred chaos. But Gabrielle refused the Kool-Aid. Loyalty had its limits. She had learned her lesson.

Despite Gabrielle's initial reluctance, she and her husband ventured to church for their fourth RCIA session. In the soft glow of the sanctuary, they found solace. Scriptures came alive. The priest's tales wove through the air, binding the congregation in a shared journey of faith.

The liturgical dance, sitting, standing, kneeling, was a delightful puzzle Gabrielle embraced. Her notes, a testament to wisdom shared. Together, they stumbled toward grace.

The next day, her back still inflamed, Gabrielle returned to the doctor. No imaging, just a change in medication. One pill a day, a bridge between pain and possibility. She dialed Doris's voicemail: "Off work until further notice." The irony made her chuckle. She emailed the office administrator. Silence.

Back home, Gabrielle and her husband celebrated their anniversary. Quiet hours ahead. Their shared gimpy bodies became an unseen benefit, whisper, muted laughter, love a balm for weary souls.

Then Jeffrey etched into her heart. Memories wrestled, hope lingered. *Destiny, hurry up*, she whispered. *Bring him back or teach me to live without him.* Ten months. His absence reverberated. The unsent letter weighed heavy in her outbox. *What if he dismissed her? What if silence was his answer? Why wasn't she good enough?*

The question echoed. Jeffrey locked her out. Gabrielle prayed. Jeffrey was a note in the symphony of her life. A hug, an embrace, could mend the rift. She held space for him, for paths to meet, for prayers to find their echo.

Then news arrived: mediation yanked back five weeks. Her attorney relayed the twist, a new lawyer, a blurred date. Mediation held her captive. Another settlement offer wrapped in legal jargon. *Bullshit*, Gabrielle thought. Why this tango? If they held damning evidence, why not litigate? Payroll persisted. Gabrielle remained ensnared. Twenty-nine days. Could she rise from the ashes of paperwork and pain?

The workers' comp liaison called Gabrielle. Doctor's appointments? Granted with caveats. A nurse would orchestrate her medical ballet. Her husband stood sentinel, recording the symphony of legality. Would they honor her doctor? Suspense lingered. Her back bore the weight of uncertainty.

Ten days. A lifetime of discomfort. Healing tiptoed. Meds lulled her into oblivion. She cocooned in solitude. The doctor would examine her. A return part-time was a tentative promise.

Later that evening, RCIA session five. Sacraments unfolded: baptismal plunge, whispered penance, Eucharist feast, anointed confirmation, matrimonial vows, holy orders, anointing of the sick. Portals to the Infinite. Gabrielle pondered their role in her life. Resolutions danced in candlelight, for her job, for Jeffrey, for destiny's threads to weave him back.

The next morning, sunlight filtered through the doctor's window. Her second visit. Pain still clung. "MRI," he said, a glimpse into the labyrinth. Gabrielle dialed workers' comp; they would orchestrate the scan.

She texted Doris: *Still off work.*

Doris replied: "Wishing you a swift recovery."

Gabrielle's silent retort: *Yeah right, you fake bitch.* The corporate veneer cracked, resentment pulsed, but Gabrielle held her tongue. Survival demanded it.

Later, an email from her attorney: the settlement offer, a reluctant concession. Negotiations were a tightrope. They stood at opposite ends of a chasm, terms and expectations yawning wide. Mediation loomed. Twenty-four days. Each tick echoed her impatience.

The workers' comp emissary called: "MRI this coming week." Gabrielle wondered at the delay. Did they harbor secrets with her spine? Did they hope her pain would vanish? She chuckled, twisted humor.

Monday arrived. The MRI machine awaited. Not life and death, but life in limbo. A month of pain meds. Chemical embrace. Twenty-three days until mediation. A courtroom ballet. Dollars pirouetted. Justice waltzed with impatience.

Amid the legal tango, her thoughts strayed to Jeffrey. Was he happy? Healthy? Gabrielle yearned for his voice, his counsel. But reality pierced her reverie. She was a footnote, a forgotten chapter. Her heart clung to hope. She dared not reach out. Rejection loomed.

Wednesday evening, RCIA session six. St. Michael's welcomed them. The path to Catholicism was no stroll; it was a pilgrimage, a marathon of faith.

Each Wednesday, Gabrielle found solace: gentle guidance, shared wisdom, a tapestry of understanding. Sundays became sanctuary. Quietude settled her mind, sacred space between her and the divine.

Her husband walked beside her. Gabrielle resolved to be a better wife, to cherish him as he cherished her. RCIA nudged her toward a deeper love, one that reached for the eternal.

Father James illuminated the Eucharist, the Sacrament of Initiation. Bread became grace. Wine became redemption. The Tabernacle held a treasure guarded by faith. The Eucharist, a symphony of gratitude, whispering of love's sacrifice, of mercy's embrace.

The day arrived. MRI. Sterile embrace. Mechanical arms. Gabrielle lay still. A peculiar calm settled. She prayed, not hurried, not desperate, but deliberate, soul-searching. She prayed for answers, for revelations, for validation. And for Jeffrey. Resolution. Reconnection. Threads rewoven.

The MRI's pulses synchronized with her heartbeat. When it released her, they handed her a CD, a digital relic, echoes of her prayers etched in pixels. The doctor would call. She clung to that promise.

The rest of the day blurred. Jeffrey's name surfaced. How could she reach him without shattering fragile bonds? Tears threatened. Faith whispered: *Someday. Trust the process.*

Sunday. Church. Gabrielle knelt and prayed for mundane happiness. For the ordinary to become extraordinary again. How much more could she bear? Yet in that sacred space, Gabrielle glimpsed solace. She surrendered her burdens, pondered life beyond the tumult. Happiness beckoned. She envisioned a future where joy was not a mirage.

A conversation loomed with her husband, honesty laid bare: less money, fewer benefits, more life. A trade-off she was willing to make. Gabrielle hoped for empathy, for a partner who would champion her pursuit of joy. No more misery. Just a leap into the unknown, fueled by faith and the promise of contentment.

On a serene Monday morning, Gabrielle visited her trusted doctor. The anticipation weighed heavy. Her back, an unwelcome companion. Her doctor greeted her with a reassuring smile, having studied the MRI.

The verdict: a bulging disc. A tangible explanation. Prescription: physical therapy, perhaps a cortisone shot. Pragmatic. Hopeful. As she spoke, Gabrielle felt the burden lift. A doctor in her corner. An advocate. The labyrinth of workers' comp suddenly seemed navigable. Her injury confirmed. The upcoming Monday, Gabrielle would face the workers' comp doctor, armed with confidence. The outcome veiled, but clarity beckoned.

Midweek. Gabrielle stepped into St. Michael's for RCIA session seven. Their purpose: to explore the worship space. Guided by Richard, they traced pews, marveled at stained glass, and absorbed whispered history.

In that sacred silence, Gabrielle found solace. The decision to embrace this faith felt ordained. Her husband walked beside her, his commitment mirroring hers.

Then Jeffrey. His memory had softened. Gabrielle turned inward. Maybe he grappled with his own inadequacies. Forgiveness unfurled. No anger. No bitterness. Only quiet release. Gabrielle hoped he would sense it across the chasm of silence. Their paths diverged, yet the heart held space for reconciliation. Time would reveal its verdict. For now, he lingered as her second priority, nestled between prayers and the impending mediation.

In the quiet corners of her mind, Gabrielle grappled with the weight life had placed upon her. The scale crept into the 220 lbs. mark. Her back ached. Her resolve wavered. Jeffrey lingered. A phantom ache. The *what ifs* haunted her. The mirror reflected flaws, but not the enigma of his heart. Eric, once her beacon, had gone silent. His morning messages vanished. Gabrielle let the void linger. Some friendships were meant to live in absence.

Sunday. Church became her sanctuary. Her husband held her hand. Gabrielle prayed for acceptance. Jeffrey became a prayer, a plea for peace. One day, she would speak her truth. Until then, Gabrielle clung to hope.

In the corridors of workers' comp, Gabrielle met Michelle, her nurse and guide. The verdict: physical therapy, eight weeks, two days a week. Her employer adjusted her role, surprisingly accommodating. Mediation loomed nine days away. Gabrielle prepared to reenter the workforce, bracing herself for the dual roles of patient and employee.

Her first therapy session: stretch, twist, heat. Relief. Back at work, no memo, no fanfare, just flickering fluorescent tubes. Gabrielle sat, ice pack on her back. Inbox: 210 emails. Deleted. Vaporized. Seven days to go. Her loyalty had evaporated. She would do enough to dodge the firing squad and do nothing more. Gabrielle raised her ice pack in salute. Survival. Freedom on the horizon.

RCIA session eight. Sponsor meeting. Her husband disappeared into the hallowed halls. Gabrielle bowed her head, prayed for resolution, whispered Jeffrey's name, and asked for divine guidance. The weight of uncertainty pressed, but Gabrielle clung to faith. God would lead her through the labyrinth.

As the class unfolded, they delved into the sacred art of gathering and listening. For Catholics, it was more than words, a divine choreography. Synodality emerged: collective discernment, the whisper of the Holy Spirit urging the Church to lean in. Listening became ritual. Gathering became graceful. Candles flickered. Revelation danced. Gabrielle carried this understanding.

The church doors opened. The night embraced them. Hearts attuned, ready to gather the whispers of eternity.

Halloween Eve. Gabrielle toiled from 10:00 a.m. to 6:00 p.m. Her second day back. She drifted with the current, minimal effort, tranquil acceptance. Six days remained. Freedom loomed.

At her desk, her personal laptop hummed. Gabrielle penned an email to her attorney, shaped by her employer's accommodations. Her attorney replied: "Not much longer." Mediation loomed. Legal negotiation awaited.

Within the sterile confines, no visitors came. Gabrielle became a specter, a harbinger of solitude. She mused an invisible plague. Cameras watched. Doris dissected. Gabrielle longed to rebel, to raise a defiant finger to the lens.

Then a revelation: her buddy GM called. Because of Gabrielle, corporate now sought a supervisor of leaves, a position carved from her own narrative. *At least christen it in her honor*, Gabrielle thought. A wry smile tugged. Irony danced. Her legacy etched in bureaucratic ink. She would regale her attorney and her husband. *Boo, bitches*, she'd whisper. Laughter echoing through unseen corridors. Six days remained. Gabrielle lingered, a ghostly apparition, her heart aflame.

Day three. Her morning began with physical therapy. Despite the ache, Gabrielle soldiered on.

At the office, a manager approached. "You're not at full capacity," he said, "but having you back brightened my day." His words resonated. Ironically, he had once been the recipient of her disciplinary actions. His tenure under Gabrielle's supervision spanned five years, diligent, dependable, and a quiet force.

But her absence had taken its toll. In a moment of vulnerability, he confessed his discontent: Doris, the office, the looming specter of layoffs. Gabrielle listened, appreciated his candor, but withheld her truth. Mediation loomed. She would not be returning, not after the ink dried. She navigated the corridors, her secret tucked away.

Day four. The office hummed. Gabrielle danced the bare-minimum ballet, illusion of productivity, maximum survival. Assigned to the assembly line: monotony, repetition. But Gabrielle had an audience: security cameras. She leaned in, feigned exertion, winced dramatically. Oscar-worthy.

At home, her husband floated a dream: "Let's sell everything and move to Florida." Tantalizing. Terrifying. A fresh canvas. Could they flip the page? Mediation loomed. Excitement and anxiety tangled. Gabrielle clung to the promise of a fresh start.

Day five. Two more days. Sweet liberation. Post-work: Dress Barn. The mission: armor for mediation. Her *kiss-my-ass* outfit. Her husband, her lighthouse, love unwavering, pessimism persistent. She adored him, flaws and all. Three days to go.

Jeffrey tiptoed into her thoughts. Should she reach out or let silence stretch? Fear whispered. She deferred action.

Homebound at 5:00 p.m., fatigue clung, anxiety and hope brewed. Her attorney would wield the wand. Gabrielle trusted her. Three more days. Each tick a heartbeat. She whispered to the ceiling: *Let this end well.* Dreams of closure. A courtroom gavel. Fresh beginnings. *Three more days. Three more days. Three more days.*

Day six. Her final physical day at work, a bittersweet ballet. Clock-watching, quiet rebellion. Her team, refuge. She, the pariah. The invisible plague. She purged her digital existence: emails gone, traces erased, artifacts boxed. A silent farewell. Cleaning? Not her concern. Her heart whispered: *Leave it better than you found it.* Her ego jeered: *Go out with a bang, bitch.* At 3:00 p.m., she stepped out, hopefully for the last time. The air tasted different. Peace settled.

Homebound. Nails were freshly painted. Grocery aisles blurred. Mundane tasks her lifeline. Jeffrey lingered, uninvited, unshakable. She spoke to him as if he were standing beside her. Her heart wrestled: wait, reach out, let silence stretch. Life played discordant notes. She needed rhythm. Three more days. Each a universe. Sleep tangled in longing. *Guide me*, she whispered. Her heart vowed to cooperate, even if it took a symphony of patience and courage. Jeffrey, her unfinished melody. She danced on the precipice, ego and grace, letting go and holding on.

Wednesday morning. The phone rang. Her attorney: urgency and reassurance. Doris and Amanda would be present at mediation, a power play, intimidation. But they wouldn't speak. Her attorney gave her shield. Gabrielle swallowed indignation, focused on the practical. She didn't need to say much; her truth was already stitched. Still, their presence gnawed.

After the call, Gabrielle shifted gears. Her back led her to physical therapy, grueling, promising. Movement returned, pain receded. A small victory in the grand scheme. She hoped these sessions would soon be memories, not milestones.

Evening found them at church. RCIA class awaited. Candlelight flickered, a silent promise of continuity and hope. Gabrielle prayed for strength, for mediation, for the courage to turn the page.

Jeffrey's memory surfaced unexpected comfort, not ache but echo. The class focused on the Eucharist, a celebration of Thanksgiving, a spiritual journey that mirrored her own. Introductory rites. Liturgy of the Word. The gathering. The listening.

Then, Liturgy of the Eucharist, the heart of the Mass. Bread and wine transformed, shared. Once a maze, now a map. Gabrielle saw her life in the rhythm of the ritual: confusion to clarity, turmoil to peace.

As she left the church, the lesson lingered. The Mass had become a metaphor, a mirror. With each step, Gabrielle felt more prepared to close the old chapter with grace, to begin painting a new, brighter story.

The day dawned with weighty significance. A career's closing chapter, etched in Gabrielle's life. Her husband stood beside her as they entered the mediation room. Once proceedings commenced, he was ushered out, leaving her to face Doris, Amanda, and the company attorney. Their presence loomed, threatening yet impotent. Her attorney never wavered. Gabrielle met their gaze with steely resolve, refusing to be cowed.

The clock ticked past 8:30 a.m. Anticipation thickened. Mediation was slated for 9:30 a.m., but bureaucracy danced to its own rhythm. By the time they convened, the sun had climbed higher, casting harsh light on the negotiation table.

They gathered, rearranged themselves for the final gambit. Gabrielle and her attorney were escorted to a smaller room. Negotiations began, a delicate dance of words, concessions, and veiled threats. Hours blurred. Back and forth they swayed.

At 2:15 p.m., the scales tipped. Gabrielle settled for less than she had hoped, but the shackles fell away. Freedom awaited. Her hard-fought victory would materialize in a month's time. Then, with a sigh, Gabrielle would close the chapter, a bittersweet farewell to a familiar narrative.

Post-mediation, Gabrielle and her husband sought refuge at Red Lobster. Dim lighting softened reality. She handed him an unofficial copy of the settlement. Relief washed over them both.

Back home, fatigue settled. Twenty-four years of corporate tides had shaped her. Now, her phone lay dormant. No urgent calls. No emails. Peace enveloped her. The next day, Gabrielle vowed to cleanse her digital slate. Apps would vanish. Memories erased. The company's imprint would fade, replaced by the promise of new beginnings.

That night, Gabrielle nestled in bed. Jeffrey's ghost lingered. *This is your threshold*, he seemed to say. *Cross it with grace.* She surrendered to sleep, ready to awaken to a world unbound by corporate chains. A few loose ends remained, like the keys to her former workplace. A symbolic gesture. Gabrielle prepared to unlock new doors.

The night before was a revelation, the best sleep in months. No deadlines. No demands. Just rest. The next morning, there was a different kind of therapy. Her back found solace in skilled hands. Knots unraveled. Tension released.

Lunch with her husband, mundane yet celebratory. A toast to possibilities. Then: the movies. Popcorn. Darkness. Laughter. The grocery store. Aisles of promise. Home. Afternoon sun painted soft hues.

Evening arrived. Spontaneity sparked. The casino beckoned. Gabrielle booked a two-day stay. Her husband's eyes widened. She promised restraint. A spa massage awaited. He chuckled, resigned. "*Okay*," he said.

As Gabrielle lay in bed, peace settled. No anxiety. No depression. Just her, her husband, and the quiet rhythm of their breathing. For the first time in ages, her heart knew only stillness.

Day two of freedom. Gabrielle awoke with anticipation. Sun streamed through the curtains. She and her husband began with church, seeking solace and stillness. He let her take the wheel on their drive to the casino: unexpected trust.

The road stretched ahead, winding through picturesque landscapes. They stopped for lunch at a roadside diner: comfort food, warm air, easy laughter.

The casino loomed, a realm of possibility, luck, chance. He played blackjack; she, the slot machines. Luck eluded her, but the thrill remained. Fueled by excitement or free drinks, Gabrielle overindulged. The alcohol blurred her edges. She stumbled back to their room, giddy and nauseous, crawling into bed, the room spinning. Outside, snowfall danced in the glow of streetlights.

In the quiet darkness, her mind wandered. Florida. His suggestion echoed, a fresh start, a warmer life. Exciting. Terrifying. To leave familiar faces, to know only a few. The weight of decision pressed.

At 4:00 a.m., Gabrielle lay awake. Unemployment settled in. The journey was far from over. She closed her eyes, listening to the snowfall, wondering where life would lead.

The next morning whispered serenity. Room service arrived: coffee, croissants, a tray of delights. They descended the grand staircase. The spa waited. Their therapists greeted them. Knots unraveled, muscles surrendered. Beside her, her husband sighed. They shared a glance, a silent treasure.

After the spa, the hot tub beckoned. They sank into warmth. Back in their room, they napped, cocooned in softness. Dinner arrived by candlelight. They showered, washed away the day, slipped into bed, fingers entwined.

They whispered gratitude for the day, for each other, for the quietude. Reality would return. But for now, they lingered, vowing to carry a piece of this peace back home. To pray more. To nourish their bodies. To cherish stolen moments. Her husband's eyes met hers. They had created a sanctuary.

The sun peeked through the curtains. Rumpled sheets. 9:00 a.m. Their journey home a blur of mundane moments. The miles stretched before them, a ribbon of asphalt leading nowhere and everywhere.

Homecoming was bittersweet. They settled on the couch, cocooned in blankets, gazes fixed on the flickering screen. The TV played mindless shows, but their minds were far from idle. They were suspended in limbo, waiting. The final settlement loomed, a transaction, a severance, a permission slip to move forward.

Jeffrey haunted her thoughts. Gabrielle yearned to reach out, but fear held her captive, fear that her words would fall into the abyss. So, she clung to silence. Her heart echoed the void. Tears came, familiar paths down her cheeks. She mourned not only what was lost but the impossibility of reclaiming it. The past was a locked door. Gabrielle fumbled for the key, knowing it was forever out of reach.

Yet hope lingered. Maybe fate would intervene. Maybe Jeffrey would respond. Maybe silence would break. Or maybe life would unfold indifferent to her desire. Gabrielle whispered her plea to the universe, surrendered her heartache to God's hands. *If it is meant to be*, she murmured, *"let it be."* Then she released it.

But the hardest battle lay within, to convince her heart to let go, to prepare for the moment she might reach out, to be done with the ache, the loop of shattered hopes. It was a war waged silently in the chambers of her soul. Gabrielle waited. The road ahead uncharted. But she clung to faith.

Day five of freedom. Life unfolded in unexpected ways. Morning sun cast a hopeful glow. Physical therapy: skilled hands, knots unraveled, relief, apprehension. Returning home, a certified letter: *Return the keys.* Curiosity mingled with annoyance. Why not just call? But maybe there was poetry in the bureaucracy. Gabrielle entertained a wicked thought:

certified mail as a proclamation of defiance. Her inner rebel yielded to reason. She would save her pennies and her peace.

Twilight painted the sky. They ventured to St. Michael's. Gabrielle had an appointment with Richard. Her husband waited, exchanging pleasantries with Father James.

Meanwhile, Richard and Gabrielle engaged in soul-searching. "How is your relationship with God?" Gabrielle spoke of peace, the kind that settles in wooden pews, which echoes ancient hymns. She and her husband navigated RCIA's labyrinth. Wednesday evenings became sacred date nights. Mass dissected, mysteries parsed, solace found in shared faith. Their bond deepened. In this spiritual odyssey, they discovered not only God but each other, a communion of souls.

For nine days, Gabrielle's life took a different rhythm. She peeled away layers of work-related stress. Her phone now rested lighter in her pocket. Only the team member app remained, soon to vanish with the final paycheck. No frantic calls, no desperate pleas, no chaos. The nights became sanctuary. Restful slumber cradled her. Peace settled into the chambers of her heart, a long-overdue guest. *Why didn't I do this sooner?* she whispered.

The next day marked the beginning of transformation. Diet. Exercise. Determination. Her goal: reclaim her body, shed weight, stand below 200 lbs. by January 1st. A milestone etched in resolve. The echoes of rock bottom still reverberated, but Gabrielle was ascending. The new year would be her solid ground. She would plant her feet, recalibrate her compass, march forward.

Jeffrey occupied her mind. Their paths had diverged. A letter existed only in her mind. Would she ever transcribe it? Would she reach out? Would he respond? Or would silence swallow her words? Her heart quivered.

The sun dipped below the horizon. Jeffrey's name lingered in the sacred space of whispered pleas. Gabrielle knew God heard her. She felt it in the quietude that followed. *When the time is right*, she murmured, you will put him back in my life. The wooden pew cradled her weary soul. Eyes closed, seeking solace. Patience, they said, was the key.

After church, Gabrielle returned home. The unemployment handbook lay on the kitchen table, a roadmap through the labyrinth of bureaucracy. She never imagined financial stability would be so intricate. Filing for benefits became an odyssey, mirroring the twists and turns of her heart.

Jeffrey's memory was a persistent companion. Almost a year had slipped by, yet his absence felt raw, as if the calendar had not turned at all. Sundays became sanctuary. Gabrielle knelt, implored the heavens. *Put him back in my life*, she whispered. *Send me a sign.* Longing. Regret. Hope. She wondered how he would react to her life now. Would he understand? *Why?* she asked. *Why does he linger?* Maybe Jeffrey was her unfinished chapter, a story waiting for its final lines. That year swept away her job, her routines, her certainties. But it gave her clarity.

Amidst the chaos, Gabrielle glimpsed purpose. *Trust the process,* they said. So, Gabrielle stepped forward, placed herself at the forefront after years of self-neglect. Yet worry clung. Would everything align? Would life stitch its frayed edges into a seamless whole? She didn't know. But she clung to faith. Gabrielle prayed. Each word was a fragile vessel launched into the divine. *Guide me*, she whispered. *Show me the way.* And in the quietude that followed, Gabrielle found solace.

Wednesday. Their tenth RCIA session. Gabrielle and her husband delved deeper into Mass. The Liturgy of the Eucharist: bread and wine, life and labor, transformed. The Great Amen. The Lord's Prayer. The exchange of peace. Holy Communion, a profound moment of unity with Jesus. Gabrielle felt more connected. The structure, the meaning, the rhythm of reverence.

Richard urged them to prepare for Mass by reading Scripture in advance, not just following the Missal but entering the mystery with open hearts. Gabrielle chuckled. New homework, but she welcomed it.

Day sixteen of unemployment. A curious blend of liberation and uncertainty. The clock ticked. The day waltzed. Gabrielle found solace in the rhythm. She laced up her sneakers, three miles at the gym. 200 lbs. by January 1st, a whispered resolution, a pact with her soul.

The treadmill hummed. Gabrielle pushed forward. Afternoon sun dipped low. Fatigue tugged. A nap, a luxurious indulgence.

In that hazy space, Jeffrey materialized. His name reverberated. The letter was penned but unsent. Ink drying. Emotions suspended. To send or not to send? His standards towered. Gabrielle traced the contours of her imperfections. But she persisted. Mentally she sharpened. Physically she sculpted. Emotionally she mended. Would their paths cross again? She whispered her hopes to the wind, a silent prayer. *Someday*, she murmured, *he'll meet a different version of me.* Patience became her mantra. Sundays became sanctuary. Hymns lifted her spirit.

But another calling tugged: the fitness industry. A vision unfurled, Gabrielle, a certified trainer, guiding others toward their best selves. Her husband, the gatekeeper of this dream. How would she convince him? Her transformation would be her testimony.

The next day, her inbox bore weight: an eleven-page draft settlement. Her attorney's email, ink and paper, months of negotiations, sleepless nights, quiet desperation. Gabrielle marveled at the dance of legalese. Clauses pirouetted. Provisions bowed. They had parsed every comma. This time it felt different. Finality loomed. *Did we miss anything?* she mused. They hadn't missed a beat. Gabrielle typed: *I am okay with everything.* Her heart echoed the words. A fragile hope blossomed. Maybe the saga would find its denouement by week's end. But realism tempered her. Justice never favored haste. She exhaled a silent prayer. *Hold on*, she whispered. *Hold on a little longer.* The finish line loomed. She clung to faith. Trust the process. Trust the unseen gears grinding slowly.

As the sun dipped, her thoughts wandered to Jeffrey. His name haunted her solitude. She missed him. Regret gnawed. Why had he pushed her away? She replayed their moments, his laughter, her hesitation. *What if?* she wondered. One night they could have rewritten their story. A year had slipped away. Why wasn't she enough? Would their paths ever converge again?

That night, Gabrielle penned a letter. Words woven with vulnerability, inked with longing. She hesitated. Rejection loomed. Maybe she'd tuck it away. Maybe she'd press send. For now, Gabrielle sat there, a settlement in one hand, a letter in the other. Straddling legality and longing. The week waned. The year stretched ahead. Fingers crossed, heart open. Somewhere, amidst the clauses and constellations, resolution awaited.

The Season of Becoming

"To everything there is a season, and a time for every purpose under heaven."

—Ecclesiastes 3:1

Happy Thanksgiving. Twenty-one days of respite, no dash to work, no exile from family warmth. For twenty-four years, duty had yanked Gabrielle away, but not this time. She and her husband journeyed to her brother's home, arriving at midday, departing at sunset.

Then came the Black Friday safari. Gabrielle and her sister braved Kohl's and Walmart. Her stoic husband endured. Her sister clashed carts, bruises earned, victory claimed. As Walmart's doors slid shut, her husband declared, "Never again." Gabrielle reveled in the absence of haste. Liberation tasted sweet.

The next day, on the way to physical therapy, Gabrielle glimpsed her old workplace. She chuckled, imagining herself as a casual customer but resisted.

Saturday. Mass. Advent whispered: anticipation, quiet hope. Would this be Gabrielle's renewal? Memory pressed in. A year ago, Jeffrey had entered her orbit, quick wit, kind eyes. They danced on the edge of friendship. December unraveled. Longing remained.

In her room, Gabrielle poured a tear-stained confession. *Read this. Understand.* Courage wavered. Doubt gnawed. Would he dismiss her? Silence loomed. Yet a fragile flame persisted. Soon, the Rite of Acceptance at St. Michael's. If he read it, he would know: his friendship was a compass, his laughter a hymn.

Sunday. Gabrielle stood at a crossroads of vulnerability and restraint. Should she reveal her departure? The cursor blinked. Resolve wavered. She chose grace, resisting raw candor. Thoughts fermented. Prayers wove through tangled threads.

Monday. Clarity in a sterile office. Six months etched their mark. The verdict: no more medications. Her body, unshackled from tension, breathed relief. Her husband rejoiced. Yet a shadow clung: the specter of regained weight. Her doctor dispelled doubt. "Be kind to yourself," she said. "Three months. Diet. Exercise. Grace."

Over breakfast, her husband leaned in. "Florida," he said, a vision of permanence. Gabrielle stood at a crossroads. Her mother, a compass. Another voice surged: "Hell yeah." Neighbors would change. Friends remain etched in memory. Was his invitation real or ephemeral? Gabrielle squinted at the horizon, seeking clarity.

Wednesday. St. Michael's again. The liturgical calendar unfurled. Doubt clouded. A handout appeared: *Rite of Acceptance.* Saturday loomed, a threshold. Gabrielle's heart fluttered. Nervousness pirouetted with anticipation. She chuckled, imagining God's bemused gaze. *Better late than never*, she whispered. Missed chances, grace-laden detours had led her there.

Illness and emotion intertwined. Memory swept her back to the message she wished erased. His resounding "no" echoed. *Yes*, she had hoped. Even for one night, she would have bartered everything. Regrets? None. Jeffrey remained her weakness. His absence haunted her. Letters bled ink and tears. *Knock*, her heart urged. Would he open? Gabrielle beseeched the heavens. The only response: ache.

Saturday. The Rite of Acceptance. Gabrielle and her husband rose early, shared breakfast, and stepped into church. Mass loomed. Her husband's presence offered comfort, yet nerves danced.

Sister Katherine guided their retreat, radiant in pink Crocs, gentle wisdom. "God's presence is everywhere," she said. The retreat culminated in a sacred exercise: a letter to their future selves. Gabrielle held a candle, its flicker God's unwavering light. With pen in hand, she poured reflections: uncertainty, farewell, Jeffrey. During quiet reflection, she composed an email to Jeffrey. She prayed he would respond.

Evening Mass began. Gabrielle stood, heart poised between hope and trepidation. Threads of connection and closure were woven. Within the church's embrace, she discovered God's light shines even in crevices of doubt. The candle she carried home cradled hope, forgiveness, transformation.

Gabrielle's email to Jeffrey was a reckoning, a confession, a thank-you prayer. She named the wound, the gift, his absence, the catalyst for rebirth. She told him: *You were the wise man.* She prayed for him daily. She hoped if paths crossed again, he would see the new version of her. And then, she pressed send.

Jeffrey responded. Simple. Kind. Blessing her journey. Calling her "friend." It was enough. Gabrielle exhaled. The thread had softened.

That same day, she posted her farewell. A month had passed since she left her career. Rumors swirled. She chose truth. From $6.50 an hour to manager, from debt to degrees, from fluorescent lights to freedom. She spoke of colleagues as family, friendships outlasting paychecks, meeting the love of her life. No bitterness. No regret. She honored legacy, integrity, and care. She quoted the wise man: *Our moments define us.* She signed off: *That is my side of the story.*

Four days later. Gabrielle sat in the hush of the doctor's office. Her back carried hope. The nurse smiled. *Healing is not a race.* The doctor prescribed gel, four applications a day. Pain meds history. Tylenol occasional. Grace daily. Her husband raised his brows. "Maybe this ordeal has a silver lining," he said. Gabrielle agreed. The company wouldn't contest her injury, a small victory.

That evening was their final RCIA class of the year. The parish hall hummed. They explored the Rite of Acceptance, ancient rituals, centuries of believers. The Mass unfolded, Eucharist a thread between earth and divine. Then the Christmas story: angels, mangers, stars. Mary, luminous and steadfast.

The next day, Gabrielle's kitchen became a sanctuary. Flour dusted her apron. Fudge, potica, truffles, each treat a testament to friendship. Her husband declared, "No sharing the potica." Gabrielle laughed. Generosity would prevail. She compiled her list of friends. Her husband hesitated. "We can't afford it."

"We can't afford not to," Gabrielle replied.

Friday. Physical therapy, three sessions left. Relief on the horizon. Then Christmas shopping. Her husband trailed a scrooge-shaped cloud. Gabrielle snapped: "Enough! I deserve a merry season."

Back in the kitchen, candy-making soothed her nerves. Neighbors would smile. That would be her reward. Then came challenge coins, tokens of camaraderie. Jeffrey's name appeared. Gabrielle didn't pry. He delivered gifts. Neighbors beamed. Spirit flickered anew.

Later, a message: settlement paperwork untangled. Dinner and a movie followed, but Gabrielle yearned for Christmas lights. Her husband accelerated past, muttering "Florida." Each year she clung to fragile hope. Maybe this time he would pause. Reality proved stubborn. Church became sanctuary. Gabrielle prayed, hoping hymns would soften his heart. Frost remained.

Sunday morning. They entered church. Gabrielle felt burdens lift. Homecoming was metamorphosis. They shed Sunday best. The gym awaited. Redemption beckoned. 199 lbs., a milestone. But storms came. 227 lbs., faltering steps. Gabrielle berated herself. Missed chances echoed. This time, the battle was hers. The coming year would be her anthem for the woman in the mirror hungering for validation.

Christmas beckoned. Gabrielle baked with devotion. Tin boxes awaited. Her husband's grandchildren would unwrap joy. Amidst flour-dusted chaos, a specter lingered: Jeffrey. Gabrielle prayed for him. Forgiveness was elusive yet essential. Could she forgive herself for faltering?

His absence gnawed, an unfinished melody. His smile haunted her solitude. *What if?* The question ricocheted. What if their bond had defied fate? Life carved its path. Gabrielle grappled with memories and whispered intentions to the stars, a fragile melody cradling her weary heart.

Monday. A twist. Her husband wished to deliver gifts to dear friends, Jeffrey among them. Gabrielle crafted messages. Friends responded. Jeffrey remained silent. They delivered cookies to a church pantry.

A friend whispered, "Jeffrey is here." Gabrielle followed, hesitant. His presence radiated indifference and curiosity. Two hugs, entry and exit, fleeting, profound. His eyes swept over her. Words eluded. Eye contact a chasm. Her husband mediated. Minutes stretched. Was his aloofness defense or disinterest? Did she project insecurities? Maybe he wrestled too with unspoken narratives.

They left swiftly. The car cocooned her. Gabrielle exhaled, breath of unanswered questions. Jeffrey remained an enigma. The gift felt like a bridge suspended between past and present. God whispered: *Not yet. Threads need time to weave.*

The next day dawned with celebration. Gabrielle's mother turned eighty. Laughter filled the room, wrinkles etched stories, eyes sparkled with mischief. Gabrielle marveled at her compass, her anchor. A year ago, fear had gripped her. That day, she stood radiant. Candles flickered. Gabrielle vowed: *If I reach eighty, let me wear my years with elegance.*

Evening brought gratitude. A thank-you arrived. The challenge coin played its part. Jeffrey remained silent. *Why persist? Why crave validation from someone who saw her as less?* Doubt etched itself into her bones.

The next day: resilience. Breakfast with old friends. Laughter wove the air. Gabrielle offered a vague explanation, a mutual parting of ways. No questions. A truce.

Later, Jeffrey's message arrived, polite, measured. Her husband extended an olive branch: breakfast. Jeffrey declined. "Why bother?" Gabrielle asked. Her husband shrugged: "Busy. No malice. Just life." His nonchalance baffled her. Gabrielle wore armor too, fragile, patched with insecurities.

Physical therapy ended. Muscles kneaded, whispered kindness. Freedom, yes, but also a void. Each lift had been a step toward strength.

Home welcomed her with quiet. Her husband slept. Gabrielle melted chocolate, glossy, reflective, a mirror of emotion. Peach Jim Beam. Patrón. Unlikely companions for a solitary celebration. She molded chocolates for the grandkids and her brother's house.

Jeffrey's memory crashed over her. Would he have stood beside her? Apron-clad? Laughing? Or snoring softly, unaware? Tears mingled with chocolate. *Would she ever be enough for Jeffrey, for herself?*

Unemployment beckoned. Gabrielle filed paperwork, a lifeline across uncertainty. Settlement money hovered. Bills whispered. Worker's comp held the key. Progress trickled. January loomed, a fresh canvas. Would it bring closure?

Saturday sun streamed. Anticipation. Her husband's kids and grandkids awaited celebration. Beyond tinsel and gifts, urgency. Christmas morning would unfold beneath Florida's sun.

St. Michael's stood serene. Her husband chose a spot near the altar. Gabrielle followed, discomfort a silent companion. The Eucharist, a bridge she could not yet cross. Her heart ached as she watched others partake.

Jeffrey, a fragile prayer on her lips. He had reappeared briefly, enough to ignite hope. Gabrielle thanked God for that moment. She was not ready. Jeffrey's indifference wounded. Did he know how she clung to stolen moments?

The priest's voice rose. Gabrielle listened. *Why hold on? What invisible thread bound her?* She could not unravel the mystery. As the hymn swelled, Gabrielle bowed her head. The congregation rose. She was both captive and willing prisoner.

The church doors opened. Her husband's hand found hers. They stepped into the night. *Why Jeffrey?* The question echoed.

The sun traced its arc. The house hushed. Her husband's laughter echoed from afar, go-karting with his boys. Gabrielle had expected a day together. The boys rewrote the script. She felt a pang. He dismissed it: "No big deal." She nodded, swallowed discontent.

The clock ticked. She poured Patrón. Solitude settled. Intoxication blurred thought. The house echoed with absence. Gabrielle wondered: *Where was Jeffrey*? Whose laughter accompanied him? She longed to whisper *Merry Christmas* across the void. Reality tethered her fingers. Silence remained.

The year ahead loomed. Would it hold forgiveness? A bridge back? Had she become a footnote? Gabrielle prayed. God bore witness. She was a speck, a forgotten constellation.

The boys returned. Laughter trailed. Her husband watched, eyes holding questions. He said nothing. Gabrielle retreated to sleep. Darkness cloaked the room. Jeffrey's name whispered through her mind. She clung to the night, her heart fragile.

Christmas Eve. Tradition guided them to her brother's house. Her husband sought forgiveness. Gabrielle granted it. But the echo lingered. Her family gathered around the tree. No stress. No deadlines. They lingered, the last to leave.

The night held magic. Stars emerged. They made their way to St. Michael's. Midnight Mass yielded to practicality. Florida beckoned. Her husband chose the earlier service.

The church doors opened, flickering candles, children's choir. Gabrielle knelt, fingers tracing the pew. Jeffrey etched on her heart. She prayed for him, as always. His absence tugged. Did he know? Could he sense her plea?

After Mass, they returned home. Suitcases ready. 4:30 a.m., bleary-eyed travelers. Gabrielle hoped to sleep on the plane. Her secret wish: Starbucks open. Her mood would shape his. Their unspoken pact. The wheels would lift them toward warmth, palm trees, promise.

The new year, not just a date, a canvas. Redemption. Hope. Jeffrey remained distant yet present. Would he forgive her? Would paths converge? Gabrielle clung to hope.

As the clock ticked toward morning, she surrendered to sleep. The plane awaited. Florida beckoned. Maybe it would be a great start to a new year, a chapter where wishes bloomed and hearts found home.

Christmas Day. The sun had yet to stretch across the horizon when Gabrielle roused herself. 3:45 a.m. Her first holiday adventure. Her sister whisked them to the airport. Gabrielle imagined tranquility, but the terminal buzzed.

5:00 a.m. The concourse teemed with wanderers. A full flight awaited. The airline offered $200 to delay. Gabrielle clung to her seat, torn between cash and cheer. She settled into her cramped spot, reached for music, no Wi-Fi. Sleep eluded her. Her husband, stoic, endured the three-hour flight.

9:00 a.m. They touched down. Friends awaited with wide smiles. Christmas dinner unfolded. Neighbors joined. Laughter bloomed.

By 7:30 p.m., Gabrielle surrendered to sleep. But Jeffrey lingered. She wished him *Merry Christmas*. His silence spoke volumes. To be part of his life, Gabrielle vowed to become good enough.

Day two. Her husband announced their mission: not vacation but exploration. Houses. A claim in paradise. Gabrielle scoured listings. One beckoned. Three miles from friends, quiet, promising. They stepped inside. Hearts quickened. It lacked a few things, but it was close. Her husband's eyes mirrored hers. They had found their canvas. Yet shadows danced. Fueled by liquid courage, he wavered. Was this certainty or performance?

That evening, in their friend's bathroom, Gabrielle faced the scale. 238 lbs. Jeffrey's rejection left scars beyond weight. Her job, her life, unraveled. Gabrielle stood. Maybe here she'd find solace, a fresh canvas, a chance to reclaim worth.

Day three. The gym. Treadmill. Thirty minutes. Each step a promise. Massage bed. Twenty minutes. The gym whispered: *If you stay, I'll be your brushstroke.*

Post-workout, her body rebelled. Swollen feet. Swollen hands.

Later, they turned their gaze to the house. Almost everything they wanted. Her husband, usually measured, declared intent. Surprising. The house back home was legacy, his parents' memories. But maybe this was the time, a new chapter.

They met the realtor. Their offer was lowballed. Cautious, but a start. Would the sellers bite? Deposit. Signatures. Closing date: end of January. Gabrielle doubted but hope lingered.

Morning arrived crisp. Deposit made. Contract signed. The sellers had until day's end.

Afternoon brought clarity. Offer declined. A counteroffer: $5,000 concession. Closing pushed to February. Twenty-four hours to decide. Her husband weighed the scales. Friends converged. Laughter echoed. Their secret was unveiled. Curious friends asked to see it. Permission granted. A second viewing. The house stood ready.

Evening descended. Glasses clinked. Camaraderie warmed the air. Then, delight: their friend's pontoon boat beckoned. They glided along the canal. An evening etched in tranquility. A decade of New Year's Eves spent toiling faded. This was different: no work, no obligations, just possibility. Gabrielle sipped her drink and felt the weight of time.

Morning again. The house awaited. They talked about price, furniture, fate. Closer to asking price, they would make their stand. Inspection loomed. Paperwork piled.

Welcome to the new year. A year to evaluate resolve, marriage, and sanity. The gym became Gabrielle's launchpad. Goal weight: 120 lbs. Another resolution tugged: Jeffrey. Even as a social media friend, she wanted him back. As midnight struck, she wondered who Jeffrey was wishing *Happy New Year* to.

Sanibel Island welcomed them. Soft sand cradled her feet. She envisioned weekly walks, shells as tokens for their new home. She promised her husband videos. His enthusiasm waned.

Back from Sanibel, paperwork arrived. They signed. Commitment sealed. Next step: inspection. Gabrielle doubted issues.

Now came the hard part: breaking the news. She texted friends, shocked yet unsurprised. Her pool was a magnet. Her mom had sensed the change. Their old house would soon be someone else's haven. Florida, their new canvas.

On a sun-kissed afternoon, they stepped into St. Therese Catholic Church. Father Michael awaited, smile genuine. They spoke of becoming parishioners, weaving lives into the faith community. He listened, eyes steady, and the words were wise. RCIA. Baptismal waters. Renewal. Gabrielle felt belonging. "When you arrive," he said, "I'll bless your new home." His words resonated.

They embarked on their journey: change, growth, trepidation. Stress settled. Gabrielle pondered: should she reach out to Jeffrey? Would he care? Mutual friends would carry whispers. Would they reach his ears?

God's plan, they say. Gabrielle chose trust. Jeffrey would find his place in the unfolding narrative.

Her husband made lists. Pen scratched. *We need this. And this.* Lists multiplied. Gabrielle watched with admiration and exasperation. The lists haunted her. *She will fold the linens. She will sort the memories.* Gabrielle, keeper of sanity.

Two months, she whispered. Days stretched. He moaned about furniture, cursed cords, fretted heirlooms. Gabrielle, conductor of this chaotic symphony: packing tape, bubble wrap, grace. Jeffrey lingered. Would she see him before the curtain fell? Would he offer closure? Or remain a question mark? *Lord help me*, Gabrielle prayed. Maybe Jeffrey would step into the spotlight once more.

Inspection day. The realtor met them, welcoming. Beside her, the homeowner. They stepped across the threshold. Footsteps echoed. The air smelled of possibility. The realtor led them through each space. They measured nooks, envisioned furniture. Meanwhile, the inspector worked, meticulous, keen-eyed. Findings were minimal. A report would arrive the next day.

One more day before returning to familiar soil. They hadn't planned to buy so swiftly, yet there they were, standing at the precipice of change. *If not now, then when?*

The plane touched down. Evening flight. Familiar soil. Indecision settled. Gabrielle clasped her husband's hand to steady herself, or to silence swirling thoughts. Their current abode: roots of a lifetime. Memories etched into every corner. Practicalities whispered: no job, a husband whose dreams danced southward. The timing opportune.

Yet Gabrielle gazed out the window—the church, her best friend, the one who knew her secrets. How could she leave her behind? In Florida, just a handful of faces. Could they fill the void? Was this more than geography? Maybe it was the answer to whispered prayers. God's plans intricate, woven with purpose. Jeffrey, wherever he was, would find her when the time was right.

On a sun-kissed afternoon, her husband burst forth: "We bought a house! We're moving!" The secret danced in the air. Boxes stood ready. Lowe's became their first stop, moving boxes eager to pack their lives. The basement was the starting point. His lists played havoc with her thoughts. *Do this. Do that.* Enthusiasm was contagious and overwhelming. Her head throbbed.

Church was a blessing. RCIA a reprieve. They drove past Jeffrey's workplace. Gabrielle whispered hopes to the heavens, a plea for understanding, forgiveness. But deep down, she knew she was a footnote in his story. He cared less. The truth stung. Christmas had passed. Silent prayers.

Richard revealed a countdown: thirteen classes to baptism. St. Michael's waters promised renewal. Gabrielle hesitated. Florida-bound dreams veiled. Jeffrey's name echoed.

RCIA explored marriage, covenant beyond contracts. Gabrielle broached the topic. His refusal was swift. Past off-limits. The marriage's validity hung in balance. "Why," she implored, "do we attend church if you selectively adhere?" Frustration bubbled. His promise cryptic: "After your baptism." Gabrielle sensed evasion. But she knew the reckoning would return.

The sun peeked over the horizon. A whirlwind of emotions. Anticipation hung, exhilarating, nerve-racking. Gabrielle shuffled into the kitchen. There they were: those lists, scattered across the table. What to pack, what to leave, who to notify. The weight settled, threatening resolve. Her husband stood, pen poised, stubborn. Gabrielle recalled their last move. He had sworn, "Never again." Yet here they were. She chuckled at his broken promise.

Then came revelation: the financial advisor had spoken. He needed Florida residency, taxes, license, truck title. Logistics multiplied. Another trip loomed. Reality set in. Unease followed: inspections, signatures, paperwork's delicate dance. Could love withstand pressure, or would it crack under cardboard and legal jargon?

The next day, her husband regaled everyone: "We're moving to Florida!" The news echoed. Their house was a silent witness. Down in the basement, Gabrielle packed. Boxes yawned open. How had they accumulated so much? The weight pressed, a reminder of the life they were leaving.

Yet Gabrielle clung to belief: upheaval would yield beauty. A new state. A new house. A chance to rewrite the script. And then, the message to Jeffrey. Regret cascaded. One keystroke, a chain reaction. She cursed the digital echo. But maybe this move was her lifeline, a purge, a healing.

Sunday. St. Michael's. Regret whispered. Jeffrey the catalyst. In her thoughts, he sat beside her. His devotion chipped away at skepticism, revealed longing. Why hadn't they come sooner? Maybe timing was divine.

Jeffrey's presence ignited her faith. As the choir sang, Gabrielle bowed her head, whispered a prayer. God listened. Grace would find its way.

Wednesday evening. RCIA. They shared their secret with Richard. "We bought a house in Florida. We're moving permanently." Richard listened, eyes crinkled. Gabrielle longed to complete baptism at Easter. "We'll work it out," he said. Their secret became shared plan.

Her husband stood: "We're Florida-bound!" Applause erupted. Gabrielle flushed but felt belonging. RCIA had become sacred space, faith and love intertwined.

Amidst excitement, a weighty topic resurfaced: marriage. Richard led the discussion. Gabrielle glanced at her husband, hoping to broach it. He changed the subject to boxes and Florida sun. Gabrielle let it slide but knew it would return.

The week was a whirlwind. Rustling boxes, packing tape, basement organized. His lists, guiding stars, greatest vexation. The garage was a maze of boxes. Walls whispered: *No more room.* Yet they persisted.

He oscillated between calm and frenzy. To friends, he exuded confidence, a man with a mission. But alone, his tone shifted: *We must do this. We need to tackle that.* Amid chaos, solace bloomed.

Sunday Mass. Hymns swirled, peace settled. Gabrielle felt affirmation. St. Michael's was refuge. Side-by-side, they sat, worries suspended. The priest's words wove hope. Gabrielle prepared for baptism. A desire stirred: Jeffrey. Could she invite him? Courage eluded. She prayed. Maybe vulnerability would pave the way.

Wednesday evening. RCIA again. Seekers gathered. Gabrielle stole glances at her husband, comforting, perplexing. Why engage in dialogue when his beliefs diverged? His skepticism tightened within her.

Yet there they were, two souls navigating faith. Gabrielle yearned for a different sponsor, someone receptive, curious. His stance left her craving safe dialogue, a haven beyond the kitchen table.

After class, there was a nocturnal odyssey. Their truck hurtled down the highway. Gabrielle drove, tires humming her thoughts of Jeffrey. Should she reach out? Fractured connection. Hastily typed words. Digital regret. She longed to rewind, to restore warmth. Tears blurred. Miles blurred. Gabrielle prayed, pleas echoing against the windshield. The heavens remained silent. Jeffrey's heart sealed.

Dawn painted the sky. Palm trees welcomed them. Jeffrey's absence loomed. Gabrielle yearned for closure, a fleeting encounter. But reality clung. Burned bridges rarely rise. She drove on, her husband's breaths rhythmic beside her. The road whispered. Gabrielle listened. Tears lost in the wind. Jeffrey was a chapter unfinished, a melody unresolved.

1:00 p.m. The storage unit. Cardboard boxes, plastic bins, belongings spilled. Friends joined. Laughter echoed through narrow corridors. Sandwiches, stories, dreams. Evening a haze of relaxation. Gabrielle sank into the couch, eyelids heavy.

Morning dawned. His decision was sealed: Florida resident. The tax collector's office. Paperwork, stamps, license exchanged. The Sunshine State gleamed. He shared the moment online: *Shit just got real.* Likes poured in. Comments overflowed. One more task: toll roads. A pass for smooth journeys. That night, laughter again. Cozy living room. Midnight struck.

At 4:00 a.m., darkness cloaked the world. Her husband gripped the wheel. Florida's palms waved goodbye. Georgia opened its arms. Gabrielle's turn. Cruise control: 77 mph. The highway stretched.

Then, flashing lights. Rearview panic. Adrenaline surged. Gabrielle pulled over, heart pounding. The officer stern: "91 in a 70." Gabrielle knew better. Cruise control held steady. She protested. He remained unmoved. Ticket scribbled. Injustice. Her husband seethed. Four hours of colorful language. Gabrielle dialed a lawyer. "Fight it," her husband urged. They resolved to battle.

Midnight. Home. Exhaustion tugged. Gabrielle collapsed onto the couch. Dreams. And in the quiet, Jeffrey. His name whispered. A secret longing. Before the move, Gabrielle yearned to see him, to bridge what was and what could be. Courage eluded. Fear clung. She prayed. Maybe, just maybe, Jeffrey would appear.

Morning sun. Phone buzzed. The ticket mocked her. Legal labyrinth. Georgia lawyer. $350. A racket, she thought. More frustration.

Then, her husband unearthed the secret: two credit cards siphoning funds. His reaction was explosive. Transactions dissected. Gabrielle the villain. His tirade echoed. Enough. Gabrielle fled to the dollar store. Texts arrived, apologies, pleas. But she had reached her limit.

Next stop: Subway. Fresh bread. Driving home, sandwich bag beside her, Gabrielle pondered. She could have erupted but chose a different path.

Back home. Kitchen table. Silence. Wrappers crinkled. Later, bed. His apologies hung fragile. Gabrielle wondered how long peace would last. Next day, measured words. He promised to be better. She vowed transparency. A fragile alliance forged.

Days passed. Gabrielle watched. Would he revert? Countdown continued. Leaving family bittersweet. Maybe she'd find passion and purpose.

That evening, packing. Jeffrey surfaced. Missed chances. Lingering ache. His stance resolute: *No room for you in my heart.* It cut deep.

Wednesday evening. RCIA. Sacraments of Initiation:

- Baptism, the beginning. Grace bestowed.
- Confirmation, strength. The Spirit fortifying faith.
- Eucharist—union, a sacred meal.

They pondered original sin, Adam, and Eve's fall. Sin. Confession. Baptism a fresh start; confession a humble conversation with God. Richard recommended patience: "We'll go deeper when the time is right."

As the sun dipped, Gabrielle felt the weight of their move. Boxes waiting. The basement echoed emptiness. Her husband paced, sorted, and tackled the garage. But the heart of the home remained untouched. Memories clung. Gabrielle loved him fiercely, but his complaints grated. Their daily symphony of grievances had become soundtrack. How many times had she wanted to scream, "Why can't you see the beauty in this chaos?"

Monday morning. A deep breath. The "For Sale" sign unfurled. Gravity settled. The house was a cradle of memories. Built in 1965, his parents the architects. Selling tugged, but practicality nudged. Two houses, double responsibility. "One house," he declared. "One home."

The listing went live. Countdown begun. Inspections. Negotiations. No turning back. Their daughter-in-law's husband, a fresh-faced realtor, navigating the market. They cheered him on.

Tuesday. Doctor's office. Her back aching. The physician proposed injection. Urgency, the move. She wanted to mend before crossing state lines. Was it necessity or pressure? The nurse offered hope: "You can transfer your case to Florida." Reassurance.

Back home: boxes and tape. But one name persisted: Jeffrey. Regret settled. If only she could rewind. Ill-fated messages. Connection severed. She yearned to undo it all. Should silence have preserved the bond? Answers lost. Packing containers filled with belongings and missed opportunities.

Wednesday morning. Sun peeked through. A day of transition. Cardboard, bubble wrap, memories packed. A photographer arrived. Snapshots danced across screens. Footsteps echoed in empty rooms.

Gabrielle and her husband shared glances: nostalgia, anticipation. They were leaving more than a house, a repository of whispered secrets, late-night talks, children's laughter. The lens froze those memories.

Evening. St. Michael's. RCIA. Richard their guide, words a delicate dance. Continuity promised. Florida loomed. Gabrielle sat, longing stirred. St. Michael's where baptism awaited, immersion in community. Faces in RCIA companions. Stories wove a tapestry.

Her husband surprised her; his enthusiasm outpaced hers. Early mornings, he stood at the church door, laughter echoing. Gabrielle prayed silently for his joy, for permanence. Wednesday nights, Sunday mornings grace enveloped them.

But once doors closed, reality seeped in. His optimist turned skeptical. Negative Nelly. Debbie Downer. Gabrielle yearned for lasting transformation.

In class, they delved deep: sacraments of initiation, confirmation, Eucharist. But confession stirred the room. Questions fluttered: *"What if?" "What must be confessed?" "What if we forget?"* Richard stood at the helm. Was confession a labyrinth or a simple path? Richard smiled: "Fret not. It's not a riddle. It's a conversation. A dance."

He leaned in: "You'll know when it's time. Not a thunderclap, just a quiet tug at your soul." *The class leaned in, hungry for solace.* "And if your sins are murky?" Richard's eyes crinkled: "Fear not. Our priests are guides. Lay bare your heart. They will listen."

Gabrielle felt the weight of her own transgressions. But baptism, a beacon of hope. Grace would cradle her. Still, a mischievous thought: how long until she faltered again? She chuckled. The human condition, frailty, and redemption in perpetual dance.

Thursday morning. The spine group. Procedure day. From bulging discs to arthritis bewilderment. Hope clung as she lay there. Would this finally quiet the ache? Her husband went with her. Their path had been rocky lately with arguments and misunderstandings. But that morning, a glimmer: "You're always so calm," he said. "I didn't know how deeply you felt." Gabrielle chuckled inwardly. Calmness her armor. She didn't unleash tempests; she weathered them.

Back home, a bruise bloomed, testament to the needle's precision. Her husband retreated. Gabrielle cocooned in solitude. Sleep came and went. Each position a negotiation with pain. "Give it a few days," the doctor had said. Fingers crossed, she waited.

Next morning. A subtle ache. Plans? Venture out or stay in? She chose to rest. Florida awaited. Her back a question mark: would it endure the journey? She made a pact: rest, rejuvenate. Their travel bag modest, just a change of clothes. The truck laden with life. The house exhaled. Walls sighed.

Golden sun stretched. Anticipation hummed. Road trip. Gabrielle's back held up, but he insisted she relinquish the wheel. His concern touching. Gabrielle cocooned in dreams. Thoughts of Jeffrey wove through her mind. How would she summon courage? She concocted a plan: a farewell soiree hosted by her dearest friend, a pretext to invite Jeffrey. Worst-case? He wouldn't come. Just a wistful sigh. Pit stop in Georgia, respite. He waved her away: "Rest." His thoughtfulness a balm.

Then, the storage unit. Boxes spilled forth. Evening held magic: reunions, laughter echoing through corridors of time. Friends persuaded her husband to extend their stay.

As the sun dipped, he found solace in old company. Laughter echoed. Not as spry as they once were; 18-hour road trips etched lines on their faces. An extra day gifted by fate.

Gabrielle coaxed her husband into a beach escapade. He had other plans, porch swing and cold beer. "The beach," she insisted. "We need the waves." He grumbled, reluctant. But love was persuasive. Off they went, his discontent simmering.

Their journey was a mirror of marriage: laughter, bickering, unexpected twists. Then the universe intervened: a bird, a splatter of white on his beloved truck. Instant karma. Gabrielle stifled a laugh, snapped a photo.

Finally, the beach. Sand yielded, waves whispered. His irritation melted. Sanibel Island, her happy place. Seashells dotted the shore. She posted: *I found my happy place.* Dinner was simple, quiet contentment. The beach had worked its magic.

The sun peeked. A new day. They hit the road. He drove first. Miles stretched, fatigue settled. Gabrielle drove, 17, 18 hours. Each mile a lifetime. Radio hummed. Silence companioned. Thoughts swirled. *Was this move right?* Unemployment loomed. Would bonds withstand the miles? 1:00 a.m. They pulled into the driveway. Exhaustion clung. No unpacking. The house echoed.

Morning. Snow. Gabrielle muttered, "Total bullshit." Two days ago, Florida sun. Now betrayal. She posted her disdain. Friends chuckled. Meanwhile, their house listed. Two showings. Hope clung. Fingers crossed.

Later, Gabrielle met Richard. The rite of election loomed. *Do you still desire to become Catholic?* Gabrielle didn't hesitate. *Yes.* Her relationship with God deepened. Yet uncertainty lingered. "If I don't throttle my husband during this relocation, we're golden," she joked.

Richard laughed. Then solemn: their marriage not confirmed by the church. Gabrielle confessed. The annulment loomed. "I'll nag him into submission." Richard smiled: "Good luck."

Dinner followed. Quiet warmth. Her husband posted: *Having dinner with my love.* A simple caption.

The next day, Jeffrey. His memory clung. Gabrielle replayed their messages, dissected each word. But reality was unyielding. He had blocked her. Erased her. The void gnawed. She posted: *I miss you, my douchebag friend. You know who you are.* He wouldn't see it. But maybe the universe would conspire.

Sunday church. Gabrielle pleaded with God: *Rewrite our story. Reunite our paths.*

Wednesday RCIA. Hope clung. Packing. Cleaning. Jeffrey's ghost lingered. Tears blurred as she folded memories. Two years, still raw. His words: *No room for you in my heart.* The ache defied time. Maybe one day the stars would align. She'd whisper: *Forgive me.* For now, Gabrielle clung to prayer.

Valentine's Day. Her husband orchestrated affection: flowers, Stella Rosa, sweet notes. They chuckled. She posted: *Chocolates are passé. Our love blooms brighter.* Dinner at Red Lobster, his favorite haunt. For once, no work obligations. Just each other.

The next night, the rodeo. Tickets gifted to grandkids. Tradition: experiences over possessions. Gabrielle snapped photos. Beneath joy, truth lingered. Florida would stretch the miles. Her husband revealed a softer side. He, too, grappled with second thoughts.

Morning sun. Half-packed boxes. The move loomed. The workshop beckoned. Crafting became refuge. Gabrielle carved seashells, painted driftwood, wove fragments of the past into tangible pieces for their new beach room. But Jeffrey's absence, a cavern no tape could fill. His laughter lingered. Would paths meet again? Her husband granted carte blanche: "Make it yours." She chuckled. Permission sweet, but unnecessary.

The calendar fluttered. One month until embrace. Eleven days until signatures. Boxes multiplied. His quirks, once endearing, now danced on her last nerve. Maybe stress. Maybe love's evolution. She had promised to stand by him, but the promise weighed heavy. Faith whispered louder than doubt.

Wednesday morning. Doctor's office. Her back a canvas of discomfort. Follow-up. Final verdict: "We've done all we can." Words hung with finality. Emotions swirled. The move loomed. The doctor's haste was suspicious, but truth appeared: her doctor, too, sought respite. Loose ends tied before leaving. "As long as my back heals," Gabrielle mused, "I am content."

Twilight. St. Michael's. RCIA. Bittersweet reality. Florida cast shadows over their spiritual journey. Richard extended grace: "Miss a few classes and still be baptized." Sadness and joy danced within her.

They delved into Lent—six weeks of fasting, repentance, self-denial. Ash Wednesday ignited the countdown toward Holy Thursday, toward transformation. Prayer. Scripture. Ancient rhythms of penance. Easter Vigil loomed, a celestial theater. Souls stepping into the spotlight. Candles flickered. Hope woven into sacred tapestry. They would rise baptized, tethered to resurrection. Days unfurled. Cardboard. Memories. Packing tape. Florida beckoned.

Ash Wednesday. Their pilgrimage to the closing table. Keys passed. Dreams found earthly abode. Excitement warmed her. Adventure whispered. But sadness lingered. Friends and family would become distant connections. Laughter distilled into farewells. "One last visit," Gabrielle vowed. Hugs. Whispered secrets. Shared meals. Family her compass. The house half-packed mocked her efforts. The clock ticked louder. Resolve stirred.

Ash Wednesday. St. Michael's. Early light through stained glass. Richard marked their foreheads, ashes, renewal. Transformation promised. But this was prologue. Their hearts pointed south. The truck bore dreams.

As they drove, Gabrielle's phone buzzed. Her best friend's regret: no farewell soiree. Life's demands eclipsed at that moment. Fragile strands of friendship frayed. Gabrielle clenched the wheel. 1,100 miles. A new chapter.

Her husband listened, eyes steady: "Perhaps she was never the friend you believed. This move is the litmus test." His words stung but rang true. No gathering. Just individual farewells. And Jeffrey: his absence gnawed.

No laughter. No goodbye. Gabrielle vowed to weave memories into her bones.

The sun rose with purpose. Their new house awaited. Mattresses first. Comfort whispered of dreams yet dreamt. Friends stepped forward: "We'll be your mattress custodians." Gratitude bloomed.

Next, the pool. Her husband slipped an envelope: "Start the service."

Then the house itself. Footsteps echoed anew. Realtor. Champagne. *To new beginnings.* Keys received. Evening draped the world. Gabrielle, exhausted, surrendered to sleep.

Morning. Title office. Fresh documents. Signatures. Promises in ink. Unexpected solitude. Just them. Then it happened, the keys were theirs.

Outside, Florida sun embraced them. Photos snapped. Palm trees framed joy. *The real just got real today.* Social media bore witness.

The storage unit awaited. Four trips. Boxes. Furniture. Forgotten trinkets unearthed. Garage a maze.

Their friend arrived, airport bound. The plan: leave the truck. Fate had other ideas. The garage door yawned. The truck was stubborn. Anxiety gripped. Boxes shifted, furniture rearranged, the truck coaxed inside, barely. Victory tasted sweet.

On the flight home. Exhaustion and exhilaration. They were homeowners in Florida. Responsibility settled. Packing, organizing, logistics. Their existing home needed new occupants. Strangers would walk through rooms filled with memories. Her heart ached. And Jeffrey circled. Would she see him before the move? Could she talk to him? Fear gnawed. But there was value in trying. Maybe a conversation would bring closure.

As the plane descended, Gabrielle made a promise: she would find a way to talk to Jeffrey before Florida became home. Whether fleeting or heartfelt, she needed to bridge the gap.

Goodbye and the Grace of Arrival

"He brought me out into a spacious place; he rescued me because he delighted in me."

—Psalm 18:19

The sun dipped low. It was the eve of the Rite of Election, a moment poised to alter Gabrielle's life. The next day at 5:30 p.m., she would step forward, pen trembling, ink etching her name onto sacred parchment. Surrender felt both weighty and liberating, a quiet offering, a bold leap into grace.

Earlier that afternoon, the RCIA retreat offered a spiritual oasis. Gabrielle sat beside her husband, his presence grounding. She inhaled deeply, then exhaled truth: the messages, Jeffrey, guilt gnawing relentless. Her husband listened, then spoke his own shadows. Secrets. Soft confessions. Forgiveness bloomed.

They vowed to weave God into their marriage, to be more devoted, more forgiving as they prepared for Florida. Regret, relief, and hope stitched together by grace. Gabrielle found solace in his eyes. He knew her mistakes yet held her close.

Their home, now an open house, stood silent, waiting for a new chapter. Offers would come. Negotiations would dance. Soon, they'd be weeks away from a permanent move. In the quiet of the church, Gabrielle whispered gratitude. The weight of confession had lifted, replaced by redemption's promise.

Neighbors orchestrated a farewell. Laughter mingled with bittersweet tears. A cake adorned with miniature houses and a fondant moving truck became the centerpiece. Hugs exchanged, promises made, addresses scribbled on napkins. They were leaving the cul-de-sac but carried friendships that transcend fences.

Monday morning. A farewell visit to her doctor. "You've come a long way," she said, prescribing three months of weight-loss medication. Gabrielle folded the paper into her pocket. The extra weight had crept back since her triumphant 199 lbs. "This time," her doctor emphasized, "we'll do it right." Later, an eye appointment, new lenses, a quiet sense of completion.

That evening, St. Michael's Church. RCIA class. Father James spoke on Reconciliation, a sacrament of renewal. Gabrielle's heart stirred. She wondered: *When is the right time to confess?*

His voice was gentle: "Child, your sins await their homecoming. Fear not. The baptismal font shall be their sanctuary. On that sacred eve, forgiveness shall descend like gentle rain."

He spoke of venial sins, deadly sins, the balance between imperfection and redemption. "Monthly confession," he advised, "but listen to your heart."

Sunday morning. Gabrielle sat in the pew, mind adrift. Jeffrey's name danced in her heart. Should she invite him to witness her baptism? She turned to her husband. His answer was soft and sure: "Yes. A thousand times yes." The decision was made, but the words? How to shape them?

Days passed. Gabrielle grappled with syllables, each one a brushstroke on the canvas of possibility. She prayed but did not send.

Wednesday evening. Another RCIA class. Another pilgrimage. The topic again: Reconciliation. Richard guided them through intricacies, mystery, mercy. They pondered remorse, redemption, the threads weaving earthly stories into celestial tapestry.

The RCIA calendar dwindled. They stood at the edge of the first scrutiny. Sunday. 8:30 a.m. Mass. They would step forward, eager, open, ready. Richard sent the email. Excitement danced within them.

The next day, Gabrielle sat with dear friends. The clink of cutlery, the hum of laughter, a symphony of farewell. Their last lunch before the move. The thought of parting tugged at her heartstrings. Yet hope flickered.

They would return, shuttling between their new home and familiar streets. "Back and forth," Gabrielle mused. Their absence was never absolute. Still, the bittersweet taste of goodbye lingered.

That evening, anticipation bubbled. A house showing loomed. "Sold," Gabrielle whispered, willing the universe to align.

The next morning. Gabrielle and her husband met their financial advisor. The office was sterile, calm. But his eyes wandered, focus fractured. Dissatisfaction simmered. They left unresolved questions trailing behind.

Over breakfast, Gabrielle met her work friend. They chatted about deadlines, and promised to stay connected. But truth hung heavy: this was likely their last rendezvous. "Visit us," Gabrielle urged. Her friend nodded, eyes holding promises of reunion. Gabrielle wondered if fate would allow their paths to cross again.

Late the next morning, an email from Richard. The scrutiny was cancelled. The archbishop had dispensed the faithful from Sunday Mass obligations. Coronavirus.

Later another email: RCIA cancelled for now. He prayed the Easter Vigil would still hold their sacred initiation.

The sun dipped below the horizon, casting a warm glow over their backyard. It was meant to be their farewell celebration, a final hurrah before Florida. But fate had other plans. The pandemic gripped the world. Excitement waned. Safety took precedence.

With heavy hearts, they cancelled the gathering. No laughter. No clinking glasses. Just silence where memories were meant to bloom.

Yet life unfolded. That day, a glimmer of hope: an offer on the house. The realtor's voice crackled, urging them to keep showing. "You never know," he said. "A higher bid might come." So they opened the doors again and whispered silent prayers for a favorable outcome.

The sun painted the sky in soft hues. Gabrielle stood at the threshold of their church. It felt surreal not to step inside, to miss polished pews, hymns woven into Sundays. Services cancelled. The pandemic rendered sacred space unsafe.

Yet hope found new avenues. Bells fell silent but digital chimes rang. The congregation gathered virtually, prayers shared from home. The priest adapted, vestments before a webcam. The Eucharist, once consecrated on the altar, now streamed through Wi-Fi.

Beyond the spiritual, practical matters tugged. They were moving in two days. Boxes lined up in the hallway. Would the company remain operational? The world folded inward, businesses shuttered. The pandemic became a universal pause button. Would the trucks roll? Would the men who lifted sofas be furloughed?

Gabrielle pondered fragility. The illusion of permanence stripped away. The world shut down, but hearts remained open to hope, to faith, to the promise of doors swinging wide once more.

Two days later. Movers arrived. Boxes cocooned memories. Furniture thudded. Her husband paced, eyes flicking between movers and headlines. "Coronavirus," he muttered. "We must not dally."

Eighteen hours blurred. At 3:00 a.m., they arrived bleary-eyed, clutching essentials. The shower washed away dust. Rest elusive. The pool crew arrived, laughter echoing: "Happy St. Patrick's Day."

Morning. Movers punctual again. Boxes spilled forth. Sofa here, dining table there. Outside, the world shut down. Inside, they lingered. Grocery shelves bare. Toilet paper was elusive. Resolve unshaken. Her husband vowed a pilgrimage to Sam's Club, stockpiling provisions like a prepper.

Sunlight warmed Gabrielle's laptop. She registered for CPR certification, a step toward becoming a trainer. Chest compressions, rescue breaths, daunting, invigorating.

Later, Zoom chimed. RCIA gathering. Faces in little squares, faith shared across pixels. "Did you settle in okay?" they asked. Virtual smiles bridged distance.

Next morning. Best Buy technicians danced through the living room. Four TVs found places. "Entertainment hubs," her husband declared.

Friends arrived, curiosity leading them to the doorstep. Amid conversation, couch and recliners arrived. They sat, reminiscing. Promises to catch up.

Their car disappeared. Gabrielle and her husband stood in the driveway: new home, new rhythm.

Friday. Respite. Garage sales, breakfast. Boxes loomed. Then excitement: their grill arrived. Soon, cookouts on the lanai. A stitch of joy.

Saturday. Xfinity arrived, weaving a web of security. A fortress stitched with blinking lights. Satisfaction on his face was worth every wire.

Sunday dawned with hope. Richard's email offered RCIA via Zoom. Bittersweet consolation. Despite disruption, they remained woven into faith.

Monday. Boxes surrounded them. Unpacking became ritual. But the sun beckoned. Backyard awaited. Solar panels glinted. Soon, the pool would bask in generosity. Gabrielle floated, weightless, watching ripples carry stress away.

Her inbox pulsed. Richard's emails guided them. RCIA adapted. Zoom sessions were condensed. Confirmation. Anointing of the sick. The Easter Triduum. The archbishop decreed Palm Sunday and Holy Week silent.

Yet St. Michael's would stream sacred moments. Wednesday's Zoom delved deeper. Pandemic shadows loomed. They discussed anointing the sick, timely in a world aching for healing.

Thursday. A call from their financial advisor. Familiar voice, thin connection. Aloof, detached. They decided to seek someone new. Local. Present. Engaged.

Another email from Richard: Neophytes awaited initiation. Timing rested in God's hands. "All in God's time," he reminded.

Easter. Friends invited them for lunch. Laughter. Warmth. Yet beneath joy, a quiet ache. Gabrielle should have been immersed in sacred waters. But life had its rhythm. Divine timing.

Lately, Jeffrey occupied her thoughts. Gabrielle took a leap. An email, simple, playful, laden with unspoken hopes.

May approached. A month stitched with celebrations: Mother's Day, birthdays, graduations. Jeffrey's name surfaced. His birthday beckoned. She crafted a note, a smart-ass plea for parole from the Jeffrey social media prison.

Subject: Request for Parole Hearing. To: Lord Master Warden.

Dear Lord Master Warden,

I am writing this correspondence to express my support for the release of Inmate #5555 (a.k.a. Gabrielle) from the Jeffrey social media prison (a.k.a. being blocked on all platforms). She has now served 508 days in solitary confinement, no lights, no visitors, no other prisoners, not even a glimpse of sunlight.

Inmate #5555 is almost certain that the Lord Master Warden never checks on his prisoners, nor is he particularly concerned with the conditions of confinement. On behalf of my client, I am requesting a parole hearing or, better yet, full pardon. She feels she has served sufficient time and is no longer a threat to society or to Lord Master Warden himself.

She has, for the most part, respected the request to be left alone. But in her defense, telling an Irish girl to leave you alone works about as well as trying to baptize a cat. Still, she tried. So hard, in fact, that she moved 1,100 miles and five states away. The odds of crossing paths again are now about as likely as taking a fat girl to an all-you-can-eat buffet and telling her she can't eat anything: not impossible, but nearly.

Inmate #5555 is willing to negotiate her release, provided it doesn't involve automotive parts or cash (unless fuzzy dice or a dashboard hula girl count). Florida now consumes most of her assets, but she's open to creative offers.

Finally, while her request is genuine, she hopes this email made Lord Master Warden chuckle. That was the intention. She hopes he's doing okay and staying safe during this pandemic. She imagines the stress he faces daily, telling clients that normal services are suspended. She's sure he's still going above and beyond.

She was told 508 days ago that healing requires humor. That laughter helps the heart, mind, and soul stay healthy. She hopes she offered a little of that today.

May peace be with you always, and may God hold you in the palm of His hand.

Stay safe, Gabrielle.

She hit send. And waited. No response.

On a sunkissed Tuesday, Gabrielle embarked on a bureaucratic odyssey. The tax collector's office was her gateway to Floridian legitimacy. Masked and determined, she navigated pandemic hurdles with grace.

The queue stretched, a silent testament to patience. Her husband stood beside her, mission clear: update his license, anchor their address in Florida soil. And then, it was done.

Gabrielle emerged clutching her freshly minted Florida driver's license. Plastic. Official. Hers. Her husband captured the moment, Gabrielle framed by her car, license plate gleaming. Social media became their stage. Likes rolled in. Comments danced. But one absence tugged at her heart: Jeffrey.

The next day. Focus shifted from bureaucracy to beauty. Their house awaited its finishing touch. Her husband, fueled by caffeine, orchestrated landscaping, rocks, curbing, a fortress against weeds. Gabrielle watched earth tones embrace their home. "Mission accomplished," he declared.

But peace was fleeting. That night, a sudden boom shattered slumber. A shelf collapsed under Gabrielle's overzealous stacking. Lowe's beckoned. Brackets, drills, determination. Their friend restored order, reinforcing shelves like a maestro. Balance returned.

As twilight painted their screens, RCIA unfolded one last time via Zoom. Smiles exchanged. Pixels bridged distance. But melancholy lingered.

This was the final act. *Who is who in the Catholic Church?* Saints, bishops, martyrs, threads binding centuries. Yet as the meeting ended, no baptism date. "His time, not ours," they were reminded.

Gabrielle clasped her hands and waited. Her inbox remained silent. Jeffrey had yet to break his silence. Blocked lists held her captive. She scrolled through old messages, seeking clues. Nothing. "Continue to pray," they said. So she did.

May arrived. Sunny and full of promises. Gabrielle embarked on a mission: thirty-one gifts in thirty-one days. Her garage became sanctuary. Wine bottles transformed into art. Shells adorned trinkets. Bottle caps became whimsical accents. Each creation held a piece of her heart.

Mother's Day approached—ten friends and her mom would unwrap handcrafted offerings. Her husband raised an eyebrow at shipping costs. Gabrielle smiled. "Joy is worth every cent."

Sanibel Island called. Dawn painted the horizon. They strolled; sand cooled beneath their feet. Gabrielle captured moments, shared them online. Likes fluttered. Comments danced.

But one absence gnawed: Jeffrey. Blocked. Estranged. Haunting her notifications. Then, a twist, she searched for his name. Unblocked. His private profile revealed little, but joy unfurled its wings. Even a glimpse was sunrise after a storm.

Saturday shimmered. Gabrielle passed her CPR test, a step toward becoming a certified trainer. Yet life's whirlwind consumed her days. Textbooks gathered dust.

The pool shimmered. She surrendered to its embrace. For the first time in months, Gabrielle felt happy. Then came a digital whisper: Jeffrey unblocked her. Hope bloomed.

Gabrielle sent Jeffrey this message through social media:

Free at last, Free at last, Thank God almighty I am free at last! I never thought I would see the day the Lord Master would have a change of heart from his hardheaded stubborn douchebag self and release me from the blocked list. Finally, as the New Yorker that you are, I am sure you have been called a "mother" a few times throughout your lifetime, so wishing you a happy "Mother's Day" tomorrow! May peace and humor be with you always. Stay Safe!

No response.

The silence settled. But Gabrielle had spoken. She had reached across the chasm. Her days unfolded in gentle rhythm, unpacking, organizing, crafting. Mundane tasks held quiet magic.

Crafting became refuge. Each handmade creation carried a piece of her heart, destined for friends near and far. Twenty gifts had sailed forth. Eleven awaited their voyage. In the garage, surrounded by half finished projects and forgotten tools, Gabrielle found peace.

Mid May. A tantalizing prospect beckoned: two weeks of adventure, reunions, the Indy 500. But Covid19 intervened.

The race, once a public celebration, unfolded behind closed doors. Her husband's frustration simmered. He vowed never to invest again in an event that denied him engines' roar and camaraderie.

Suitcases gathered dust. Disappointment tugged, yet Gabrielle realized safety trumped wanderlust. They cocooned themselves in familiar walls, finding solace in the everyday.

Captiva and Turner Beach offered sanctuary. Empty sands, rhythmic waves, gulls crying. Shells became treasures woven into her crafts.

Friends arrived from Tampa. Together, they traced familiar paths, laughter mingling with tide's erasure.

Then the boat, gliding canals, engine hum echoing.

In quiet corners, Gabrielle built a sense of anticipation. Giving became her symphony. Parcels adorned with ribbons embarked on journeys that transcended distance.

Notifications chimed: *Delivered.* Joy spilled forth. Social media became a gallery of gratitude.

But one recipient held a special place: Jeffrey. Gabrielle poured creativity into his gift. Rum Chata bottles transformed, miniature cars from caps, a hula girl swaying, fuzzy dice dangling. Whimsy. Memory. Hope. Her husband nodded: "You've outdone yourself." Gabrielle sealed the gift. It was a fragile bridge spanning silence.

Days passed. Confirmation arrived: Jeffrey's gift had reached its destination. Would he acknowledge the effort? Or would silence stretch its arms once more? Gabrielle waited. The mailbox became her oracle.

The beach became sanctuary. "Love the beach," she murmured. Her husband nodded.

Then came Jeffrey's birthday. His name tugged. Had he unwrapped the layers? Silence echoed. Gabrielle clung to possibility.

Another tide swept in, baptism. The date etched in her heart. They would fly home. The Eucharist beckoned. "Sounds kind of dumb," she confessed. Her husband smiled. He understood. It was about rebirth.

Then, shadows across social media. A message arrived. Jeffrey broke his silence: *Thank you for the birthday present.*

He messaged her husband. *You're welcome. I'll pass it along*, her husband replied.

Jeffrey added: *I thought it was your talent that made these.*

Her husband chuckled: *I try not to let my secrets out. But I did help with the rum.*

The conversation ended. Indirect gratitude stung. Why bypass her? Was it deliberate or forgetfulness? *End of conversation*, her mind whispered. Yet emotions lingered. The gift had not carried her closer to Jeffrey's digital shores.

Still, a flicker of hope remained. Jeffrey had responded even if through her husband's proxy. As the tide rolled in, Gabrielle cradled disappointment. The sun traced its arch.

That day she cast aside routine, embracing the pool. Beside her, her husband shared the sun's warmth. They floated, suspended between mundane and miraculous.

A job, Gabrielle mused. Masks clung to faces. Should she venture forth, masked and wary, or linger by the pool?

"Sell your crafts," her husband suggested. The farmer's market beckoned. Could Gabrielle set up her stall? May had unfurled its petals. Thirty-one gifts carried pieces of her heart. Responses warmed her soul.

But Jeffrey stood apart. His silence puzzled her. "Ask him," her husband urged. Gabrielle hesitated. "He was not overjoyed because of who sent them." Her husband brushed it aside. "I will reach out." Gabrielle wondered: would Jeffrey glimpse the fragile hope stitched into each creation?

On the cusp of June. Gabrielle and her husband embarked on a journey. Her baptism awaited. Flights delayed, corridors buzzing with masked travelers.

Amid departure boards, her husband messaged Jeffrey about Gabrielle's crafting and dream of farmer's markets. Gabrielle peered over his shoulder but held no illusions. Jeffrey never responded.

The celebration of her Baptism left her craving for more. No mingling, no laughter over coffee.

Instead, they dispersed, souls nourished, bonds restrained.

Richard offered blessings. Jeffrey's silence reverberated. Was her longing penance? A baptism of fire, not water?

At a café, her husband led her to a quiet corner. They dined, laden with unspoken questions. Maybe God's silence whispered truths. Maybe Jeffrey's absence was a mirror. Redemption, she realized, was not always wrapped in expected forms.

As twilight fell, Gabrielle knelt in her heart. *God*, she implored, *weave the frayed threads of our past into something whole. Restore what was lost. Bring him back not as a ghost but as presence.*

Was she pleading for Jeffrey's return or her own healing? She surrendered prayers to the night. Jeffrey remained a mystery.

Unable to bear silence, Gabrielle sent a final message:

As you know, I was baptized and confirmed tonight at St. Michael's. Thank you for giving me that push years ago. The birthday gift you received was part of my thirty-one day kindness act. I hoped it might make you laugh. Please accept my apologies if it was unwelcome. Crafting keeps me connected to my dad; it's where I find peace. Tomorrow begins a new chapter for us. I hope your friendship remains with my husband. May peace be with you always.

No response. Silence returned. Gabrielle closed her eyes. She had spoken, offered, let go. A thread was stitched, not between her and Jeffrey but between her and grace.

Sunday. They traced their way back to Florida. Her mother's absence lingered. "No more flights," her husband declared. "We shall drive come July." Memorial Day passed. Graveside adornments undone. July beckoned.

The week unfolded. Gabrielle cocooned herself at home. Study and creation became her compass. Manuals, notes, each chapter a step toward mastery.

Crafting filled the garage. Practicality nudged: downsize, sell, create space.

Friday. "To the beach," her husband declared. Shells nestled in her palm. The kitchen project was near completion.

Sunday. Their new church welcomed them. Father Michael extended his hand. "Welcome." Communion tasted like grace. Yet Jeffrey lingered in her prayers. Silence met her plea. Were some prayers meant to be carried by the wind?

Monday dawned. Sanibel Island stretched before them. Gabrielle walked, collecting shells. Jeffrey's absence echoed. She longed for resolution.

Later, she penned a reflection online: *We all have pasts. None of us are innocent. But we get a fresh start every day to be better than yesterday.*

Tuesday. Adventure called. The Shell Factory, souvenirs, zoo of wonders, mini golf. For a while, they were carefree children chasing balls across emerald greens.

Inside, shells adorned every nook. Her husband dubbed it a "knick-knack shop." Gabrielle reveled in its chaos, gathering a few more for her kitchen project.

Wednesday morning. Sanibel Island called again. Gabrielle sought missing pieces, shells to complete her creation. She walked, collected, marveled. Pictures snapped of her happy place, her favorite person by her side.

Later, their great room plunged into darkness. The TV had breathed its last. Urgency gripped her husband. Best Buy, then Walmart, a pilgrimage for a new screen. The Geek Squad arrived. Relief washed over him when the screen flickered to life. Entertainment restored.

The week unfolded. The pool beckoned. They lounged, floated, sun treading across their skin.

On the lanai, something extraordinary: a cloud materialized, etched with a face, a silent witness. Gabrielle captured it. Her husband shared it online, a moment suspended between heaven and earth.

The weekend. Friends from Tampa returned. Lighthouse Beach cradled them at sunrise.

Later, more friends gathered at Nervous Nellies, Fort Myers Beach. Cutlery clattered, stories warmed. It felt like coming home.

July 4th. Quieter celebration. Their backyard blazed with splendor. Neighbors raided fireworks aisles. Explosions painted the sky. Their sleepy neighborhood transformed into a theater of light.

Summer unfolded with joy. Her husband's grandkids arrived. Laughter echoed. The beach became sanctuary: sandcastles, seashell hunts, salty breezes.

A pirate cruise transformed their boat ride into swashbuckling escapade.

Back home, the pool beckoned. Marco Polo until sunset. Laughter echoed. The house, once quiet, now hummed with life.

After the grandkids left, a family reunion called. Gabrielle's mother tugged at her heartstrings. "I missed your baptism," she pleaded.

Gabrielle negotiated: "Three hours in the air versus eighteen on the road." The scales tipped. They soared above clouds. The reunion awaited.

But Covid cast shadows. Only ten souls attended. Cautious smiles masked uncertainty. Gabrielle, accustomed to Florida's laissezfaire, navigated a state where caution reigned.

Her husband's longing to reconnect remained unfulfilled. Yet pockets of connection emerged: dear friends, familiar laughter, grandkids resilient. Her mother wrapped her in warmth.

Sunday. St. Michael's stood as a beacon. In person Mass returned, masks donned. Father James greeted them. "Welcome back," he said. His laughter echoed.

Amidst silence, her husband reached for his phone. Jeffrey. The message: *We are here thinking of you. Lunch?* No reply. Gabrielle knew better. Jeffrey's silence was not about a virus. It was about her. She imagined him reading, hesitating, dismissing. Had her husband been alone, Jeffrey would have replied.

Her husband dismissed her intuition: "Overreacting. Busy, perhaps." Yet Gabrielle sensed truth: Jeffrey chose silence over awkwardness.

Time slipped. They explored familiar streets, laughed until sides ached. Her mother reveled in their presence. The reunion, though diminished, held its own magic.

August unfurled with reckoning. Their former financial advisor's indifference ignited her husband's ire.

Enter Brian. A phone call, a meeting, competence incarnate. Brian dissected accounts with precision. "Here, the glitch, an easy fix." Her husband nodded. Gabrielle squirmed. Brian glimpsed her vulnerability. Part time job," he advised. "You are young."

Gabrielle bristled, pride wounded. Yet she knew the safety net was frayed.

Two hours unfolded, a tapestry of numbers, projections, possibilities. "Maximize," Brian urged. "Invest." And then: "A part time gig won't hurt." They left impressed, contemplative. The switch was made. Their financial sails adjusted.

Later that week, Father Michael graced their doorstep. Their home awaited his sacred touch. Pandemic rhythms had made visits rare, reserved for the sick. But on this day, he arrived.

Friends and neighbors gathered, six souls beneath their roof. Gabrielle prepared appetizers. Father Michael blessed their feast, weaving hope and solace into their home.

Then the ritual: holy water sprinkled room by room, from kitchen to study. Gabrielle, reverent, forgot the camera. The sacred moments uncaptured. Later, the absence gnawed.

Days flowed: beach breezes, poolside laughter, dinners with friends.

Tampa visitors returned. In that semi-retired reverie, Gabrielle reveled in the ordinary. Yet beneath sundappled days, a quiet knowing lingered. The world would awaken. A job awaited.

Gabrielle embarked on a pilgrimage to her new doctor's office. The waiting room bore witness to the pandemic's grip. The scale revealed truths she had danced around. "Overweight," the doctor said. Gabrielle nodded. The move had disrupted her rhythm. The gym lay dormant. Her husband proposed a pact: a return to movement.

At Autumn's cusp. Gabrielle faced a pivotal moment. The certified trainer test loomed. Twice deferred, now unavoidable.

In a frenzy, she crammed months of material into a week. Textbooks became nocturnal companions. But deep down, she knew she wasn't ready. The move to Florida had shifted her dreams. Jeffrey, the ghost behind the mirror, lingered. She believed shedding pounds might make her appealing.

She battled her body, counted calories, sweated through workouts. But the mirror reflected stubborn curves. Jeffrey drifted away. The irony stung, sacrificing wellbeing for a love already lost.

The exam room revealed inadequacy. As the proctor collected answer sheets, Gabrielle knew she no longer desired the title. "Certified trainer" was no longer her destination. The dream had withered.

October settled with relief. After birthdays, anniversaries, dolphin dances, Gabrielle, and her husband embraced stillness. The pool shimmered. Their lanai became sanctuary.

Sixteen years of marriage, six months in Florida, a lifetime unfolding. The cement hands, hardened and displayed, stood as testament, not just to love but endurance. Her husband, once skeptical, now admired their creation with pride.

The Catholic Ladies Auxiliary remained a gentle echo. Carmella's kindness, the lunch table's probing, the door ajar. Gabrielle knew she wasn't ready. Her plate was full of study, healing, and rediscovery.

The gun permit class had been a curious detour. Gabrielle chuckled at the irony. Florida's laws, her indulgences, the absurdity of imagining herself as a stoned action hero. Cheetos and couch cuddles, not combat. Still, the permit was earned. A box checked.

Mid October air shifted. Days unfolded with quiet grace: beach walks, shell-collecting, sunsets painted in forgiveness. Gabrielle no longer waited for Jeffrey's reply. She had written her final message in the language of healing. Now she listened for God's whisper in waves, laughter, silence.

Yet her mind wandered to Jeffrey. Elusive, a social media unblock, a gesture revealing nothing. His profile offered no clues. Was he well? Was he happy? The unanswered messages hung in digital ether.

After a few Margaritas, Gabrielle decided to test the waters once more. Her fingers danced across the screen, crafting a message with equal humor and heartbreak.

Message to Jeffrey:

Dear Diary:

Several months ago, out of the goodness of my heart, I sent a douchebag a gift. As I floated on my floaty in the pool this afternoon, sipping my margarita, I couldn't help but think of that gift. Eighty-nine degrees, the sun shining bright, a light breeze swaying the palm trees, not a cloud in sight, just sunshine and lollipops. . .

Then suddenly, concern struck. The hula girl. Did she make it to the dashboard? Did she get to do her hula? Is she living her best life? Or was she pimped out to turn tricks to pay the rent? Worse, was she tossed in a junk drawer? Or at the bottom of a landfill, suffocating in her packaging, never given a name? I saved and saved my sixpence allowance to afford her. And now, I fear I sent her into the abyss. I'll never know how she turned out. I'll always have more questions than answers. . . Lesson learned, dear diary. Lesson learned. . .

Gabrielle was proud of her message. Surely, he would find it humorous. Surely, he would respond. But again, to her heartbreak, there was no response.

November arrived, crisp and golden. Gabrielle and her husband embarked on their civic pilgrimage. The polling station buzzed with anticipation. Gabrielle cast her vote, a whisper of hope in democracy's chorus. But anxiety gnawed. Would others uphold their bargain?

As the sun dipped, results unfurled. Joe Biden ascended. Her husband, fueled by cable news and conspiracy theories, embarked on a post-election odyssey.

He devoured headlines, dissected scandals, chased ballot shadows. "They cheated!" he exclaimed, eyes ablaze. "The Democratic Party, a cabal of cunning strategists!" *Gabrielle*, the voice of reason, countered, "Evidence, my dear. Evidence is the currency of truth."

But her husband was a tempest. The television blared. Pundits pontificated. Gabrielle braced. *Joe Biden is our president*, she reminded him, mantra against the gale. She perched on the precipice of four years of discourse. Would her ears endure? Only time would tell.

Late November. A tech adventure beckoned. Phone upgrades promised convenience and savings. Her husband's transition was seamless, data migrated, bill lowered, satisfaction palpable.

Gabrielle's phone, too, made the leap, but fate intervened. Locked out. Social media was gone. No tweets. No stories. No updates. Just a barren screen. Desperation led her to the virtual doorstep of the social media overlords. She penned a heartfelt email, attached credentials, a photo ID, her pixelated passport to redemption.

But the pandemic cast its shadow even here. Verification wheels turned slow. Days stretched into weeks. Each tick echoed with frustration.

The irony was not lost: a global crisis delaying her humble plea for account access. *What a tangled web*, she muttered. *A virus conspiring with bureaucracy to thwart digital desires.* In the grand scheme, it was a minor inconvenience. Yet as Gabrielle stared at her dormant phone, she could not help but mutter: *What a bunch of bullshit.*

The Reckoning of Joy

*"Weeping may endure for a night, but
joy comes in the morning."*

—Psalm 30:5

As the year ended, Gabrielle and her husband received an unexpected call. Her brother's voice, somber yet resolute: "Thanksgiving and Christmas are cancelled. No super-spreaders in this family."

Caution prevailed, leaving Gabrielle adrift in disappointment. "Well," her husband sighed, "looks like we'll celebrate in Florida." Sunshine instead of snow. Palm trees instead of pine.

Determined to share love across the miles, they compiled a list, homemade treats, heartfelt crafts, emissaries of affection. "Jeffrey," her husband insisted. Gabrielle hesitated. Jeffrey had been elusive, ignoring messages and requests. But her husband's faith nudged her forward. "He'll appreciate it," he assured.

December arrived. Packages embarked on their journey. Thank-you notes trickled in, laughter echoed through phone calls. Social media lit up with kindness, her husband reading posts aloud, bridging the gap for Gabrielle, whose accounts remained locked.

Days later, their washer and dryer retired without warning. Lowe's beckoned. Shiny appliances restored domestic order. Her husband declared the upgrade Gabrielle's Christmas gift, posting a photo captioned: *Forget diamonds, nothing says love like a fresh spin cycle.* Friends chuckled.

A week before Christmas. A digital missive arrived. Jeffrey. His words settled gently into her husband's inbox: *Thank you. Your thoughtful package arrived.*

But beneath gratitude, a boundary: *I shall wait to unveil this treasure when my children gather.* Subtext folded within the lines: *Kindly refrain from further offerings.* Jeffrey pirouetted between appreciation and polite refusal.

Her husband, offended, replied: *I am sorry to have read this, and sorry we bothered you. My wife was right; we will remove you from our list. You might want to open the box, though: there are perishables and a letter I put in the card. You can disregard that. Merry Christmas. Enjoy your children."*

Jeffrey answered: *Let me know when you are in town next. I would like you and I to sit down and talk. Merry Christmas.*

Her husband responded: *We will not be in town for a while. It's okay, we don't need a sitdown. I harbor no hard feelings. If you had read the letter, you would have known that. We will respect your request. You will not hear from either of us anymore. Take care.*

Jeffrey replied: *I have not opened the box. I will tomorrow.*

Her husband closed: *Take care.*

Three days passed. No word.

At church Sunday, her husband handed Gabrielle a copy of the letter he had placed in Jeffrey's card. It spoke of grief, anger, redemption. It honored Jeffrey's role in their darkest chapters, the death of a son, the loss of a mother, the near collapse of a marriage. It revealed reconciliation, forgiveness, faith rediscovered in the pews of St. Michael's. It named Gabrielle's longing, her need to make things right. Her belief that those who help us become better should never be cast aside.

It was a letter not meant to be answered, only understood. Gabrielle cried when she read it. "Why did you send this?" she asked.

He looked at her, voice steady but soft. "I knew Jeffrey meant a lot to you. I thought maybe he wasn't responding because of me. Maybe he feared how I'd react to a friendship between you two." He wanted Jeffrey to know it was okay. If he wanted to be her friend, he had his blessing.

After church, silence pressed on her husband. Jeffrey had not responded after opening the package. That was unusual. Jeffrey had always replied to him. Feeling guilty, her husband sent another message.

He spoke of offense taken too quickly, assumptions made too fast. He described the package as gratitude woven into tradition. He spoke of Gabrielle, not as a woman reaching out inappropriately, but as someone carrying two years of guilt and heartbreak for a mistake she could not undo.

He painted her as a woman who had found peace because of Jeffrey's words, who had changed her life because of his influence, and who had been denied even a simple coffee conversation to make things right.

He admitted it was he who had insisted on including Jeffrey this year, stepping out of his comfort zone, putting ego aside, writing a letter he hoped would bring peace.

Instead, it had blown up in his face. *I will always consider you a friend, even from a distance. I don't need a sitdown to confirm that.* He offered a meal, a gesture of friendship. But if Jeffrey saw him only as another customer, he would respect that too.

He spoke of Gabrielle with reverence: her heart, he said, was bigger than both of them. He asked Jeffrey to consider giving her friendship another chance, to set boundaries of trust, to see her not as a mistake but as someone who had grown. And if not, that was okay too.

Merry Christmas, he wrote. *I hope you and your kids enjoy the package. I wish you nothing but health and happiness.*

Thirty-five days in digital exile ended with validation. Gabrielle reclaimed her social media throne, posting with humor: *Back from the void! Let the memes flow!* Likes and comments cascaded, a chorus of welcome.

New Year's Eve. They went to Mass, a quiet ritual to close the year. Her husband, still carrying the weight of Jeffrey's silence, confided: "Maybe we shouldn't have sent the package." He sent another message. Jeffrey did not respond.

On Sanibel's serene shores, they ushered in the New Year. Tradition etched into sand: the date and "Happy New Year." Social media bore witness.

Her husband posted: *Starting the New Year off right.* But Gabrielle's heart whispered a name: Jeffrey. Her husband, tinged with regret, confessed the ache.

Gabrielle felt guilt settled in. She had penned the messages, tried to mend the thread. Her husband bore the weight of her actions. *Pray*, she whispered. *Listen to your heart.*

Back home, they settled at the kitchen counter. Father Mike Schmitz beckoned them into the *Bible in a Year* podcast. For Gabrielle, this was uncharted terrain.

Baptism had left questions, a sense of incompleteness. Could the Bible bridge water and spirit?

They pressed play. Genesis 1 and 2, the cosmic overture. Psalm 19: "The heavens declare the glory of God." Gabrielle listened. Her soul echoed the refrain. The kitchen became sanctuary. Each verse a brush-stroke, each chapter revelation.

Later, her husband confessed he had prayed. Then he sent one final message to Jeffrey. He apologized for assumptions, for judgments, for trying to wrap forgiveness in a Christmas box.

He acknowledged Jeffrey's burdens, the mortuary, reputation, family, sacrifices. He spoke of envy, admiration, the hope his gift might spark joy in Jeffrey's sons. He thanked Jeffrey for not deleting him, for not engaging in argument. He offered, one last time, a sitdown. A meal. A moment. Again, no response.

Weeks passed. Her husband posted a tribute to his late mother on her heavenly birthday. He thanked Jeffrey and the mortuary for the beauty woven around her memory.

Jeffrey responded with a single heart emoji. A digital nod. Her husband saw peace. Gabrielle saw ambiguity. "We all allocate time to those who matter," she said. "Jeffrey had none to spare for us."

Her husband's disappointment lingered, but he vowed not to let it gnaw. Gabrielle loathed stoicism, silent acceptance. She yearned for clarity, a language beyond emojis. So, she posted: *Communication should be about seeing things from another's perspective, not about who is right or wrong.*

January descended. Sleepless nights returned. Motivation eluded her. Unemployment loomed. Gabrielle refused to return to the wellworn path of discontent. Twetny-four years had etched weariness into her soul.

She stood at life's crossroads, grappling with the question: *What would kindle happiness?* The trainer dream had fizzled. Neighborhood strolls hardly counted as workouts.

In this slump, Jeffrey lingered. She prayed for him each Sunday, wove his name into petitions. The heavens remained silent.

One moondrenched night, scrolling her feed, a post appeared: *When you cannot sleep at night . . . maybe that was God's way of saying, we need to talk.* The words clung. In the hush of midnight, Gabrielle knelt. She asked God for a compass, to guide her purpose beyond bills and obligations.

Another verse surfaced: "Whatever you ask in prayer, believe that you have received it, and it will be yours" (Mark 11:24). Was it a sign? A cosmic nudge? Gabrielle didn't know. But she listened. And she believed.

February unfurled with familiar rhythm. Mornings began with Father Mike's podcast, a steady heartbeat in their kitchen sanctuary.

Gabrielle and her husband became tourists in their own lives, wandering Florida's sunlit corners, collecting moments.

Yet beneath the warmth, a quiet storm brewed. Unemployment loomed. The job market offered no solace. Gabrielle knew she needed work.

Then, a website beckoned: real estate. The words danced in her mind, a siren call to reinvention. She shared her revelation. Her husband surprised her with unwavering support. The classroom was virtual. Covid had silenced lecture halls. Self study became her mantra. The exam waited, a threshold to a new chapter.

As Lent approached, its significance reverberated through Gabrielle's heart. She yearned for a meaningful endeavor, something to deepen her connection to the church and fill her days with purpose.

Then she discovered *Busted Halo*, a digital sanctuary for imperfect seekers. Their Lenten challenge beckoned: a photographic pilgrimage, one image a day, each guided by a theme. Gabrielle accepted, not just to post but to reflect, to grow.

Ash Wednesday marked the beginning. Forty days stitched with light, longing, and grace. Each day became meditation, a pause to see the sacred in the ordinary. Some prompts were playful; others cracked her open. Sacrifice, healing, grief. Through it all, Gabrielle found herself not just documenting Lent but living it.

She saw her baptism anew. She honored her father's memory with laughter frozen in a photograph. She let the ocean become her confessional, the sunset, her psalm, the rice bowl, her prayer.

Her husband, ever her anchor, appeared in snapshots of gratitude, forgiveness, shared meals, quiet walks.

The challenge became rhythm, a sacred beat carrying her through March.

As Holy Week neared, Gabrielle felt something shift. She wasn't just participating. She was transforming. Bottle caps became palm trees and crabs. The brick outside church became a station of the cross.

In quiet moments, poolside reveries, backyard meditations, video chats. Gabrielle found God in the gentle. Lent had always been about giving up. This year, she gave herself permission to be present, imperfect, seen. Grace was not earned, but received one photo, one prayer, one breath at a time.

Day by day, Gabrielle stitched a tapestry of devotion. Each photograph, each caption, each quiet moment became a thread in her spiritual quilt, a visual liturgy of Lent. From hibiscus blooms to fish sandwiches, baptismal candles to bottle cap crabs, Gabrielle chronicled not just the season but her soul's unfolding. She captured sunsets like benedictions, crosses like anchors, her own face veiled in joy or restlessness. The challenge began as outlet but became sacred rhythm, a daily invitation to reflect, remember, and receive.

When Easter arrived, Gabrielle stood at resurrection's edge with gratitude and longing. She had not missed a day. Yet something felt incomplete.

On the Easter Vigil, as eight souls stepped into baptismal waters, Gabrielle watched. Her own baptism, a pitcher's pour at the altar, now felt like a whisper compared to the cascade she witnessed. "I missed out," she confessed. Was it punishment, humility, or simply pandemic timing?

Her husband's counsel was gentle: "Pray. Seek the priest's wisdom." Even as bunny rabbits greeted them in the driveway, Gabrielle's heart remained tethered to something deeper.

Easter Sunday. Gabrielle posted a picture, its caption echoing the empty tomb: "He is not here, for He has risen."

Easter unfolded at a friend's house. Neighbors gathered. Laughter mingled with fragrant dishes. Stories flowed. In that communion, Gabrielle found solace.

Her Lenten challenge concluded, a mosaic of pixels spanning February to April. She had not missed a day. Yet a quiet void lingered. Jeffrey, once a wound, now a specter in her prayers. He no longer evoked tears but remained a name whispered in silence.

April. The real estate exam arrived, a threshold to reinvention. Doubts crept in, but her husband's encouragement became her compass. "You've come this far. Don't stop now." Gabrielle pressed on, seeking purpose beyond pixels and prayers.

May. Nostalgia stirred. Gabrielle and her husband packed their truck. This time, they chose the road over the skies. Her husband refused the mask bound rituals of air travel, so the highway became their pilgrimage, eighteen hours of asphalt and anticipation.

Gabrielle took the wheel at times, her fingers tracing the contours of the steering wheel, her thoughts tracing the contours of Jeffrey's absence. Would she find courage to seek him out? Would he even want to be found?

The following day, celebration. Her husband's grandson's birthday unfolded in bursts of laughter and frosting. They hugged the little ones, joy contagious. The oldest grandson drifted toward adolescence and independence.

As the sun dipped, Gabrielle's side of the family gathered. Stories flowed around a long table. Her mother beamed, her smile a lighthouse in the fog of time.

Mother's Day dawned golden. St. Michael's Church stood radiant, its steeple catching morning light. Gabrielle and her husband stepped into the sanctuary, a place that had once held their confessions, their beginnings.

Father James greeted them, eyes crinkling: "How fares Florida?" They stood on the threshold of normalcy: no masks but still a cautious dance of space. Gabrielle knelt. Her whispered prayers rose like incense. Jeffrey's name lingered, a plea to the heavens. Could God hear the echoes of longing?

Outside, the church yard basked in warmth. Her husband wandered, nostalgia guiding him. The old neighborhood unfolded, doors knocked, memories stirred. Some neighbors welcomed him, others hesitated. Covid had woven threads of caution, and he respected them.

Days blurred, a patchwork of hellos and goodbyes. Her husband reconnected with old friends. Gabrielle found solace in their temporary abode. Her mother and sister became companions. Friends flitted beyond her grasp, work, distance, life. But her mother filled the gaps, her presence a quiet comfort.

The next morning: Cracker Barrel. Her mom's eyes sparkled as she ordered pancakes. They lingered, stretching time. Departure loomed. They hugged her mom, her embrace a harbor against storms.

As the sun dipped, they climbed into their truck. The road stretched ahead, leading them back to Florida. Jeffrey remained a phantom. Gabrielle wished for more time, more chances to mend frayed connections.

They drove through the night. Stars winked above. Her husband hummed a tune. Gabrielle, nestled in the passenger seat, whispered her final prayer: *Maybe someday, Jeffrey.*

Sunday. Stained glass filtered light. They sat in the hallowed embrace of church, liturgy unfolding like a familiar song. But Gabrielle's heart was elsewhere. Jeffrey's name echoed, a fragile prayer. She knelt, murmuring: *"Jeffrey . . . please put him back in my life."*

After Mass, her husband hesitated, gift and card poised. Their friends, new homeowners, received a housewarming gift: a prayer of

Saint Benedict. Protection. Peace. They posted a snapshot online, a testament to friendship and connection. Gabrielle and her husband felt the warmth.

Then came Jeffrey's birthday. Gabrielle's cursor hovered. *Happy Birthday, douchebag*, she typed. Delivered. Seen. No reply. Silence, a familiar companion. Jeffrey's page lacked the birthday feature, a secret he kept. Her husband, too, hesitated. Maybe Jeffrey wanted no fanfare. So he held his wishes.

As the day waned, Gabrielle imagined Jeffrey somewhere out there, caught in life's currents. Did he feel the echoes of her whispers? Frustration bloomed.

Gabrielle posted: *No response is a response. If they wanted to, they would have. Not everyone has the same heart as you.* Later, sadness returned. Another post: *Not everyone is meant to be in your future. Some people are just passing through to teach you life's lessons.*

June arrived. A month of blooming flowers and whispered secrets. Friends gathered at their home. The grill sizzled—steaks, potatoes, charred perfection. Laughter flowed. Stars bore witness to camaraderie.

The next day, Tampa friends arrived. And then, the unexpected: a Tshirt, bold and cheeky, *House Bitch.* Crafted for her husband. Jealousy tinged with admiration. He was no ordinary participant in domestic duties. He danced with the broom, waltzed with laundry, and painted walls with precision. Cooking was Gabrielle's realm. A pact they had made: she was the chef, he the cleaner. A choreographyof partnership.

Their friends had stories of their own. One husband, a phantom in his home. His wife, the caretaker, served him meals, filled his plate, tended to his every need. A silent contract. She was the martyr; he was the invalid.

Gabrielle listened, her heart a mosaic of empathy and defiance. "Choose your battles," they said. But this was Gabrielle's battle. Her husband stood beside her, a testament to equality, shared responsibility, love moving in both directions. Their marriage built not on tradition but on truth. Not on roles but respect.

On a sunny July morning, Gabrielle's determination paid off. The Mustang convertible, her dream, had danced on the edges of conversation for eighteen months. She dropped hints at breakfast, slipped brochures onto his desk, and admired their neighbor's gleaming ride.

Her husband, ever the pragmatist, resisted: "Our vehicles are paid for." But Gabrielle persisted in gentle persuasion, raised eyebrows, wistful sighs. Slowly, his resolve cracked.

That morning, the sun kissed the driveway. Keys cool in her palm. Top down. Gabrielle slid into the driver's seat, heart a symphony of joy.

Her husband smiled with surrender and pride. The engine purred. It wasn't just a car. It was a promise fulfilled. Freedom. Joy.

The Mustang arrived, pristine white, black ragtop. Not the color she'd dreamed of but everything she needed. His caption said it all: *She finally wore me down and got her midlife crisis vehicle!* Teasing comments rolled in. Spoiled, indulgent. Gabrielle didn't care. She had earned this moment.

Then, contrast. The rain came. A tempest turned their neighborhood into a waterlogged wonderland. Streets shimmered like rivers. Driveways disappeared. But their home stood firm, no damage, just raindrops on a grateful roof.

Coincidence or divine timing, the flood arrived as her husband's children and grandchildren descended. Thirteen souls, a cascade of laughter, chaos, family bonds.

Morning of the airport run, streets submerged, but their truck plowed through. They emerged soggy but triumphant, ready to welcome his youngest son.

Lunch leisurely, reunion sweet. By the time they returned, floodwater receded, leaving damp memories and dry laughter.

Then came the rest: daughter-in-law, her husband, grandkids exuberant, untamed, a symphony of tiny feet and big emotions. Their quiet home became sanctuary of sound.

The following day dawned with rolling suitcases and airport itineraries. Her husband, now a seasoned shuttle driver, embarked on a marathon of pickups: first, his oldest grandson and girlfriend; then, under afternoon sun, his son's girlfriend; finally, twilight painted the sky as his oldest son arrived, weary and grateful. By the time he returned, he resembled a cabbie on his final shift, eyes bleary, heart full.

Their three bedroom abode was transformed into refuge for multitudes. Air mattresses bloomed. The great room became playground. The den cradled his oldest son. The dining room morphed into a nest for the grandson and girlfriend. Chaos reigned, smelling of sunscreen, sounding like laughter.

Then, a twist of fate. Gabrielle handed the Mustang keys to her oldest grandson. His eyes widened, awe and adrenaline. The engine roared, wind tousled his hair. He became master of the sleek white steed. The other grandkids clamored for rides, joy echoing down sunlit streets. Gabrielle snapped photos, delight etched on faces. Her caption: *My chauffeur for the day* ❤❤❤.

The rest of the day unfolded lazily. The boys teed off at the golf course, camaraderie infectious. The others basked by the pool, sipping cool drinks, sharing tales. As the sun dipped, they gathered for dinner, a chorus of voices, a table full of stories.

Next morning, beach day. Her husband's daughter-in-law, fueled by wanderlust, proposed an outing. Gabrielle suggested a secluded state park, but her heart was set on North Captiva Island, visions of pristine shores and hidden coves. North Captiva, accessible only by boat, beckoned with promises of serenity.

The daughter-in-law paid the fare. Saltkissed breeze, sundrenched smiles. Reality shifted: no taxis, no shuttles, only golf carts reserved for guests. Panic fluttered. Belongings weighed heavy.

Enter the local hero, a sunkissed islander, eyes glazed from more than sun. Her husband struck a deal. The man's golf cart carried their cargo, sobriety elusive. Her husband climbed aboard, bags stacked like a Jenga tower. The rest trudged the sandy path, frustration woven into each step.

The beach appeared, a sliver of paradise. Azure waves, swaying palms. But it was private. They relocated to the public section, a postage stamp of coastline.

A family photo captured exasperation smiles masking tempest. No restrooms. No relief. The dock, a distant mirage. Bickering erupted. Gabrielle declared escape.

The boat schedule mocked impatience. 1:00 p.m. loomed. She sought solace at the bar. Margaritas soothed. Her husband joined her. Laughter mingled with clinking glasses.

Lunchtime, the sole restaurant. Laughter echoed across sand.

As the boat neared, choices crystallized. Her husband, his oldest grandson, his girlfriend, and Gabrielle boarded. The mainland welcomed them. Gabrielle vowed never to take solid ground for granted again.

Back home, tales spilled forth. Dinner became celebration. Despite chaos and misadventure, they reveled in absurdity.

The sun rose over their Florida home. Grandkids chased each other through halls, laughter bouncing off walls. Gabrielle brewed coffee, heart full despite fatigue. The pool sparkled, a magnet for splashes and cannonballs. Gabrielle watched from the lanai, cold drink in hand, snapping photos of sunkissed faces.

Next morning, golf and goodbyes. The boys teed off, camaraderie effortless. Her husband resumed airport chauffeur duties.

First, his son's girlfriend departed. Then the oldest grandson and girlfriend. The house began to exhale. Air mattresses deflated. Towels hung to dry.

Conversation softened. That evening, the remaining crew gathered for dinner. The table brimmed with laughter, stories of the beach, golf swings gone awry, Mustang joyrides.

The next day, farewells. Gabrielle and her husband escorted his youngest and oldest sons to the airport. Hugs long, goodbyes bittersweet. Her husband declared: "Never again!" Eyes twinkled with exhaustion and affection.

They chuckled, knowing "never again" meant "until next time." Dinner on the way home, a quiet meal. The house waited, silence startling. Linens laundered, memories folded, air mattresses tucked away. Exhaustion palpable, gratitude deeper.

The following morning, bags packed. A promise to Gabrielle's mom awaited: the garage, the yard sale, the pilgrimage of memory.

That evening, as the house settled into stillness, her husband sighed: "Quiet. I kind of miss the chaos." Gabrielle smiled. Chaos had its charm, but quiet held grace.

The next day, on the road again. Truck tires hummed against asphalt, retracing familiar route. Spirits threadbare, energy sapped by laughter and logistics.

Twilight settled as they pulled into her mom's driveway. Porch light flickered, a beacon of welcome. Her mom's embrace awaited.

Next morning, St. Michael's. Sunlight filtered through stained glass. Gabrielle and her husband sat side-by-side, Mass unfolding like a familiar song. Her husband discreetly snapped a photo, a quiet moment shared with the world.

Yet Gabrielle's mind drifted. Jeffrey. That church had been the backdrop for their conversation during her mother-in-law's funeral. His grief had mirrored hers. Their shared vulnerability etched indelible marks. Gabrielle bowed her head, offering silent prayer.

After service, she toyed with suggesting a visit. Hesitation held her back. Would he even want to see her? Instead, they returned to her mom's house.

The garage, once a repository of forgotten treasures, resembled a battlefield. Cardboard boxes teetered, contents spilling. Her husband surveyed chaos with horror and determination. He rolled up his sleeves, ready to wage war.

But as afternoon sun slanted through dusty windows, he surrendered. The clutter had won. He retreated to the cool interior, seeking refuge in television's glow. Meanwhile, Gabrielle and her mom sifted through remnants.

The next day, purpose. The garage beckoned. Armed with resolve and nostalgia, they stepped into the dust. Footsteps stirred motes. The air smelled of memories. A walking path emerged. Her mom, a keeper of miscellaneous items, had amassed a curious collection.

Her siblings, well intentioned but elusive, had promised to help. But as the sun climbed, excuses multiplied. One had a migraine. Another, a deadline. Figures, Gabrielle thought. Their absence a familiar ache. She and her husband soldiered on, fueled by purpose and stubborn resolve.

Later, a cemetery pilgrimage. Rows of weathered headstones. Her husband's parents rested side-by-side. His son lay nearby, memory of a fragile bloom. They placed wreaths, handmade in Florida, woven with reverence.

Then, another cemetery. Another chapter. Her dad's grave, adorned with fresh flowers. Gabrielle knelt, tracing the letters of his name. The wreaths found their place there too.

She had made wreaths for two friends as well, one for a softball player chasing dreams, another for a friend's son who played football, not baseball. The extra wreath lingered. Jeffrey surfaced. Her husband reached out. A message sent into the ether: did Jeffrey want the spare wreath?

Her husband messaged Jeffrey, including Gabrielle in the exchange.

Husband: *I'm not trying to be in your business but was wondering if your sons are still playing baseball.*

Jeffrey: *Yes, he's doing well. Wants to give up travel ball as his interest is elsewhere.*

Husband: *What are his team's colors, and what's his jersey number?*

Jeffrey: *Red and blue. Number twenty-four. Plays first base and catcher. Does well for a boy who lost interest. Lol.*

Her husband sent a photo of the wreath—red, white, and blue. *Trying to find it a home. No pressure.*

Jeffrey replied he would send the picture to his son's mother and asked how much.

Husband: *It's yours if you want it. No charge.*

No reply followed. Gabrielle guessed he was waiting on his ex-wife.

That evening, the county fair. Cotton candy stalls, Ferris wheels spinning lazily, carnival games humming. First stop: the car show. An oasis for her husband's passion. His eyes sparkled as he admired vintage classics, muscle cars.

Armed with his camera, he captured chrome and combustion. Later, he shared those moments online. Friends marveled at his keen eye.

The following day, garage cleaning. Her mom unearthed a list of son-in-law duties. Armed with a toolbox, he changed bulbs, filters, anything needing attention. As he balanced on a ladder, Gabrielle chuckled. Guilt or not, he completed each task, earning brownie points in the family ledger.

Evening brought reunion. Dinner at Texas Roadhouse with his oldest grandson and girlfriend. They laughed, reminisced, savored togetherness. Before parting, her husband insisted on a group photo. Smiles wide, he shared another slice of life online.

Back at her mom's house, a message awaited.

Jeffrey: *First, let me thank you for offering. She just returned my message and said she's not interested. Thank you, it's a nice wreath. Frankly, I wouldn't have a place to display it. Thanks again.*

Her husband had already given up. Gabrielle's sister found someone who wanted the wreath. He replied: *No worries. My wife's sister found a home for it. Take care.*

No response. Gabrielle had anticipated convergence. Surely, her husband would extend an invitation. But it remained unspoken. When she questioned him, his eyes flickered with guilt and defiance. Her defense: "Pictures, my dear. Pictures on social media. Jeffrey surely saw we were here."

Beneath hashtags lay truth. Christmas had left her husband's heart marinated in resentment. Still, he left the door ajar. Jeffrey remained silent, cocooned in his own world.

The next evening, Gabrielle and her husband embarked on what she believed would be a majestic hot air balloon ride. It was etched onto her bucket list.

At the launch site, anticipation bubbled. The balloon stood proudly against the fading sky, its envelope billowing. Gabrielle imagined drifting over hills, glimpsing distant lakes. The world would shrink beneath them.

As the balloon lifted, she peered over the edge, expecting the ground to recede. Instead, they hovered just above the fairgrounds, tethered by an invisible thread. They ascended to a modest height, three hundred feet. It was as if the balloon whispered: *Fear not, for magic exists even in the mundane.*

The view, though not the sweeping panorama she'd envisioned, held charm. From above, the fairgrounds transformed into a miniature wonderland. Her disappointment softened into quiet acceptance.

As they descended, burners roared, casting a warm glow. The fairgrounds welcomed them back. Gabrielle laughed with relief and contentment. It wasn't the grand voyage she'd imagined, but it was shared. Etched into memory.

Later that night, she scrolled through her phone, selecting snapshots from their tethered flight. She posted them with a caption: *When life offers you a balloon ride, even if it's just a few feet off the ground, take it. You'll find magic in unexpected places.*

The next morning, there was a transformation. The garage stood neat. Rows of stacked boxes. Swept corners. Open space beckoned. Pride swelled. Each item had found its place. You could walk through it unhindered. The air carried whispers of freedom.

The garage sale remained a dream. Her siblings, bound by their own lives, couldn't lend a hand. Gabrielle and her husband were a team, but even together, a sale required accomplices.

Later that afternoon, there was a café conversation. Her friend arrived. They sat across from each other at a cozy table. She spilled her heart's triumphs, setbacks, mundane miracles.

And then, inevitably, Jeffrey. Gabrielle listened, her silence a sanctuary. Her friend recounted the encounter at her father's service, painting Jeffrey's eyes, the lines etched by time, the quiet gravity of his presence. Gabrielle didn't interrupt. She nodded, a witness. Jeffrey was a chapter in both their lives. Though Gabrielle hadn't seen him, his presence lingered.

Across town, her husband embarked on his own journey. Old neighbors welcomed him. Gabrielle glimpsed nostalgia in his eyes, the same eyes that had watched their departure from familiar streets. They had traded the known for the unknown, routine for reinvention. And while he never admitted it, Gabrielle sensed melancholy. The neighborhood they left behind was more than houses and lawns. It was a tapestry woven with laughter, whispered secrets, everyday rhythm.

As the afternoon waned, Gabrielle and her friend parted, promising to meet again. Her husband returned, footsteps heavy with memories.

The sun peeked over the horizon. Their departure was swift, fueled by the promise of home, Florida waiting at the end of the road. No urgent matters pulled them back.

They surrendered to the rhythm of the highway, letting miles carry them toward rest and reflection.

Morning tiptoed in. The road unspooled, a ribbon of recollection. Conversations flowed, laughter mingled with quiet contemplation.

Then, home. They stepped inside. The laundry basket beckoned. Suitcases disgorged their contents.

Her husband's eyes lingered on familiar houses. He wouldn't admit it, but Gabrielle saw it, the ache of leaving. Florida was their new chapter. But the old one remained etched in their hearts.

The Grace That Found Her

"Surely goodness and mercy shall follow me all the days of my life."

—PSALM 23:6

JULY STRETCHED BEFORE THEM. Gabrielle and her husband embraced it fully. Their Mustang became a chariot, its convertible top folded down as they cruised sundrenched roads. The engine's purr harmonized with laughter. Gabrielle reveled in the wind whipping through her hair, her husband in the sheer joy of top down driving. Their roles were clear: Gabrielle, the navigator. He, the conductor.

August arrived with a yearning for something new, a hidden beach, a treasure waiting to be discovered. They veered toward Casperson Beach, a lesser known gem near Venice. The salty breeze greeted them.

Gabrielle scanned the shoreline for shark teeth, tiny fossils peeking from the sand. She snapped photos and shared them online. Friends tapped hearts, left comments.

As they left, a sign caught their eye: *Red Tide Warning.* Dead fish scattered along the shore. They dismissed it, a mere footnote in their escapade.

Back home, laughter gave way to discomfort. Her husband tested positive for Covid. Medications arrived. Their home became a sanctuary of care. Gabrielle followed suit.

Ten days of quarantine stitched together with uncertainty. Her husband paced, muttering about red tide and conspiracy theories. Gabrielle sipped tea and watched the days unfold.

And then, her husband emerged. Labor Day beckoned. He strutted around. "Back to normal," he declared.

Their friends had other plans. Unvaccinated, they were pariahs, lepers of the social circuit. His fury brewed. "Lepers," he muttered.

So, their weekend shifted. They fired up the grill. Their lanai became sanctuary.

But the road called them to Marco Island. The Mustang's engine hummed. He snapped photos, the sunset, the seagulls, their dinner. Each click a declaration: *We exist. We thrive.* As waves lapped their toes, they reveled in defiance. His vow: stay away, a self imposed exile.

Days passed. His anger softened. Then fate intervened. A thump, a wobble, the Mustang's tire groaned.

They pulled over, hearts sinking. Modern Mustangs flaunt sleek lines, but spare tires are relics. Instead, repair kits and optimism.

The dealership beckoned. A tow truck hoisted their steed. Gabrielle snapped a photo, captioned with a sad emoji.

Friends, the very ones who spurned them, were distant constellations. They hailed an Uber, rode home in silence. The Mustang's absence was a quiet ache.

Days later, the dealership worked its magic. Tire resurrected, spirit intact. Her husband seized the moment. Social media beckoned. "Back in business," he declared. The Mustang gleamed. The road awaited. His fury softened. Maybe, just maybe, their friends had meant well.

September neared. Gabrielle's anticipation grew. Her 50th birthday loomed ahead. Her husband had dropped a hint: "The Mustang is yours."

But celebrations were impossible. Friends and family scattered. Gabrielle had a secret wish: a bulldog puppy. Wrinkled faces, waddling gait melted her heart.

Her husband shook his head. "Not ready for that commitment." Undeterred, Gabrielle compiled a list of desires, road trips, and adventures.

Days passed. Then, a package arrived. Her husband's excitement bubbled. "Open it!" Gabrielle tore through wrapping, revealing a tiny ceramic bulldog. "Gizmo," he announced. "Your very own puppy."

Gabrielle chuckled, touched. "Well Gizmo, you may not wag your tail, but you've stolen my heart."

The mailbox overflowed. Her husband had orchestrated a covert operation. He rallied their tribe: "Send her a card for her 50th." And so they came. Familiar handwriting, long lost signatures.

Gabrielle placed them beside Gizmo, who seemed to nod with approval.

The eve of her birthday arrived. Her husband whispered promises of a surprise, a road trip into the unknown. "Trust me," he said.

They hit the open road. Curiosity bubbled. "Where are we headed?" Gabrielle asked. His grin held firm. Then they veered toward the airport. Her heart sank. Airports were for departures, not arrivals. Yet there they were.

Inside, against bustling travelers, stood her mom and sister. Her jaw dropped. Her mom, who had never flown, stood wideeyed. Beside her, her sister grinned.

Tears blurred Gabrielle's vision as she enveloped them in a three way hug. "How?" she stammered. Her husband beamed. "A plea for birthday cards turned into flights. Fifty cards for fifty years." Her mom clutched her hand. "I flew," she whispered. "For you."

The sundrenched days unfolded. Her mom and sister graced their home. Together, they toured Florida—palm lined streets, hidden gems, powdery sands. At the water's edge, Gabrielle watched her mom's eyes widen. "This," she murmured, "is paradise."

Then, the day arrived. Gabrielle sat at the coffee table, surrounded by love. Her husband grinned. "Fifty cards. Just like your fifty years."

Gabrielle opened each one, a cascade of well wishes, laughter, heartfelt sentiments. Tears blurred her vision as she realized her heart had cast a wider net than she ever imagined. Friends near and far had woven themselves into her story. This, she knew, was the grandest celebration of all.

That evening, her husband whisked them away to her favorite rib joint. The menu offered comfort in smoky promises. As the first rib met her lips, Gabrielle tasted not just barbecue sauce but the sweetness of love.

Midway through their feast, the doorbell chimed. A basket of goodies lay at their doorstep, a symphony of chocolate, scented candles, handwritten notes.

Back home, Gabrielle clutched it to her chest, heart swollen. The basket sat on the coffee table, its contents spilling warmth. She traced the edges of each item, chocolate wrapped in gold foil, candles infused with lavender, notes penned in familiar hands. Her heart swelled. Not from grandeur but from grace.

The days that followed carried a gentle rhythm. Her mom and sister lingered. Her mom marveled at Florida's skies, declaring each sunset a masterpiece. Her sister snapped candid photos, sunlit smiles destined for albums and recollections.

And then, as all visits must, the time came to part. Gabrielle stood at the airport beneath the weight of goodbye. Her mom hugged her tightly. "I flew for you," she whispered again. Her sister winked, promising another adventure.

Gabrielle carried their love home, tucked between birthday cards and scented candles, between ribs and road trips, between Gizmo's ceramic smile and the Mustang's steady purr.

Back home, Gizmo sat proudly on the coffee table, surrounded by birthday cards that refused to be tucked away. Gabrielle paused, fingers grazing the edges of one with handwriting she didn't recognize.

Even the unknown had found her. But amid the cascade of kindness, one silence still echoed. Jeffrey. Her husband had included him in the invitation, fifty cards for fifty years. But no message arrived. Gabrielle's heart cracked, just slightly, beneath the celebration.

Days passed. The birthday glow softened into routine. Another milestone approached: her husband's birthday. He had two steadfast loves: lobster and chocolate cake.

Gabrielle swept him to a cozy seafood joint where butter was pooled in tiny dishes. Across the table, his eyes sparkled.

Then came the cake, sinfully rich. They savored it slowly, forks clinking, laughter rising.

Back home, a gift waited, new clothes chosen with care. His gratitude was quiet, but Gabrielle saw it in the way he fingered the fabric.

Then, the digital world intruded. A message from Jeffrey: *Happy Birthday, my friend. Wishing you a wonderful day! Peace be ours, brother.* Her husband's reply was simple: *Amen.* Gabrielle leaned across the table. "What's the story?" He chuckled. "Man code. It means all is forgiven." Jeffrey had resurfaced. Not for her. But for him. And somehow, that was enough.

A few days later, Tropicana Field. Great seats by the Rays dugout. Gabrielle clutched her foam finger. *This is where magic happens.*

The game unfolded. Her husband turned photographer, capturing smiles, scoreboard winking. He posted: *Still celebrating her 50th birthday. How many days does one celebrate turning fifty? Asking for a friend.*

Gabrielle laughed. *As long as she wants*, she whispered. He grinned. "In baseball and birthdays, there are no limits."

Sunday morning, familiar pews. The sanctuary glowed with stained glass. Father Michael stood near the altar, eyes crinkled, posture thoughtful. Nudged by celestial forces, he turned toward them. "How have you both been? It's been too long since I last visited your home."

Gabrielle's husband blurted, "Father, would you honor us with dinner?" Father Michael's eyes twinkled. "I would be delighted."

Their ordinary Sunday was stitched with anticipation. Gabrielle's anxiety took flight. What would they serve? Could mismatched plates suffice? Her husband reassured her, "He's just a man, love. A man who happens to wear a collar." But Gabrielle knew he was more—a vessel of grace.

On the cusp of October, there was another celebration. Seventeen years of marriage. Their favorite BBQ joint welcomed them. "The usual?" the waiter asked. They nodded. Ribs, brisket, cornbread, a feast of memory.

Between bites, they reminisced about their wedding day, the tremble in his hand as he slid the ring onto her finger. Seventeen years later, that same hand held hers across the sticky tablecloth.

Dessert arrived, a molten chocolate lava cake. As they split the center, the years melted away. He posted their story online, a sepia wedding photo beside a recent snapshot. *Happy 17th anniversary and counting.* Notifications chimed, a chorus of hearts and congratulations. Each one a stitch in their shared joy.

A few days later, Father Michael arrived. Their home carried the lingering warmth of anniversary laughter. The scent of roasted pork and shared stories danced in the air. Gabrielle's culinary symphony was humble but heartfelt, pork roast with golden potatoes, carrots, and cornbread.

Father Michael, eyes crinkling in approval, requested seconds. Amid the clinking of forks and flicker of candlelight, conversation deepened. Their church back home became the topic.

Over dessert, Gabrielle poured out her heart. "Father, I felt cheated. Covid stole my chance at a traditional Easter baptism."

Father Michael's gaze held her. "You are not alone. The pandemic reshaped our rituals, but it need not dim your faith. Perhaps there is another path."

Then came the invitation. Unexpected. Sacred. He asked Gabrielle to join the RCIA program. The woman who had guided him had moved away, leaving a void. "Help me," he implored. "Your baptism was merely the prologue. RCIA can be your epiphany."

He extended the invitation to her husband as well. "A team," her husband had declared. Now, that bond was extended into ministry. They agreed without hesitation.

The days marched toward their first RCIA class. Gabrielle reread the binder, its pages a map of mystery and meaning. Doctrine, sacraments, liturgical seasons, words she had once skimmed now felt like sacred invitations.

The dinner had been more than a meal. It was a doorway. "He knew," Gabrielle whispered. "Father Michael knew all along."

As she washed dishes, her hands moving through warm water and memory, she whispered: *Thank you for this unexpected grace.*

Sunday arrived, golden morning. The bishop led the liturgy, his voice steady, his eyes holding centuries of faith. *May your journey be blessed*, he said. Gabrielle felt the words settle into her bones.

After Mass, Father Michael guided them to the RCIA room. Five souls awaited, seekers in search of sacred ground. Gabrielle and her husband were introduced not just as participants but as guides.

The session unfolded gently, the Holy Trinity, mystery wrapped in unity. They weren't just learning. They remembered something ancient.

At the end, Father Michael handed them a guide. "You'll lead together," he said. "He'll manage attendance. You'll foster dialogue. Together, you'll help them find their way."

Back home, Gabrielle laid the binder on the table. Pages meticulous, each lesson a thread woven with intention. She took notes, chronicling their pilgrimage. Sundays were no longer ordinary. They were marked by revelation, by shared questions, by the sacred rhythm of seeking.

The morning of the real estate exam arrived with unfinished dreams. Gabrielle sat in the testing center, surrounded by desperation and fluorescent lights. She hadn't studied much, just a frantic cram session.

The questions came fast: zoning laws, escrow accounts, terms memorized but not mastered. Her fingers trembled.

The verdict: four points short. Gabrielle walked out into sunlight, but it didn't feel warm. "Maybe destiny has other plans," she whispered.

On the drive home, her husband pointed to a construction site. A sign caught her eye: *Farmer Joe's Coming Soon!* "You should apply," he said. Gabrielle mourned the dream that hadn't bloomed. But later that evening, she filled out the application.

The next morning, an email arrived. *Interview Invitation.* Gabrielle blinked. It was happening fast. She ironed a blouse, tucked nerves into her purse, and walked into the interview with a borrowed smile.

The questions were simple. The manager was kind. The offer came quickly: deli team, part time. Gabrielle accepted with quiet resolve. Her husband's pride was palpable, a balm to her bruised ambition. Inside, she still longed for freedom, but this was a beginning. Not the one she had planned. Perhaps the one she needed.

On a tranquil Sunday, Gabrielle and her husband met in the sanctuary. Light filtered through stained glass.

Their second RCIA session began. Her husband recorded attendance. Gabrielle prepared the space, straightening chairs, lighting candles.

Dialogue unfolded gently, touching upon her unique RCIA journey, shaped by the shadow of the pandemic. She spoke of her postponed baptism, the ache of waiting. Yet faith had anchored her, not in ceremony but conviction.

Father Michael stepped forward, voice calm, presence steady.

The topic: *Who is Jesus Christ?*

In candlelight, they explored Christ's many facets:

- The Inviter: Jesus, who walks beside us, guiding us beyond ritual into relationship.
- The Promise Keeper: He assures eternal life, filling our souls with hope and renewal.
- The Path of Relationship: Through prayer and sacrament, we draw nearer to the divine, to the mystery of the Trinity.

As dusk fell, they parted ways, their hearts ablaze with new understanding. Gabrielle felt something shift in her spirit. This was no longer a class. It was a pilgrimage.

The following Sunday, they transitioned from the solemnity of Mass to the vibrant RCIA classroom.

A new presenter awaited them. Jack, with a warm, resonant voice, welcomed them into the world of Scripture. He unfolded the Bible like a map of sacred terrain:

- The Pentateuch: The genesis of the Israelites and the divine covenant.

- Historical Books: Tales of wanderings, battles, and divine intervention.
- Wisdom Books: Reflections on human nature, suffering, and joy.
- Prophetic Books: Proclamations of justice and the relentless love of God.
- The Gospels: Four lenses, one Savior.
- Acts and Epistles: The early church's heartbeat and the teachings that shaped it.
- Revelation: The triumph of Christ and the promise of eternity.

Gabrielle listened, each verse unfolding like a thread woven into her understanding. The Bible, once a static text, became a living guide, a path to be walked, not just read.

Inspired, she and her husband began a new ritual. They discovered the *Bible in a Year* podcast with Father Mike Schmitz, a daily immersion into Scripture. Each morning, they listened together, hearts open. They shared this discovery with their RCIA peers, inviting them to join the journey as pilgrims on a divine odyssey.

The next sacred Sunday arrived, bathed in morning light and quiet reverence. Gabrielle and her husband entered the sanctuary, their steps familiar, their hearts open. It was their fourth RCIA session, and the classroom had begun to feel like sacred ground, a place where questions bloomed and faith was stitched together one thread at a time.

Father Thom stood at the front, his Indian heritage woven into every word, his cadence rich with warmth and wisdom.

The day's topic: *Divine Revelation*. He spoke of God's voice, not booming from mountain tops but whispered through nature, prophets, and Scripture. "God's Revelation," he said, "is like a friend confiding a secret. Not to overwhelm, but to invite intimacy."

Gabrielle felt the words settle into her chest. She scribbled notes as Father Thom continued:

- God's Revelation: The Divine unveiled through creation and prophecy.
- Hearts Unveiled: The Bible as a love letter, inviting eternal friendship.
- Winding Journeys: Faith's path is not linear but always accompanied by God's steadfast presence.

Then came the question. A woman, new to the group, her Baptist roots evident in her posture and tone, raised her hand. "Why do Catholics call their priests 'Father'? Isn't God the only Father?"

The room paused. Father Thom's eyes softened. He began to answer, his words gentle but tangled in translation. His English bore the threads of his homeland: beautiful but not always precise. Gabrielle felt the tension. Not confrontation, but confusion.

Gabrielle stood, her voice steady, though her heart fluttered. "In our Catholic tradition," she began, "we address our priests as 'Father' for many reasons. It's a sign of respect, a recognition of their sacred role."

She glanced at the woman, whose arms were folded, her brow furrowed. "They are spiritual leaders," Gabrielle continued, "entrusted with the care of our souls. Like a father, they guide, correct, and nourish us."

She spoke of the priest's mantle, the shepherd of the parish, the spiritual head. "In return, we view him with affection. He becomes our confidant, our guide through life's labyrinth."

And then, the ancient echoes. "In the Old Testament, the father of the household was the spiritual leader. He shaped the family's faith. Our priests inherit that legacy. They are the fathers of our parish family."

The woman's expression shifted, not to agreement but to contemplation. "Shouldn't they be called 'Brother'? Like in other churches?"

Gabrielle nodded gently. "Indeed, that's one way. The path of brotherhood. But the Catholic Church, with its ancient rituals and traditions, sets us apart. 'Father' is not just a title. It's a thread connecting us to generations of faithful seekers."

The room was silent. Gabrielle stepped closer. "Open your heart," she said softly. "See this class not as a battle of words, but as an exploration. Let the nuances seep in. Let the layers of faith speak."

The woman sat back, her heart a locked chest, but the key now resting nearby. Father Thom resumed, his eyes still searching, his voice steady.

As the session ended, he approached Gabrielle. "Thank you," he said. "You built a bridge today."

Her husband leaned in, his voice low. "You put her in her place kindly." Gabrielle smiled, but not with pride. "I didn't want to win," she said. "I wanted her to feel welcome."

November's first light unfurled. Gabrielle sat at her kitchen table. But that day, her fingers danced across a different surface, the keyboard.

Indeed.com blinked back at her, a constellation of possibilities. Though she had agreed to join Farmer Joe's, her spirit craved something deeper, a calling that stirred her soul.

She searched for roles that whispered purpose. The solemn allure of funeral homes was the first to call to her. There was something sacred in the idea of helping others say goodbye, to be a quiet witness to grief's choreography.

But her heart wandered further, drawn to the quiet grandeur of hotels. She imagined herself as the harbinger of welcome and departure, weaving each guest's experience into a tapestry of comfort.

Each résumé she sent was a silent entreaty. She wondered: *Could her touch soothe the bereaved? Could her presence become part of someone's journey without ever knowing their name?*

And then, Sunday arrived again. The sacred rhythm resumed. Their fifth RCIA session unfolded beneath the soft glow of sanctuary light.

Rachel, the new director of religious education, stood before them, her voice warm, her presence grounding.

That day's topic: *Prayer and Catholic Traditions.* Rachel's words painted a mosaic of devotion:

- Prayer: A sacred dialogue where hearts meet God beyond the limits of language.
- Forms and Steps: Like a symphony, prayer moves through rhythms—Liturgy of the Hours, Examen, Jesus Prayer—each note a soul's offering.
- Solitude and Community: Whether whispered alone or spoken in circles, prayer touches eternity.
- God's Meeting Place: Amid joy, sorrow, doubt, or certainty, the Divine Artist paints our lives with presence.
- Rosary: Rachel's beads whispered secrets—Joyful, Sorrowful, Glorious Mysteries—each one a thread in Christ's story.

At the close of the session, Rachel gave each of them a rosary. Crafted by Catholic women in the parish, the beads shimmered with intention. Gabrielle's set, made from Florida's beaches, a symbol of the ebb and flow of life and faith.

After class, Gabrielle lingered. She confided in Rachel about the Baptist woman's absence. "I fear I drove her away," she said.

Rachel leaned in, her voice gentle. "The daughter yearns for Catholicism. Her heart beats with curiosity. But the mother seeks reasons to withhold permission. You did right by explaining."

Father Thom had spoken with Rachel too. He had sensed the tension, the resistance. Rachel predicted their departure. The mother, firm in her Baptist roots, had drawn a line. But the daughter lingered in spirit. A fragile hope remained.

As Advent approached, Rachel shared her vision. Gabrielle and her husband would now guide seekers through the Mass readings, offering context, inviting reflection, becoming stewards of Scripture. They would miss the Eucharist during RCIA, but Rachel reminded them, "Your commitment is profound. Attend another Mass. Receive communion. But know your presence here is a form of grace."

The week unfolded with a hush. Gabrielle's inbox remained silent, her applications drifting into the digital void. She considered reaching out to a recruiter, but her husband's voice—steady, practical—reminded her of her commitment to Farmer Joe's. "Let's not chase shadows," he said. "You've got a start date. Let's see where it leads." Gabrielle nodded. She wasn't sure if deli counters and name tags were where her spirit belonged, but she was willing to show up.

Then came the unexpected call. The manager's voice was upbeat, inviting her to a preopening meet and greet, a gathering for team building, training discussions, and a glimpse into the rhythm of the storetobe. The date was still floating, but Gabrielle agreed, her eagerness subdued, her heart cautiously open.

Sunday arrived and with it, the sixth RCIA session. The sanctuary welcomed them.

Father Thom stood before them, his presence calm, his words rich with meaning. That day's lesson: *The Liturgical Calendar.* They journeyed through the sacred seasons:

- Advent: A time of waiting, of quiet anticipation.
- Christmas: Joy incarnate, God with us.
- Lent: A pilgrimage inward, a mirror held to the soul.
- Triduum: Three days of solemnity of sacrifice and silence.
- Easter: Resurrection's triumph, the dawn of hope.
- Ordinary Time: The deep teachings, the sacred woven into the everyday.

Father Thom then unveiled the Gospel cycles—Years A, B, and C—a divine choreography that ensured every voice of Scripture was heard in time.

They explored the Mass itself, each part a step in the sacred dance of worship. From the opening rites to the final blessing, Gabrielle felt herself not just attending Mass but entering it.

As the session ended, Father Thom lingered. His eyes met Gabrielle's, and something passed between them, a silent recognition. She remembered her own RCIA journey—the waiting, the wondering. She nodded. No complaints. Only hearts ablaze.

Later that week, Gabrielle's job search resumed, her screen aglow with possibility. She applied to funeral homes again, drawn to the sacredness of farewell.

A coastal drive with her husband offered a balm: the Mustang's purr, the ocean's whispers, a tapestry of peace. And in that quiet, Jeffrey surfaced in her thoughts. Was he safe? Would he ever accept her again? Did friendship have a resurrection?

Sunday returned and with it, the seventh RCIA session. Father Michael led them through the sacred spaces of the Catholic Church. They explored the baptismal font, the altar's golden glow, and the ambo's resonant wood. Each element spoke of faith, of history, of belonging.

A new member joined them, her silence loud with story. Together, they wandered through the sacristy, the choir loft, the vestibule, a shared pilgrimage. Father Michael's teachings elevated each step, each space.

As the session ended, Gabrielle saw the new member's smile, a flicker of comfort found. And in herself, a sense of renewal. Retracing the steps of her spiritual home had rekindled something ancient, something alive.

The Return and the Whisper

"And after the fire came a gentle whisper."

—1 Kings 19:12

Thanksgiving beckoned, a tradition lost the year before to Covid's hush. This time, Gabrielle and her husband reclaimed it: to gather, to feast, to be held again by family.

Their flight hummed with anticipation. Upon touchdown, familiar ground welcomed them. A roadside eatery soothed travelworn souls before they arrived at Gabrielle's mother's house. The armchairs, stitched with years of stories, embraced them. Conversation lingered until fatigue settled.

Dawn broke and with it, remembrance. At a beloved breakfast nook, old friends awaited. They toasted resilience, laughter weaving through decades of shared history. Her husband captured the moment: *Morning with my buddies, where coffee and camaraderie collide.*

Thanksgiving lingered in warmth. At her brother's house, stories flowed. Black Friday brought Gabrielle and her sister to retail aisles, while her husband found sanctuary in her mother's quiet home. Evening drew them together over puzzle pieces, each click a metaphor for moments reclaimed.

On Sunday, they entered St. Michaels. The pews welcomed them, but guilt lingered, RCIA classes left behind in Florida whispered in their hearts. Advent had begun.

Her husband captured a photo, a digital memento of their return. Gabrielle's thoughts drifted to Jeffrey. The rift. The silence. The ache.

During the Eucharistic prayer, she bowed her head. *Please put Jeffrey back in my life*, she whispered. Her husband considered calling him, but he hesitated. "He's probably with his kids," he said. "I don't want to intrude."

Still, Gabrielle hoped that God, in His infinite wisdom, might weave their paths anew, to rekindle what was lost, to stitch together what time had frayed.

Later, in a cozy café, Gabrielle sat across from a dear friend. Laughter danced through golden light. She poured out her life's narrative—the unexpected turns, the grace that met her in unlikely places.

Jeffrey's name surfaced, a flicker, a ghost. Gabrielle's heart skipped, then steadied. She steered the conversation elsewhere.

Meanwhile, her husband wandered familiar streets, welcomed by old neighbors.

Later, Gabrielle and her friend met him at the curb. He stood steady, a quiet anchor. They drove home in companionable silence.

Christmas movies spun their magic. Her husband, wrapped in a festive blanket, leaned back with a grin. Her mother hovered nearby, cocoa in hand. Gabrielle captured the moment: *Watching Christmas movies with mom, because some traditions are timeless.*

The image joined their digital tapestry. As credits rolled, Gabrielle's gaze drifted to the puzzle sprawled across the table. With eyes closed, she whispered, *Bring Jeffrey back into my life.*

Family reunion followed, laughter and shared stories. Twilight brought them to his daughter-in-law's home, where innocence reminded them love binds beyond blood. Three generations wove past and future into the present, a bittersweet last evening, cherished and complete.

Dawn heralded their return to Florida. Friends waited at the airport, their offer to pick them up a silent truce. Breakfast buzzed with chatter.

At home, the rhythm was simple, unpacking, laundry, quiet companionship.

Yet Gabrielle's thoughts lingered on RCIA session eight, missed during travels. Rachel's voice echoed: heaven and hell, purgatory's refining fire, the scales of eternity. *Eschatology*, a word that tasted like hope. Gabrielle prayed for understanding.

December's warmth settled over their retreat. Their Christmas tree remained tucked away, yet the house glowed with understated charm. Gabrielle devised gag gifts: Tshirts labeled *Chest and Nuts, "Merry*

Christmas from a couple of nuts in Florida." A tiny flowerpot paired with a cheeky note: *A little bag of pot from Florida.* Her laughter filled the room.

Her husband included Jeffrey on the list. Gabrielle raised an eyebrow. "Why Jeffrey?" His eyes twinkled. "Because even nuts deserve holiday cheer."

Later, seizing the day's beauty, they embarked on a coastal drive. Mustang top down, freedom embraced. Gabrielle leaned toward her husband. "This RCIA program isn't the organized voyage I envisioned."

He grinned. "Organized? Perhaps not. The Lord's brushstrokes are wild and unpredictable."

"Mysterious ways?" she asked.

"Exactly. The Saints didn't follow neat outlines. They danced with the wind, wrestled with doubt, and still found grace."

"So, our role as sponsors . . ."

". . . is the flow," he finished.

"To be vessels, not architects," she said. "The Spirit guides, and we go with the flow."

Their laughter merged with the ocean's song. As they parked by the water, he squeezed her hand. "Everything will turn out fine. The Lord's currents carry us."

Days later, as Gabrielle wrapped gifts, her thoughts drifted to Jeffrey. The digital world held only his partial absence. Did he know the depth of his imprint, or was she just a passing chapter?

As Christmas neared, the desire to heal old wounds grew. Yet she paused, wary of reaching into silence. Would reconciliation flourish or falter?

Scrolling through social media, a post appeared: *If someone leaves footprints on your soul, be thankful. Even if their stay is fleeting, they've gifted you joy.*

Gabrielle hesitated, cursor poised. *This is for you, Jeffrey.* But reality intervened; he wouldn't see it. Still, her heart was clenched. She let the post linger, a whispered secret meant for his ears alone.

Another post surfaced: *There are moments when you miss someone so much, you want to pick them from your dreams and hug them for real.*

How achingly true, she thought. The screen blurred, memory surged, Jeffrey's laughter, then the ache. The craving for a hug, a bridge across absence.

She whispered: *Bring him back into my life. Not in grand gestures, but in quiet ways, a shared smile, a message that defies the silence.* She prayed, as she often did. Yet reality clung stubbornly. Jeffrey's absence left a hollow ache. He wasn't her friend online, yet Gabrielle clung to hope that someday, somehow, he might accept her.

Sunday marked a milestone. RCIA session ten and the Rite of Acceptance. The air was charged with anticipation. Though coordination was chaotic, Rachel encouraged them to embrace spontaneity and follow Father Michael's lead.

Gabrielle and her husband, novices in this realm, were given an unexpected honor: presenting the gifts during the Eucharist, bread and wine, symbols of Christ's sacrifice.

As they stepped forward, reverence settled upon them. Father Michael beckoned her husband to the Ambo to introduce the Catechumenates.

Gabrielle discreetly snapped photos, his expression a blend of excitement and solemnity. She posted them with quiet explanation. Friends glimpsed this sacred act unfolding within parish walls.

The Rite followed ancient rituals. Amid prayers and blessings, her husband was entrusted with the Roman Missal.

As the class dispersed, he led the way, carrying the sacred book. Gabrielle watched with pride.

Later, he confided that it stirred a sense of honor to play a role, to belong. A privilege beyond measure.

Post Mass, Father Michael's counsel was a balm. Their path needn't be perfect, only open. As they left, they felt the rhythm of their faith journey, assured that wherever the current of God's love led, they would follow. The topic shifted to the sacred rites that would shape their RCIA path:

- Rite of Acceptance: Their recent milestone, where the parish enveloped them with prayers and open arms.
- Rite of Sending: A spiritual convoy preparing them for the cathedral's embrace.
- Rite of Election: On the First Sunday of Lent, ancient rituals would affirm their calling—chosen by God and the Church.

And the sacraments, seven visible signs of grace soon to mark their souls:

- Baptism
- Confirmation

- Eucharist
- Penance
- Reconciliation
- Matrimony
- Holy Orders

After class, Father Michael sought them out. His words flowed like balm. They dissected the Mass, the rituals, the missteps, each thread woven with grace. Their mistakes, he assured, were insignificant.

The Divine was not bound by human stumbles. "Continue," he said, "to go with the flow. For where the current leads, there God awaits."

Gabrielle's week took an unexpected turn. Farmer Joe's manager called her in for deli orientation. She mingled with a lively crew, each sharing quirks and candy favorites.

Training was thorough: machines, sanitation, smiles. But delays loomed, casting doubt over her start date. Her husband's counsel steadied her. She pursued other prospects, each application a step toward promise.

As the holidays neared, Gabrielle prepared parcels with care. The post office buzzed with festive cheer. Each tracking number, a pledge of joy in transit.

At home, a social media post about mending friendships caught her eye. Moved, Gabrielle shared it, hoping to inspire kindness in the season of giving.

Sunday morning, the RCIA group gathered. Her husband led them from church to classroom, where Don and Rebecca shared tales of saints and sacraments.

Their passion was infectious, yet Gabrielle felt adrift, torn between admiration and her own contemplative rhythm. Baptism and Confirmation became mysteries alive. Rebecca's vivid descriptions of the Easter Vigil captivated them all.

As the session closed, Gabrielle pondered their fervor. Her husband's playful nudge, "always the contemplative," made her smile. Rebecca invited them to join her prayer group.

Gabrielle glimpsed the fire in her eyes but held back. "Don and Rebecca are devout, yes," she admitted later, "but maybe a tad too hard core for me." She craved solitude, the quietude of contemplation.

As the festive season enveloped their home, Gabrielle and her husband found themselves surrounded by heartfelt connection. The gifts they'd chosen carried silent promises to kindle joy. Jeffrey's message, though relayed through her husband, was genuine, a flicker of connection.

Yet Gabrielle longed for inclusion, a direct word. Still, she realized: his gratitude, though indirect, had reached her.

On Christmas Eve, they embarked on an unexpected adventure: midnight Mass. Despite reluctance, her husband agreed.

Inside, the choir's harmonies enveloped them. Beloved hymns bridged the earthly and divine. Later, as midnight bells tolled, they emerged, hearts full.

Homebound, they wrapped themselves in blankets. *It's a Wonderful Life* flickered on the screen, and they reveled in quiet magic.

Christmas arrived with greetings from loved ones.

Midday brought them to a friend's home. Simple gifts were shared; laughter filled the air. By dusk, they returned home, lulled to sleep by holiday films.

The next morning, they attended Mass. Afterward, a café offered reflection. Twilight fell and they wrapped themselves in peace, vowing to carry it beyond the season.

Then, a jolt. Gabrielle's phone rang. The manager at Farmer Joe's relayed another postponement. The delays tested her patience, but the promise of a new year offered hope.

An interview at a hotel on New Year's Eve: festive, unusual, welcome.

New Year's Eve unveiled possibilities. A quaint hotel buzzed with guests.

The interview unfolded easily. "Waiting," Gabrielle said, "is like brewing tea, patient, deliberate, worth the steep."

Forty-five minutes passed. The offer came: night auditor, full-time, Sunday through Thursday. Gratitude swelled. Yet hesitation stirred: the night shift clashed with church and RCIA.

Her husband's support was unwavering. "The decision is yours," he said. Gabrielle accepted. The reply came swiftly: "Begin on New Year's Day." She resolved: Monday, a new week, a new beginning.

As dawn broke on the New Year, they upheld tradition. Sanibel Island's shores embraced them. Gabrielle captured the sun's ascent. A perfect sand dollar appeared, a silent wish for reconciliation.

That evening, they joined hands in Mass. The chalk blessing marked their home: *20+C+M+B+22*. Gabrielle shared the ritual online, a digital echo of faith and hope.

Sunday morning, the RCIA congregation gathered. Mark and Ellen spoke of the Eucharist as encounter. "In the breaking of the bread," Mark said, "we meet the risen Lord." The session closed in prayer. Gabrielle felt the quiet power of change.

The next day marked Gabrielle's first shift. At sunrise, she crossed the hotel's threshold, heart fluttering. Todd, the assistant GM, greeted her warmly. Carol, her intended mentor, was out with Covid, leaving Todd to lead.

Departures unfurled, arrivals choreographed with precision. At 9:00 a.m., Allen, the GM, appeared, leaving a checklist, her treasure map.

The afternoon unfolded as a solo recital. Guests paraded before her. She welcomed them, entrusted keys, sent them off. Allen appeared now and then, offering quiet encouragement.

But Gabrielle's feet waged protest. Muscles murmured dissent, soles craved solace. *The theater of employment is no mere jest*, she sighed, surrendering to bed.

That night, she typed: *First day at the hotel, a symphony of checkins, sore feet, and whispered secrets.*

Day two began at 6:00 a.m. Todd passed the torch with silent camaraderie. "The maestro Allen will soon take the stage," he whispered.

At 9:00 a.m., Allen appeared. His mentorship was brief, his demeanor suggesting: "Trust your instincts."

Gabrielle found rhythm in elegiac goodbyes, the waltz of transactions ending. But her feet sang a ballad of dissent. Memory foam, gel inserts, anything to cradle her arches.

Allen retreated to his office, lost in administrative melodies. Gabrielle fielded inquiries, hoping her responses struck the right chord. The lobby resonated with arrivals and farewells.

Allen emerged now and then, eyes folding into vintage lines. "Well done," he signaled.

By afternoon's curtain call, Gabrielle's feet composed a requiem of discomfort. She typed: *Day two, a concerto of farewells, aching soles, and hushed revelations.*

Day three began with the 11:00 a.m. chorus. At 2:00 p.m., Greg arrived, signaling partnership. Together, they navigated the hotel's labyrinth.

Greg introduced her to the ballet of checkins. Allen's stark methods gave way to tuneful instruction, laughter, anecdotes, and woven experience.

Yet dissonance echoed; Gabrielle's feet continued their silent protest. Shoes demanded replacement. As she attuned to the hotel's rhythm, she uncovered sanctuaries: housekeeping enchantment, the kitchen's incantations. Checkins became her forte.

With evening's curtain call, Gabrielle retreated home. A warm foot bath offered relief. Then a shower, an encore to cleanse away exertions.

"Dinner?" her husband asked. "Not this eve," she murmured. "Tonight, my feet orchestrate their own requiem of weariness."

Dawn unfurled. Gabrielle stood poised at the threshold of her 11:00 a.m. to 7:00 p.m. shift. The morning's overture was a duet with Allen.

By afternoon, Greg joined her. Sunlight pirouetted through the lobby. Phones summoned her with siren calls. Once daunting, their demands now danced in rhythm.

Allen appeared, fingers garlanded with sticky notes, cryptic keys to the digital domain. Gabrielle tucked them away, meaning to unfold in time.

Each checkin exchanged a glimpse into a traveler's tale. The computer screen became a canvas. Passwords as brushstrokes, revealing mystery.

At 7:30 p.m., the curtain fell. Gabrielle retreated to her sanctuary. A foot bath, infused with soothing essences, enveloped her.

"Dinner?" her husband asked. "Not tonight," she sighed. "To chase the horizon with youth's vigor is a melody best left to the fleetfooted."

On a day of leisure, Gabrielle and her husband embarked on a suburban safari of garage sales. He longed only for breakfast banter.

They wove through streets lined with relics of lives past. A cozy café hosted their breakfast encore. Fishing tales filled the air, laughter stitched between bites. Work beckoned.

The hotel's rhythm was a relaxed waltz. Her feet found respite. Training videos whispered hospitality's ballet. Sticky notes became cryptic scores tucked in her wallet.

Evening brought her home, laughter, simple suppers, quiet hum of shared life.

Sunday's RCIA class unfolded with sacred intent. Father Thom illuminated reconciliation. The class shared transgressions, finding solace in his wisdom: through baptism and confession, they would be reborn in grace.

The session closed with promise, a soothing cadence of redemption.

After class, Gabrielle and her husband sought comfort in a familiar haven: Subway sandwiches. The aroma of freshly baked bread mingled with laughter. They savored each bite. Gabrielle curled up for a brief nap before her evening shift.

At 2:00 p.m., she stepped into the hotel lobby. Carol, absent on Gabrielle's first day, had returned. "You're in charge tonight," she whispered. "I'll be your safety net."

Gabrielle waded into the symphony of checkins and whispered passwords. Carol retreated to the laundry room, tending to sheets and towels. Gabrielle navigated the front desk.

Melissa, the bartender, appeared, her smile a warm chord. "Usually four to ten," she said, "but sometimes I stay for thirsty souls."

Her eyes held stories, late night confessions, laughter, forgotten cocktails.

She mentioned another bartender, a talkative soul.

Gabrielle sensed tension between Melissa and Carol. They moved in separate orbits. The laundry room door opened only when Gabrielle needed aid. She wondered about their silent symphony.

At 10:30 p.m., Gabrielle returned home. A shower washed away the day's dust. She sank into bed.

The next day, a day off, an intermezzo in the hotel saga. Her feet, still tender, cradled dreams of comfort. Her husband gently asked her wishes. "Let's stay home," Gabrielle mused. "Lose ourselves in a movie."

Together, they nestled into blankets, the screen illuminating stories untold. As the plot thickened, Gabrielle's eyelids grew heavy. She drifted into sleep.

Then, a text: Farmer Joe's announced its grand opening. Tuesday beckoned. But Gabrielle's feet murmured a different tune.

The hotel had ensnared her affection. Farmer Joe's struck a lesser chord. With grace, Gabrielle replied, a courteous declination. Silence followed.

The next day mirrored the last. Gabrielle found solace in their backyard oasis. As evening approached, she donned her apron and approached the grill. Succulent steaks sizzled.

A pang of remorse stirred, recent demands had distanced them. But her husband's unwavering support deserved more than acknowledgment. She served him his cherished dish.

The sun rose with leisurely grace. At 11:00 a.m., Gabrielle stepped into the lobby. Alone, she welcomed each guest, her smile a beacon.

By midafternoon, Greg joined her. Side-by-side, they ensured each sanctuary was ready. The impending night audit cast its shadow. "Master the rhythm of digits," they advised.

As twilight approached, Gabrielle reflected. Two and a half decades spent elsewhere now rippled in memory. Amidst the fragrance of linen, she pondered: was this her destined course?

The next morning greeted Gabrielle with quiet familiarity. She resumed her post, the day's cadence a solo performance. Greg's presence lingered, summoned by her messages, then vanishing again. His absences sparked curiosity. *Where did he retreat?* Gabrielle mused on these mysteries, imagining Greg navigating unseen passageways.

On the day of her final morning to evening shift, Gabrielle embraced the familiar tempo. The lobby hummed with arrivals, yet the air held poignancy. The night audit loomed.

She moved with alacrity and heartfelt attention. In the waning hours, she caught sight of Greg, his silent vigil a testament to faith in her. His unspoken encouragement bolstered her as she conducted the day's symphony.

As her shift concluded, the lobby exhaled. Gabrielle had proven herself. The absence of supervision became its own commendation. Todd would soon guide her through the afterhours maze.

Saturday dawned, soft and slow. Gabrielle retreated into the sanctuary of home. Her feet exhaled in gratitude. Eight hour marathons had left their mark.

Beside her, her husband stood as ally. Together, they nestled on the sofa, their remote their guide through dramas and comedies.

Later, they entered the sacred space of church. Mass offered collective introspection. Dinner became a shared sacrament. Nightfall beckoned them home. The day stitched itself into memory, a quiet tapestry of contentment.

On Sunday, the RCIA class gathered to explore *Anointing the Sick*. Father Thom spoke of grace woven through human frailty. A rite not reserved for life's edge but for any soul battling illness.

After class, Gabrielle and her husband found comfort in Subway sandwiches. At home, the couch offered respite before Gabrielle's first night audit.

Stepping into the lobby, she met Todd. His youthful energy belied experience. They struck up camaraderie, swapping stories between audit reports and printer hums.

Todd had held many jobs; Gabrielle, just four over twenty-four years. Her loyalty impressed him. The night audit was like babysitting a digital toddler. "Watch for anomalies," Todd advised. "The numbers tell tales."

But the real adventure awaited in the kitchen. As dawn neared, Gabrielle donned her invisible chef's hat. Bread, croissants, fruit, oatmeal sachets, coffee brewed strong. Todd nodded approvingly. "Tomorrow, it's all yours." Gabrielle snapped photos of her breakfast masterpiece. His parting words echoed: "You got this."

Enshrouded by night's embrace, Gabrielle returned home. The shower's warmth erased traces of work. Her husband preserved her peace as she slept soundly from dawn to dusk.

Awakening, Gabrielle rose, attuned to the evening's rhythm. In the kitchen, she crafted a meal. Together, they feasted, silent conversation in every bite.

Later, nestled on the couch, she lost herself in television tales, the night's duties lingering at the day's edge.

Her second night unfurled with spreadsheets and ledgers. Todd entrusted her with the solo performance. "Tonight, the stage is yours," he said. Though his visits were brief, his guidance was a beacon.

Gabrielle danced across the keyboard, vigilant, ensuring harmony between the hotel's accounts and the universe's grand design.

At dawn, Todd appeared, his approving smile a silent ovation. "Bravo," he whispered. Gabrielle embraced the solitude of her role, the night's lone custodian.

Emerging into daybreak, she left the hotel's embrace. Home was her retreat. The shower's steam her curtain call. Her bed, a sanctuary of dreams.

Awakened in evening's soft light, her husband moved with quiet reverence. Together, they orchestrated an impromptu dinner. The couch and television their audience, they reveled in serenity.

Duty beckoned once more. Gabrielle's third night loomed. Todd, a specter in the dim lobby, whispered, "Tonight, the helm is yours."

The night unfolded, a concerto of figures and fiscal narratives. Todd imparted wisdom; Gabrielle waltzed with data. His number, a lifeline in her pocket. "Trust your cadence," he said, vanishing at 2:00 a.m.

Her fourth night whispered independence. Todd left her to navigate solo. Carol, her afternoon predecessor, hinted at solitude. Checklists, once guides, now commanded with gravitas. Gabrielle stood ready to soar.

At midnight, Todd's call reassured her. "All is well," she affirmed. The audit danced forward in quiet rhythm.

At dawn, Greg appeared, astonished by her solitary vigil. He shared tales of Todd's tireless toil, his absence a rare respite. The urgency of her training was clear.

On the fifth night, the hotel's doors whispered tales of the day. Gabrielle settled in. The computer sparked to life.

Then Seth appeared, banker by day, auditor by moonlight. "Rostered tonight," he said. Todd had granted this anomaly. Gabrielle watched Seth navigate shadows. His verdict came swiftly: "You're ready." And he vanished.

Alone, Gabrielle became steward of figures, the night's minstrel.

After her shift, she returned home. Stress dissolved under the shower's embrace. Joined by her husband, they visited a friend. Breakfast chatter wove between work tales and garage sale gems.

The afternoon sun cast a golden tapestry across their backyard. The pool glinted, beckoning. But Gabrielle sank into the couch, fatigue luring her into sleep. Her husband watched over her rest.

When she awoke to evening's soft caress, the house was silent. He had retreated to dreams. Gabrielle found herself alone with her thoughts. Jeffrey tugged at the edges of her consciousness. Would he care about her new job? Why did she still think of him so intensely? She prayed for him daily. Yet reality stood firm: Jeffrey was a constellation that would never align. And yet, against reason, Gabrielle clung to hope.

Her husband's gentle call to breakfast awakened her. Waffles brought them together in morning's first light.

The day unfolded with languid rhythm. Television hummed.

Later, they stepped out to find solace in Mass. At a quaint Mexican restaurant, Gabrielle was reminded that love often lives in the simplest gestures.

Dawn broke and the fifteenth RCIA class gathered.

The day's focus: *Matrimony*. Mark and Ellen shared their saga of resilience. In the chapel's hushed glow, they celebrated selflessness, forgiveness, and the vow of faithfulness. Gabrielle and her husband found solace in Subway's embrace.

At home, she surrendered to slumber's cradle, her thoughts adrift in revelation.

As the week unfurled, the hotel's hushed corridors became Gabrielle's stage.

In downtime, she unearthed a forgotten treasure: her baseball card collection. Once tucked away, now each card became a vibrant note in her nocturnal melody. They held more than memories.

In college, when cash was scarce, cards replaced chips in poker and spades. Laughter echoed through dorm rooms, and the cards bore witness to youthful exuberance. Her husband's quiet understanding was in harmony to her melody.

Life's baton waved, and Gabrielle heeded its call for pause. The weekend beckoned with Naples's allure. Leaving behind her nocturnal vigil, she embraced the promise of a getaway. Their arrival was met by friends whose lives danced between northern retreats and Florida's embrace. Retirement had become their rhythm. The past mingled with present laughter. Tales of racetracks and dominoes, the grill's hiss, the clink of glasses. Her husband, usually steady, surrendered to the night's revelry.

As twilight approached, sleep eluded Gabrielle. She lay awake, pondering their friend's mentorship, guiding stars in their lives. In moonlit stillness, her thoughts wove a tapestry of gratitude. Her husband's contented snores a counterpoint in her wakeful reverie.

Morning light nudged them awake. The breakfast table became a canvas. Naples revealed itself as a verdant masterpiece, whispering leisure and camaraderie.

The interlude concluded. The car's hum marked their return. Gabrielle, cradled by its rhythm, surrendered to rest.

Home welcomed them with comfort and routine. Her husband's tender care underscored a love profound and unspoken.

The church's sacred call drew them from sanctuary. Mass offered reflection. The meal that followed was simple yet rich in their bond.

The day's curtain fell with warmth from the shower, and they retired to their shared haven.

Dawn's light caressed the spires. The sixteenth RCIA class met. Father Thom guided them through Holy Orders, delineating the roles of deacon, priest, and bishop, each a note in the church's grand chorus. The air vibrated with his personal odyssey.

The class delved into service, their questions unfurling. His responses painted devotion and the delicate dance with doubt. His gratitude lingered, his touch an affirmation of their shared journey.

Departing into daylight, Gabrielle and her husband carried the ember of his legacy. Subway's scent wove into their reflections.

In quietude, Gabrielle contemplated her workplace. Passwords and logins felt like keys to a clandestine realm.

Then came the thrill of her own hotel email address, a digital insignia of her role. At first, it was pride but soon became the conduit for Allen's directives. His preference for email meant her inbox bloomed with tasks.

One assignment led Gabrielle to the hotel's intranet, a trove of training videos and procedural lore. With headphones as her conduit, she absorbed streams of information, musing on how earlier access might have eased her transition. Her previous job had offered structured choreography; this role unfolded as a fluid dance of discovery. Gabrielle's task was not to critique, only to learn.

Friday's narrative ended her workweek with a wellness check. Home offered brief respite before the clinical encounter. Her husband's presence was quiet vigilance. The doctor's verdict was mixed: progress in weight loss, yet the label *morbidly obese* loomed large.

Saturday greeted them with sea air and renewal. A beachside escape, thoughtfully planned by her husband, offered solace. Their walk along the shore became a gentle nudge toward healthier living. Gabrielle's resistance, born of fatigue, met with understanding. A compromise was struck.

The ride home was liberating, wind and sun conspiring to lift spirits. A breakfast of vibrant colors marked their commitment to change.

As the sun descended, they heeded the call of 4:00 p.m. Mass. Within the church's sanctified walls, the choir's melodies ascended.

Post Mass hunger led them to Subway, where "healthy" choices sparked lighthearted debate.

Sunday's RCIA session was a journey through faith's lineage. Rachel guided them from Abraham's covenant to Pentecostal fire. Their hearts alighted with inquiry; they traversed epochs of belief. Rachel's post class assignment affirmed the vibrancy of their spiritual community, a beacon of active faith and fellowship.

The week continued, Gabrielle's night audit shifts painting her days in twilight hues. Rewarding, yes, but weekends were frayed by early alarms.

New opportunities beckoned. Job listings offered glimpses of different paths. The post office and storage facilities stood out, beacons of potential change. She submitted applications.

In the quiet of the hotel lobby, Gabrielle pondered her unfolding tapestry. Each step a thread toward an unwritten future.

Friday morning arrived. Gabrielle greeted the day from the sanctuary of her bed. Grand plans for her day off yielded to sleep's sweet surrender.

Her husband, ever the morning soul, embraced the day's offerings. Gabrielle remained ensnared in dreams, letting time slip by in tranquil haze.

Come Saturday, she emerged revitalized. The sacred melodies of the 4:00 p.m. Mass anchored her.

At home, she confided in her desire for change. Her husband offered support and sage advice, encouraging her to preserve what worked, yet remained open to new paths.

Sunday's RCIA class unfolded as a tapestry of reflection. Rachel guided them through *Christian Moral Living and the Dignity of Life*.

The session, rich with wisdom, ended swiftly. Rachel off to other commitments. Gabrielle and her husband continued their Sunday tradition, Subway's scent awaiting.

Back home, Gabrielle indulged in a restorative nap, gathering strength for the night audit ahead.

In her seventh week of employment, Gabrielle's rhythm shifted. A dear friend was on the way, ready to share laughter and stories. Gabrielle and her husband prepared eagerly.

Sunday passed in obligation, Monday followed, Tuesday danced by, and Wednesday dawned. At 6:00 a.m., Gabrielle emerged from work, exhausted yet exhilarated. Her friend awaited at her in-law's home.

The plan was simple: a few days together. But fate intervened. Her friend's husband cast a shadow, insistent calls, urgent texts punctuated their time. Over lunch, her friend's eyes darted toward her phone, torn between loyalty and obligation. "I must return," she said, and the thread unraveled.

Gabrielle's husband joined her on the bittersweet journey back. Fatigue settled on Gabrielle's shoulders.

Back home, exhaustion claimed her. She surrendered to sleep, dreams weaving disappointment and understanding.

Morning light peeked through the curtains. Gabrielle turned to her husband, already weaving plans. The hotel lingered in thought. Her fingers hovered over the keypad.

But her husband intervened. "You've toiled enough. Savor life beyond the office walls." With his blessing, Gabrielle embraced leisure.

Their Mustang awaited. Sanibel Island beckoned. They cruised winding roads, indulging in Dairy Queen. Gabrielle considered capturing the moment, but bitterness held her back.

The next day, friends joined them in a quest for hidden treasures. Garage sales unfolded. Breakfast at a quaint diner fueled their adventures.

Back home, the pool beckoned. Evening descended, the grill crackled, burgers sizzled. In those unplanned moments, Gabrielle found solace.

On Saturday, sunlight danced across the kitchen. Her husband joined her in the breakfast ritual. A call from Sarasota came. Her friend waited. But doubt shadowed Gabrielle's anticipation. The long drive for a short encounter felt hollow. With resolve, Gabrielle chose home. Mass offered comfort.

On Sunday morning, their class gathered for the nineteenth session. The discourse: *A Consistent Ethic of Life and Social Justice.* Rachel carried the mantle with quiet strength.

They journeyed through life's sanctity, Catholic teachings, moral dilemmas, forgiveness.

Later, beneath Subway's glow, Gabrielle, and her husband spoke of justice as divine balance. Their debate ended in shared resolve: to live out kindness and forgiveness.

Gabrielle entered her eighth week of nocturnal vigilance. The clock's hushed ticks marked silent hours. Her best friend's promised visit was now adrift. Gabrielle's disappointment lingered.

The specter of Jeffrey loomed. Was her friend's brief lunch a sign of allegiance to him? Gabrielle's heart ached. She chose silence, resigning to the possibility that her friend, like Jeffrey, might fade into memory.

The week donned a quilt of necessity. Her husband embarked on a sleep study, and Gabrielle became his chauffeur.

At 6:00 p.m., the hospital's corridors thrummed with life. Her husband was ushered into the realm of sleep science. Gabrielle watched him go, her heart a tapestry of worry and hope.

Weary, she retreated home. Silence draped her in solace. She indulged in Chinese takeout, a rare liberty.

Alone, she relished each bite. As night enveloped her, Gabrielle lounged in solitude. Memories of Jeffrey stirred. She wondered where life had taken him. Curiosity led her to her husband's social media. Jeffrey's life unfolded in pixels. Gabrielle lingered, an unseen guest. His refusal to accept her friend request lingered. She grappled with the ache of lost connections.

Morning cast a gentle glow. Gabrielle navigated to the hospital. Her husband emerged, a weary voyager from his wired odyssey. His hunger voiced its demand. "Bob Evans?" she offered. He nodded.

The diner's embrace was a balm to the night's sterility. Over breakfast, he recounted his sleepless vigil. "All those wires. Like a scifi movie. I barely slept." Gabrielle nodded, empathizing. They returned home, cocooned in quiet.

Wednesday brought routine. Hope flickered with an email from the post office. An online test awaited. Gabrielle pondered her worth as she dispatched her details into the digital expanse. The wait began. Her screen brimmed with prospects, remote work, customer service, data entry. Which path would lead her from the numbing glow of screens to daylight's vocation?

The post office reached out. Fingerprinting was next. Gabrielle scheduled the appointment for Friday. Could this be her escape from the night shift?

Friday's narrative unfolded. Work's shadows behind her, Gabrielle found solace at home. A shower's warmth washed away the day.

With her husband beside her, they set out. The postal sign stood firm against her uncertainty. The voice on the line, devoid of warmth, directed her to a bench, her interim haven. Time stretched. The bureaucrat, monotone and unhurried, led her through dim corridors. Inked fingertips marked the beginning of her journey. He spoke of waiting, a test of patience before the next chapter.

Back in daylight, the warehouse stood stoic. Driving away, Gabrielle pondered the man's role in this vast tapestry. She, now a thread in the system, waited with hope.

As the sun dipped, Gabrielle and her husband left fingerprinting behind. The air brimmed with sea tang and new adventures. They cruised the coastal road.

Home welcomed her back. The couch, a tender haven. Slumber crept in; dreams unfurled their gossamer wings.

With the new day's light, Gabrielle adorned herself in her apron. Breakfast became their shared act of faith.

Mass called them to reverence. Then, a foray into a Mexican eatery, where they feasted. The day wove itself into memory as they returned to the familiarity of home. Night's mantle descended, enshrouding them in soft folds.

On a tranquil Sunday morning, the RCIA class gathered for a pivotal session: the Purification and Enlightenment phase.

Father Michael introduced the theme: *Saying Yes to Jesus and Living Lent.* Lent, he said, was a time for reflection and renewal. He urged them to embrace the upcoming scrutiny rites with courage, a testament to faith. The room buzzed with nerves and hope.

Father Michael spoke of sponsors, steadfast companions on the sacred path. He reassured a latecomer, encouraging her to choose a familiar face. Grace, he reminded them, often arrives through unexpected channels.

Gabrielle, now a sponsor herself, recalled her disrupted RCIA journey during the pandemic. Excitement stirred for the upcoming pilgrimage to the cathedral, a place steeped in centuries of devotion.

Father Michael guided them through Lent's sacred rhythm:

- Jesus' Invitation: *"Will you follow me?"*
- God's Unfailing Mercy: Seeking us in our darkest moments.
- The Rite of Scrutiny: A mirror to the soul.
- Lent's Sacred Trio: Fasting, prayer, and almsgiving.

After class, a woman lingered, her eyes clouded. She sought Father Michael in private. Gabrielle glimpsed her turmoil. What secrets did she share? Father Michael approached Gabrielle and her husband, eyes crinkled in warmth.

"You," he said to her husband, "shall be the charioteer to the cathedral. Gas? Consider it covered. And afterward, dinner, a feast of fellowship."

They chuckled. His marching orders were solemn and whimsical. As they stepped into the sundrenched afternoon, Subway beckoned. Gabrielle leaned in. "Our priest, a master of divine logistics." They laughed, hearts light.

As twilight embraced the earth, Gabrielle entered the hotel lobby. The night audit loomed. Yet within her stirred a longing for the profound. The lobby whispered tales of transient souls.

In defiance of the ordinary, Gabrielle reached for her Bible. The *Bible in a Year* podcast promised connection to timeless truths. *The Great Adventure Bible* opened. Father Mike Schmitz's voice guided her through sacred text. Genesis breathed life. Exodus echoed liberation. Leviticus carried the fragrance of sanctity. Each verse drew her deeper into discovery.

Nestled in the lobby's embrace, Gabrielle annotated her revelations. Unseen by passing guests, she embarked on an internal odyssey, tracing the steps of prophets and pilgrims. "Two hours each night," she contemplated, "to traverse the bridge from ancient wisdom to contemporary hearts." Father Mike's fervent narration spurred her journey, a beacon in the night.

The Banner and the Benediction

"His banner over me was love."

—Song of Songs 2:4

At dawn, Gabrielle emerged from work, fatigue mingled with anticipation. Ash Wednesday beckoned, a solemn gateway to Lent.

At home, she cast off the night's weariness beneath the shower's purifying stream. Clad in her finest, she joined her husband at church. Father Michael marked her forehead, not with a perfect cross but a smudge of grace. "These ashes transcend form," he said. "They remind us of our shared humanity, dust to dust."

Back home, Gabrielle scrolled through social media. Ash marked faces filled her feed. She captured her own, hesitated, then posted a tentative step toward reconnection. Jeffrey's absence lingered like a shadow, a silent ache beneath the season's promise.

Saturday's 4:00 p.m. Mass shimmered with expectation. Candidates gathered to sign the Rite of Sending document, a pledge of faith's unfolding journey. A brief panic: the parchment misplaced.

Rachel appeared, calm and resolute, guiding each signature. Plans for the cathedral were finalized. Carpooling arranged. Gabrielle wondered about the absent woman, the one who had sparred with Father Michael. Would she come? Her husband doubted it. Gabrielle clung to hope.

Dawn painted the sky in hues of promise. Gabrielle prepared breakfast, teasing her husband: "Remember, you're chauffeuring a priest today. Drive like a saint." He smirked.

At church, Father Michael claimed the front seat. Laughter filled the cab as miles unfurled. "Faster," Father urged. "I'm an impatient driver." Gabrielle's caution clashed with his humor. "Ignore her," he winked. "Drive as your spirit dictates."

The cathedral rose in solemn grandeur. The Rite of Election unfolded beneath vaulted arches. Banners swayed, a ballet of faith. Her husband bore theirs, earning the nickname "Banner Boy." The bishop's blessing crowned the moment. Photos captured faces luminous with grace.

As the sun dipped low, hunger stirred. The plan: BBQ, Father Michael's smoky delight. But the restaurant teemed with patrons. "Patience is a virtue," he murmured.

They recalibrated. Bonefish Grill beckoned. Gabrielle's husband, still Banner Boy, slid behind the wheel. Father Michael had other plans. "Faster! Beat the lights!" When traffic stalled, he commanded an illegal turn. Her husband, eyes wide, muttered about tickets. "You'll pay the fine," he warned, half in jest.

Father Michael laughed. "Fear not, the collar is our shield. Unless, of course, we meet a lesbian police officer. They, my friends, harbor no love for priests." Silence rippled.

Rachel, seasoned eye-roller, gasped. Her husband sputtered, "Did that just come from a man of the cloth?" Father Michael wiped tears of laughter. "Indeed, Banner Boy. Life's too short for piety alone."

At Bonefish Grill, appetites undiminished, the server led them to their table. Father Michael ordered bang bang shrimp with a wink. Laughter lingered, a benediction of absurdity.

Dinner unfolded in warm glow. The class, diminished by absent souls, left a trio: the faithful, the curious, and the reluctant.

Father Michael zeroed in on the latter. "What stirs your spirit?" he asked. "Beyond these walls, what beckons?" Their classmate hesitated. The church had been a compass, but now the path diverged.

Father Michael hinted at uncharted territory. "Service extends beyond pews and hymnals." He spoke of the diaconate, a bridge between sacred and mundane. "You'd assist the priest," he explained. "A silent partner in the sacraments."

The stole's weight danced before their classmate's eyes. Yet he wavered. Father Michael leaned in. "Think. Pray. The church awaits your answer."

Then, with a twinkle: "Remember, the collar shields even the most audacious turns, unless you meet a lesbian police officer."

The table erupted in laughter at his irreverent humor. Rachel sighed. Her husband chuckled. "Father, you've woven a tale worthy of Scripture."

As they left, Father Michael settled the bill. "Church business," he declared. The receipt bore witness to sacred negotiations.

Twilight draped the weary travelers. Father Michael shed his shoes, loosened his collar. The truck's cab became his sanctuary. Topics flowed: politics, baseball, pineapple on pizza.

Then, the Prius. It crept ahead, electric heart beating in no hurry. Father Michael leaned forward. "For heaven's sake, turn!" he implored. "I'd be terrified too if I drove a Prius."

Gabrielle's husband erupted in laughter. The car gods, it seemed, had a sense of irony.

At the church, lights blazed. Father Michael narrowed his eyes. "Someone left the damn lights on." He requested a stop, vanished into the nave, collar askew.

The rest climbed into their vehicles. Rachel rolled her eyes. Her husband, free from Banner Boy duties, steered them home.

Father Michael's words echoed absurdity, humanity. "He's one of us," her husband mused. "A fellow traveler on this cosmic road."

Gabrielle glided to the kitchen. Coffee and bacon orchestrated a morning symphony. Her husband nestled into his chair. They lingered, laughter echoing from the day before.

Father Michael's irreverent humor lingered. "A man of the cloth," her husband mused, "endowed with a zest for mischief."

Throughout the day, his words resurfaced. Gabrielle surrendered to the cadence. Cat naps became sanctuary.

Then, as twilight beckoned, duty summoned. Gabrielle adorned herself in night audit regalia.

In the days that followed, the night audit enfolded Gabrielle in its quiet rhythm. She tallied figures, reconciled accounts. Yet beyond the dim corridors, a new quest shimmered: the post office held promise. Her application floated in the digital ether, hope affixed to possibility. The waiting game became her silent consort.

Then, serendipity sauntered in, another clerk's role, closer to home, beckoned. Gabrielle dispatched her application.

Between spreadsheets and silence, she found solace in sacred texts. The *Bible in a Year* podcast enveloped her fatigued spirit. Notebook in hand, she etched insights. From Genesis to Psalms to Revelation, the odyssey unfurled.

Friday brought respite. Gabrielle and her husband joined friends for garage sales and breakfast. Laughter stitched the hours.

Back home, water cradled their wearied forms. The grill awaited Gabrielle's touch, burgers sizzling, a sacred offering of their Friday ritual.

Saturday mirrored the day before: Mass at 4:00 p.m., dinner, a liturgy of taste, fellowship their benediction.

Sunday's RCIA class met for its twenty first session. The bulletin displayed their group portrait. Her husband distributed copies. Rachel had woven her magic, the bishop's image now graced every hand, a keepsake of their shared journey.

Rachel's voice filled the room. The absent girl had chosen a divergent path. They held her in prayer, hoping grace would rekindle her heart.

The topic unfurled: *The Ten Commandments and the Beatitudes.* Ancient words etched in stone, whispered by prophets, danced in their midst. The Law a roadmap to holiness. The Beatitudes paradoxes of blessedness. Their souls leaned toward truth beneath the cross's shadow.

Then, the unexpected—a confession, raw and unbidden. The girl stood at the precipice, her words a torrent of guilt and longing. The commandments had become her mirror.

She traced her sins: betrayal, broken trust. Her boyfriend, silent, bore the weight of her words. The room was transformed into a confessional. Heartache, struggle, the ache to forgive.

Rachel intervened. "After class," she promised. "Make an appointment with one of the priests." The girl nodded. Her footsteps echoed as the class dispersed. In the afterglow, she and Rachel huddled, whispers of grace exchanged.

One classmate invited Gabrielle and her husband to lunch. They welcomed him into their Subway ritual. Over sandwiches, his words unfurled a conspiracy of intrigue and absurdity. The girl who had dropped out became the protagonist. The FBI, he claimed, had cast its net over their church. Spies, secrets, salvation, his narrative danced.

Gabrielle had her own theory: not a spy but a soul adrift. Bad decisions, scars, shaky faith, the ingredients of her story. Her husband, intrigued, leaned in. "The Catholic Church," he mused, "is the epicenter of intrigue." His eyes traced the shadows of the pews.

But as the hour stretched, Gabrielle's patience waned. She yearned to sleep. Her husband, still captivated, dissected the conspiracy. "Did you notice?" he asked. "Some people at Mass out of place." Gabrielle had noticed the misfits, the seekers, the broken.

Beneath the moon's watchful eye, they drove home. The guy's theories, her husband's musings swirled. Gabrielle, the weary passenger, longed for silence. "Next time," she murmured, "they can unravel their mysteries without me."

Stepping through the front door, the familiar scent of home embraced her. The day had been long. She made a beeline for the bedroom, cocooning herself in sheets. Sleep claimed her swiftly.

As the sun dipped below the horizon, duty called. The night audit awaited. The lobby, once bustling, now lay hushed. She stepped behind the desk, fingers dancing across the keyboard. The ledger whispered secrets of the day's comings and goings. Guest payments reconciled. Requests surfaced: a forgotten toothbrush, a late night snack, a wakeup call.

Gabrielle navigated these constellations. The night held its rhythm. Yet as days melted into weeks, restlessness stirred. The night owl's existence left her yearning. It was time to open a new chapter, one where daylight and dreams coexisted, where her husband's smile wasn't a fleeting memory.

During the third week of Lent, their twenty second RCIA session marked a milestone. The atmosphere buzzed with anticipation. They entered the sacred rite of the first scrutiny, a pivotal moment for those preparing to join the church.

New presenter Jason infused fresh energy. He spoke of the scrutiny as a spiritual compass, a rite unveiling hidden depths, guiding the elect toward Christ's light at baptism.

Jason explored the Nicene Creed and the Lord's Prayer, distributing sacred parchments. As the final bell tolled, eager hands clutched those timeless texts, ready to carry faith beyond ivory walls.

As twilight painted the sky, Gabrielle stepped into the hotel lobby. Greg, already on duty, wore a mischievous grin. "I've got something for you when you clock in," he whispered. Curiosity piqued. Greg produced a small magnet: *Manager on Duty*, it proclaimed.

Gabrielle stifled a laugh. "Greg, I'm the only one here. Who am I managing my own shadow?" He chuckled. "Think of it from a guest's perspective. You're a guardian angel, solo but steadfast."

Gabrielle tilted her head. "So, I'm the silent sentinel, ensuring the coffee stays hot and the elevators behave?"

"Exactly," Greg grinned. "And don't forget the mysterious aura you exude while doing it."

That night, Gabrielle snapped a photo of her new title and posted it with a sly caption: *When the only person you're in charge of is yourself.* Likes and comments poured in. Friends shared tales of solo heroism.

During her shifts, she strolled past the sign, nodding sagely as if consulting invisible guests.

Friday and Saturday unfolded in familiar rhythm: garage sales, hearty breakfasts, languid afternoons by the pool. Their cozy paradise wrapped around them. But the weekend held surprises, tickets to an Air Supply concert in Naples, a rare treat.

As the sun dipped, her husband offered one more surprise. "Check the flowerpots," he said, eyes twinkling.

Gabrielle stepped outside. There they were: two pineapples. Friends had gifted the plants when they moved in, symbols of patience and good fortune. Two years later, they bore fruit. She laughed, snapped a photo, and posted: *I finally got my first crop.* Celebration bloomed online.

That night, they left their pineapple guardians and headed to the concert. Air Supply's melodies wrapped around them. Her husband captured their joy in photos, announcing their date night.

Amid harmonies and applause, Gabrielle's phone buzzed. Todd from the hotel. Seth had called off. Could she step in? She hesitated. The concert pulsed around her. Her husband's eyes met hers. She replied: *Sorry, we're at the concert. Won't be home until late.*

Guilt gnawed. They returned close to 2:00 a.m., echoes of music still humming. The hotel would manage without her for one night.

On the fourth Sunday of Lent, anticipation hung in the air. Their twenty third RCIA session began. Father Michael stood before them.

The topic: the Mass, a sacred tapestry woven through centuries. Gabrielle expected a lecture. Instead, Father Michael queued for a brief video, sacred vessels, congregants, incense, whispers of the grand symphony.

He spoke of Easter's approach, pregnant with hope. The forty hours of devotion loomed, a vigil of prayer.

Then, solemn news: Father Thom would not stand beside them at the Easter Vigil. His path led home. The Diocese had granted his return, recognizing his health and quiet yearning. He had shepherded them through spiritual valleys. Now, he would tread familiar soil.

Father Michael invited them to a farewell gathering. Faces reflected sorrow and joy. For Father Thom, it was a homecoming.

Amid fluorescent lights, Gabrielle returned to her night audit shifts. The world slumbered. She grappled with inverted days. "You'll grow accustomed," they said. But it remained elusive.

Her two days off flitted away, leaving her yearning. Then, a letter arrived, her fingerprint journey processed, cleared. Yet the start date remained vague. Time wore a cloak of uncertainty. Gabrielle settled into waiting. The night audit became both refuge and challenge.

During tranquil days off, familiar rhythms returned. Fridays were treasure hunts. Saturdays led to Mass.

But Sunday held a twist: the third scrutiny and dismissal bridged the mundane and sacred. Rachel spoke of devotion and the Reconciliation Chapel. Their names echoed with centuries of faith.

Father Thom stood at the crossroads. His tenure neared its end. Gabrielle and her husband approached. His eyes held countless prayers. He offered a prayer card and a talisman for Easter. "I will pray for you always," he promised.

They stepped into the sundappled morning. In this interplay of days and devotion, Gabrielle found solace. Father Thom's departure was not an ending; it was a return to roots, to healing, to the quiet chambers of his heart.

Amid workday rhythms, Gabrielle danced with the clock. The *Bible in a Year* podcast became her celestial companion, a thread connecting her to ancient wisdom.

Then, a call. An invitation from Sanibel Island. She accepted. An interview awaited, bridging aspirations and reality.

As the sun dipped low, Gabrielle shed her workday vestiges. She and her husband embarked on a pilgrimage to the Sanibel Island post office. The clerk's position was filled, but a mail carrier role remained. The catch? She'd need her own vehicle.

Sanibel's allure couldn't outweigh the commute's toll. The postmaster's vision of her Mustang-convertible-turned-delivery-vessel felt whimsical.

Back home, Gabrielle composed a polite decline. She embraced the mundane: quiet chores, familiar spaces. Her husband's words echoed: "Perhaps a blessing in disguise." The island's sunkissed beaches had ensnared her imagination, but the single artery to the mainland was a toll in time and patience.

On Saturday, they skipped the 4:00 p.m. Mass for Palm Sunday's grandeur. A beach walk began their day.

Breakfast at a seaside café followed, then poolside chats and grilled skewers.

On a radiant Sunday morning, their class gathered for the twenty fourth session, Palm Sunday. Clutching freshly cut branches, they entered the sacred space.

Father Michael shared the news: Gabrielle and her husband would offer bread and wine. And more, their names whispered by heaven to receive sacred oils at the Chrism Mass.

Mass unfolded. They joined the procession, reenacting Christ's entry. Palms, blessed by Father Michael, became vessels of memory and hope. Some would keep them; others would become ashes.

In the classroom, Jack wove a rich narrative. Palms still echoing, he unveiled Holy Week's heart, a crescendo of Lent's introspection.

The Triduum's significance:

- Palm Sunday & Easter Triduum: Jubilant crowds greeted Jesus, unaware of the cross to come.
- Holy Week: A mosaic of sorrow and hope—dusty roads, olive groves, upper room.
- Holy Thursday: Jesus washed feet, redefining history.
- Good Friday: A pilgrimage of heartache and redemption. Even in darkness, hope lingered.

They stepped into Holy Week's rhythm. The Triduum awaited.

At the cathedral, they would receive the sacred oils. Palms, once symbols of jubilation, now bore witness to grace's cost. Jack distributed keychains, each bearing a delicate cross. "Have it blessed," he said. Father Michael would infuse the humble token with sacredness.

The cathedral beckoned: Thursday's Chrism Mass, oils, consecrations, vows. Good Friday loomed with Stations of the Cross. Before that, rehearsal for Holy Saturday's grand liturgy, the Easter Vigil, candlelight, and alleluias.

Their motley crew assembled: Gabrielle's husband, classmates, and Father Michael. Rachel entrusted her husband with timekeeping.

Home offered respite before the night audit, where numbers replaced hymns.

Gabrielle's workweek had two chapters: Sunday and Monday. The rest was reserved for RCIA. Gratitude swelled. Allen's kindness allowed her this rhythm.

As the sun dipped, she stepped out of the hotel lobby. Work relinquished its hold. Home embraced her weariness. A nap became a prelude to the Chrism Mass. She and her husband would be anointed, vessels for fragrant oils. Father Michael's words wove tapestries of faith. No grand procession, no spotlight: the oils would come quietly, after the final crescendo. No fanfare, just blessings pressed into their hands.

The cathedral loomed. Inside, incense thickened the air. Father Michael's voice carried them through the liturgy. He led a quiet tour of hidden alcoves, forgotten corners. And there they were: the oils, vials of consecration, fragrant secrets sealed in glass.

Their seats beckoned. Father Michael orchestrated their placement, then joined the bishop's procession. Priests robed in color, voices harmonizing in ancient chants. Their seats, though vacant, held quiet anticipation.

The Mass shimmered with reverence. Gabrielle's first Chrism Mass. Her RCIA journey had once been halted by the pandemic. Now, the oils waited, earthly vessels. No photographs, just the quiet exchange of grace.

After Mass, Father Michael found them. A brief meeting with the bishop delayed their departure. "Wait," he said. They lingered, suspended between sacred and mundane.

Her husband and fellow pilgrims disappeared into the restroom. Gabrielle stood alone with her thoughts. They drifted to Jeffrey. Two years had passed since those messages strained their friendship. She whispered at the cathedral, hoping God had heard her plea.

Outside, life buzzed, unaware of the quiet drama within.

Father Michael reappeared, oils in hand. He entrusted them to Gabrielle. "Do not spill," he said. Her heart fluttered. She was a guardian of blessings, a steward of grace.

The sun cast a warm glow on the road ahead. Father Michael led them to his favorite BBQ haven. He became their culinary cartographer, whispering shortcuts, pointing out flea markets and dollar stores.

His promise of retail therapy, top down in the Mustang, elicited a chuckle. The BBQ joint welcomed them. Gabrielle chose ribs, shared her bounty with Father Michael. His eyes crinkled with gratitude, a silent prayer of thanks.

The ride home was a quiet coda. Bellies full, conversation a gentle hum. Father Michael kicked off his shoes, settling into the front seat. He and Gabrielle's husband exchanged stories.

But Gabrielle's attention wavered, she was the guardian of the oils. The vials nestled beside her, their weight symbolic. Blessings rode shotgun. She watched each turn, each bump, nerves dancing. The oils remained intact. Still, Gabrielle held her breath.

Back at the church, Father Michael reclaimed the oils. Gabrielle exhaled. A sacred duty fulfilled. Goodbyes exchanged, they stepped into the quiet of home. Exhaustion tugged at their bones.

Spy Wednesday whispered betrayal's tale. Judas's shadow loomed in Scripture. Gabrielle and her husband lingered for the Rosary, fumbling through prayers, vowing to learn.

Holy Thursday shimmered with humility, feet washed, Eucharist carried in solemn procession. Midnight cloaked the church in silence. Gabrielle knelt, heart heavy with memories of a Holy Week lost to Covid. Her husband's hand found hers. "You are not alone," he murmured.

Friday beckoned gently. Church obligations were minimal, a solitary pilgrimage to the Stations of the Cross awaited.

But first, a cinematic detour. They entered the theater. *Father Stu*, a boxer's journey to priesthood, faith, doubt, redemption. They laughed, wept, and marveled. A selfie captured the moment. "On a date with my wife," her husband posted.

After the credits, they chose a booth over pews. "Enough church for one week," he said. Bonefish Grill welcomed them. Seafood mingled with grace.

Back home, the evening settled. They slipped into bed, Friday cocooned in memories.

Saturday dawned. Gabrielle stood in the kitchen, breakfast aroma rising. Her husband shuffled in, smiling. The quiet interlude before Easter beckoned.

They drove to church. Rehearsal awaited. Doors opened to Easter egg hunts, laughter, and Father Michael blessing baskets.

The morning was a symphony. Rachel began rehearsal late. Movements mapped. "Don't worry," she said. "I'll be your compass." A prayer session followed. Whispers absorbed by church walls. Father Michael dismissed them. "Sunday best," he reminded. The Vigil awaited—fire, water, resurrection.

Back home, they paused. A quiet intermission. The day stretched. The Vigil would unfold. But for now, they rested.

Afternoon sun painted the world. They rose from their nap. The pilgrimage to church began.

In the Narthex, nerves, and anticipation. Her husband ensured all were accounted for. Front pews reserved. They stood on the threshold of transformation. Rachel offered a pep talk. "Go with the flow," she said. "Follow Father Michael's lead."

The sanctuary glowed with candlelight. Mass unfolded. Gabrielle and her husband, sponsors, stood witness. But her thoughts wandered to Jeffrey, his absence. What if he had been there, forgiving, embracing? Covid had stolen Holy Week but grace remained.

The procession led them out. Congregation trailing behind Father Michael. In the Narthex, congratulations flowed.

Back into the church, faces, snapshots of grace. Group pictures immortalized their pilgrimage. Father Michael stood with them. An individual photo, a keepsake. The clock ticked past midnight.

They stepped into the cool night air. The journey complete: a symphony of water, fire, and spirit. Driving home, the world asleep, Gabrielle thought of Jeffrey, hoping forgiveness transcended time and space.

Easter Sunday dawned. Church bells tolled, but they chose sleep. Later, they joined friends for a feast of fellowship. Laughter flowed, neighbors mingled, dinner's aroma mingled with joy.

Her husband posted a photo: Father Michael, eyes kind, stood with them. Caption: *Blessed to have Father Michael in our lives. Happy Easter.* Social media bore witness. Their hearts echoed the sentiment.

Back at the hotel, Gabrielle slipped into the night audit's quiet cadence. Greg greeted her warmly: "We missed you." Simple words, yet deeply resonant.

During hushed hours, she turned to Scripture, *The Bible in a Year* her nocturnal companion. Joel Osteen's and Joyce Meyer's voices braided hope into the silence.

Yet beneath their exhortations, Jeffrey lingered, a phantom of unfinished conversations. Gabrielle prayed: "God, grant me closure. Stitch the frayed edges, and if it be your will, reunite us as friends."

Saturday brought a surprise, hockey tickets. Their usual church routine shifted. The class, now baptized, could linger through full Sunday Mass. A subtle liberation. Gabrielle reveled in freedom.

The hockey game awaited. They transformed the evening into a date: dinner first, then the arena. Her husband posted a photo: *On a date with my wife.* Comments flowed, hearts, thumbs up, wellwishes.

But truth unfolded: hockey arenas are frigid realms. Chills seeped through their layers. Gabrielle huddled, teeth chattering. Her husband clenched his jaw, equally brave. The final buzzer sounded.

They stepped into the chilly night. Gabrielle requested, "Heat please." Her husband grumbled, but warmth soon enveloped them.

Sunday morning, they cocooned in bed. Sunlight tiptoed through curtains. Their destination: 10:30 a.m. Mass. No class session awaited, a rare gift, lingering in sacred space without discussion.

After Mass, the Mustang awaited. But a dashboard notification blinked: low tire pressure. Her husband whisked it to the gas station. Air hissed into tires. Gabrielle watched, grateful.

Then the twist: "Don't drive the Mustang," he said. "Take my truck to work tonight." Gabrielle blinked, stunned. He handed her the reins.

Sliding into the driver's seat, exhilaration mingled with trepidation. The engine roared. She navigated familiar streets. The hotel loomed. But anxiety clung. What if a careless guest dinged the truck?

Throughout the night, Gabrielle tiptoed to the parking lot. The truck stood steadfast. She whispered to the universe: "Keep it safe. Spare it from scratches."

At dawn, she returned the truck. Her husband had a plan; the Mustang would visit the tire doctor.

That evening, Gabrielle stirred from slumber, a nocturnal creature preparing for night audit. Her husband stood by the door, expressing a mix of gravity and amusement. "New tires," he declared. The Mustang had been limping on wornout shoes.

Gabrielle blinked. Her commute was a predictable loop: home to work, work to home. No offroad escapades, no tire squealing maneuvers. Yet here they were, facing a tire replacement saga.

Then it hit her, her husband's clandestine joyrides. While Gabrielle slept, he'd been gallivanting, top down, wind tousling his hair. The Mustang had become his playground. Corners taken like a daredevil, engine revving with delight. The tires bore the brunt of his adrenaline.

He documented the evidence: a snapshot of the Mustang perched on racks, underbelly exposed. Captioned cheekily: *When you drive it like you stole it, you need new tires.* Comments flowed, laughter, admiration, gentle ribbing. They shared a glance. No blame needed. The Mustang had danced between practicality and exhilaration.

Amid the daily grind, an unexpected email arrived: an interview invitation at a nearby hotel, front-desk position. Gabrielle called and secured a Friday appointment, her day off.

But fate had other brushstrokes, and the hotel rescheduled. "Monday," they said. Gabrielle sighed, anticipation deflated. Still, curiosity tugged. "Let's drive by," she told her husband.

They cruised past the grand edifice, a behemoth by the water's edge. Closer to home, yet the same traffic tango awaited. The hotel's allure clashed with practicality. Her husband nodded. "Stay where you are," he advised. The neighborhood was unpredictable.

Sunday morning, Father Michael guided the RCIA class. The topic: *Conversion, A Lifelong Process, and the Role of Laity.* Their baptismal experiences had merged with water and grace. Now, they were entrusted with a divine mission: sanctifying the world. *Be salt and light.*

Father Michael's gaze held expectations: find your niche, choir, charity, listening ears.

After class, they stepped into the sundrenched afternoon. Lunch at their favorite spot. Gabrielle retreated home for a brief respite before her shift.

Days melded into monotony: work, sleep, repeat. The night audit's solitude and the post office's bureaucracy dulled her spirit. The declined hotel interview left her craving a new chapter. The elusive 2:00 p.m. to 10:00 p.m. shift sparked curiosity and frustration. Why not her? Yet destiny hinted at a brighter path: a storage facility job, promising daytime stability. Résumé sent.

Sunday, their RCIA class gathered for the twenty sixth session. Rebecca and Don took center stage. The theme: *Discernment*, a word heavy with anticipation. Rebecca unveiled the tapestry of church activities. Each participant encouraged to reflect, pray, and find their purpose.

As she spoke, Gabrielle felt like she was watching a televangelist, waiting for the call to action, the plea for contributions. A fleeting thought, but it lingered. Rebecca spoke of spiritual gifts. Each person held a treasure, waiting to be discovered through prayer. She held the map; they were seekers.

After class, Gabrielle shared her musings with her husband. To her surprise, he'd felt the same evangelist vibes. They chuckled, appreciating the irony.

Outside, her husband chatted briefly with Don. Gabrielle opted for quiet. Rebecca's words echoed: "Listen for God's voice."

Lunch at Subway followed. Back home, Gabrielle nestled into a nap, preparing for the week ahead.

The days blurred: work, sleep, repeat. But amid the rhythm, a spark, a call from the storage facility. They wanted to interview her. Friday, her day off. The prospect of change shimmered. A new chapter beckoned.

As the week unfolded, Gabrielle found solace in the hotel's bustling corridors. Her mission: to tame the chaos of the market storage area. Boxes, forgotten supplies, and misplaced items formed a testament to neglect. No one else seemed bothered, but Gabrielle's inner organizer stirred.

During downtime, she sorted, labeled, stacked. Each item found its right place. The cluttered mess shed its skin. Shelves stood neat, supplies ready for use. No longer did she cringe, passing by during night audit. Order had bloomed from disarray.

Friday held a clandestine promise. After a brisk shower, Gabrielle donned her best attire. The storage facility awaited. Three faces greeted her, eyes assessing, questions probing. Managerial responsibilities, long hours, six days a week, a fledgling venture needing nurturing. Gabrielle listened, calculating the balance between ambition and exhaustion.

They unraveled her resume, her resilience, her adaptability. An hour passed, fleeting and eternal. "We'll be in touch," they said. Her fate sealed, not yet stamped.

Her husband waited outside, engine humming. She climbed in, his eyes searching hers. "How was it?" he asked. Gabrielle spilled the details. Manual labor, cleaning lots and units, the words tasted bitter. "Not for me," she declared. They shared a silent pact. The facility would not claim her.

Their escape led to Outback Steakhouse: sizzling steaks, blooming onions, and lifted spirits.

Back home, exhaustion enveloped her. Gabrielle sank into the couch. Her husband whispered, "Come to bed."

Sunday morning, their twenty seventh RCIA class gathered. Jack led a spiritual discussion: *Holiness and Living the Virtues.* "Holiness is not an abstract ideal," Jack said. "It's a journey we undertake together." Their baptismal experiences had merged with water and grace. Now, they were entrusted with a divine mission to sanctify the world through service, compassion, and faith.

But destiny had other plans. Her husband's oldest grandson's graduation beckoned, a celebration they couldn't miss. With regret, they informed the class they'd miss the closing session but promised to attend the dinner reception.

As the church doors closed behind them, emotions swirled: relief for lifted commitments, gratitude for wisdom gained. Her husband smiled. "No more Sunday class," he said. "Just 8:30a.m. Mass to start our day." Gabrielle nodded. Those quiet moments after Mass would be her sanctuary, a breath before the night audit resumed.

Work unfolded in familiar rhythm, a well worn melody. Unexpected notes harmonized with her days. Gabrielle waltzed into another interview, a different storage facility—same script, same questions.

But a twist: they wanted her to commute forty-five minutes each way to a location she hadn't applied for. Gabrielle hesitated. She chose a different tune. Her night audits became her nocturne.

As she sifted through numbers, she pondered possibilities. Could she orchestrate a shift change? Gabrielle resolved to approach Allen, seeking a more harmonious arrangement.

The week peaked with a soldout symphony. Hotel rooms hummed with guests. Late arrivals danced in, their tired steps echoing through the lobby.

Gabrielle kept tempo balancing reservations, inquiries, and lost keycards. Amidst the crescendo, a staccato beat appeared: they planned a pilgrimage home. Gabrielle and her husband gathered their belongings. The rhythm of packing disrupted her sleep, but anticipation fueled her steps.

At dawn, Gabrielle left the hotel, her husband at the wheel. Tennessee beckoned, a restful haven to break the journey. They planned to drive, rest overnight, then continue refreshed. Fatigue lingered from the night's work and packing. Her husband drove while Gabrielle slept.

She awoke, surprised—lunch already? Afterward, she took the wheel as he slept. Miles stretched before her. Her mind wandered to Jeffrey. Should she reach out? She vowed to consult her copilot when he woke up.

A traffic jam materialized. They sat, captive, on the interstate stage. Her husband stirred. An hour crawled by, stopping, inch forward, stop again. They arrived at the hotel at 9:00 p.m., three hours behind. Dinner blurred, showers necessary. Sleep enveloped them.

Dawn bathed the room. A modest breakfast fueled their journey to her mother's home. The road called. Her husband steered them onward. It was Jeffrey's birthday. Gabrielle paused. Social media became her canvas. She sent a message: *Happy Birthday, Douchebag.* A whisper into the digital abyss.

Their home state welcomed them. Gabrielle snapped a photo of the road sign: *We are back.* Comments flowed, welcome backs, heart emojis.

That night, they indulged in nostalgia: Pizza Hut, taco pizza, family laughter. Jeffrey's response never came, but the sentiment lingered.

The next morning held significance. Her husband's grandson stood poised, cap and gown, ready to embrace the future. They began with a pilgrimage to Gabrielle's favorite donut shop: freshly glazed pastries, laughter, and rituals.

At the high school, her husband's demeanor shifted. She would be there, the ex-wife. They chose seats on the opposite side of the gym, a physical buffer against the past.

The ceremony unfolded: caps, tassels, dreams. Only 178 graduates, yet the air brimmed with hope. Her husband's sons sat with their mother.

His daughter-in-law arrived, once married to his son, now remarried yet still family in his eyes. Labels dissolved. They sat together. Her husband watched the stage. Beside him, his grandson's stepmom. They whispered, exchanged glances, love transcending legal ties.

The grandkids clung to programs, blissfully unaware of the web around them. The ceremony stretched. Her husband's eyes welled when his grandson's name echoed. His absent son haunted the moment. Gabrielle, camera in hand, captured the reunion, the old man and the young graduate, a fragile thread across generations.

Afterward, they found the grandson. His smile radiated pride. Her husband's tears flowed freely. Words were unnecessary. Their hearts spoke a language beyond syllables, a silent symphony of love, resilience, and grace.

Outside, fate played its hand. Her husband's two sons appeared, flanking their mother. Awkwardness hung in the air. Brief words exchanged. Plans made. Then the ex-wife interjected. Her words lost to Gabrielle, but they stirred something. Her husband ignored her, striding forward. Gabrielle followed, respecting the silence that cocooned him.

Driving away, she asked about the exchange. His reply was curt, a mention of their grandson, a son's phantom presence. His anger simmered. Gabrielle understood, shared grief, divergent paths. She let it be.

The sun dipped below the horizon. They returned to her mother's house. The air held quiet reverence. They had seen her husband's grandson ascend, a beacon of hope. But beneath the surface, emotions swirled.

Inside, the cozy living room welcomed them. Gabrielle's mom embraced them. Her sister had joined the gathering.

Her husband unleashed his phone's magic. Graduation photos, captured through Gabrielle's lens, now graced his social media: *Proud of my grandson, a high school graduate.*

As evening unfolded, they faced a choice: familiar Sunday rituals or vigil Mass at St. Michael's. They chose the latter, stepping into the hallowed space. Her husband snapped a photo of them in the pew. The wooden bench cradled their shared history, whispered confessions, silent pleas. His post quietly announced their return. Then he vanished, friends awaited, laughter echoing. Gabrielle sat alone.

In solitude, she turned inward to Jeffrey. His name etched in her heart. She prayed: *God, mend the frayed threads. If it be your will, reunite us as friends.* Fear held her captive. Would he welcome her words?

Mass began. The priest's voice washed over her, a rhythm of faith. As she knelt, Gabrielle surrendered her longing to the divine.

The final chimes scattered the faithful. Her husband lingered, laughter weaving through old friendships. His eyes sparkled with nostalgia. Jeffrey's name lingered. His workplace stood nearby.

Breaking the silence, her husband mused, "Wonder how Jeffrey's doing." Gabrielle masked her feelings: "He's probably busy."

They entered the deli. Each bite a culinary overture. In silence, Gabrielle offered a prayer for Jeffrey, for courage, for a bridge across silence.

Dawn unfurled. Her husband ventured out: gokarts, sons, grandsons, shared mirth. Gabrielle remained in her mother's embrace. Her mother understood her cadence, the longing for serenity, for stillness. Her sister appeared. Together, they settled into sisterly communion. Jeffrey's name lingered, unvoiced yet omnipresent.

Her husband returned, eyes alight. "Good day with the kids," he said. Gabrielle absorbed his joy, her heart resonating. As night draped the sky, Gabrielle reclined in bed. Jeffrey's visage appeared. She murmured her hopes, a silent vow to keep faith, a whisper that their paths might intertwine again.

Morning rose. Gabrielle and her husband joined her mom and sister. A shopping adventure, unsuspecting of the drama ahead. First stop: the Amish market, a pilgrimage through countryside vistas. Her mom's anticipation radiated. Scents of bread, hum of conversation, an hour well spent.

Next: the department store. Her sister twirled in dresses. Gabrielle's husband offered opinions, his eyes yearning for the exit.

Then: the tractor supply store. Among feed bags and gardening tools, fate intervened. A cowboy hat beckoned. Gabrielle slipped it on, mischief in her reflection.

And then he appeared. "Looks good on you," he said. A stranger, a spark. Her husband erupted, jealousy twisting his features. He railed against boundaries, against men who dared flirt.

Caught in the crossfire, Gabrielle teased, "Maybe if you paid more attention, they wouldn't!" Her mom and sister laughed. Her husband did not. Scowls etched deeper. They fled the Rural King, cowboy hat abandoned.

At Dairy Queen, spoons scraped silence. Her sister sensed the tension, announced her departure. Evening settled. Television flickered. Quietude returned.

The sun climbed higher. Her husband hoped to reconnect with his estranged grandson. But life intervened. The ex-daughter-in-law's lunch plans shifted the day. A call revealed that the grandson chose to stay with his dad. Three years of silence weighed heavy.

Still, her husband made the call. "McDonald's," the boy said. They went, a trio bound by blood and unspoken griefs. At the golden arches, smiles were etched in pixels. The boy had grown. He talked, filling the space between bites.

After lunch, they drove back. Her husband's frustration simmered. His son's absence loomed. Gabrielle and her mom exchanged glances. Back home, her husband posted: *Lunch with my not so little grandson.*

The next day dawned. They embarked on separate missions. He revisited old neighbors; she reunited with former colleagues. Lunch with the girls was a balm. Her husband's reunion stirred nostalgia, waves across driveways, familiar faces. Not enough to return but enough to warm his heart.

Back at her mom's house, they picked up the matriarch. Taco pizza awaited. Laughter punctuated bites. Then her sister arrived. Her husband, still salty from the grandson encounter, vented. The room crackled with tension.

The sun peeked over the horizon. A pilgrimage began, to honor those who had left their mark. Breakfast at Cracker Barrel. Her mom joined them. They visited cemeteries. First: his grandparents. Tombstones stood, a testament to generations' past. They lingered, whispered gratitude. Next: the aunts. Stories woven into family lore. Flowers placed, memories brushed.

Finally: Gabrielle's dad, a bittersweet reunion. His memory was a mosaic of laughter and life lessons.

As the sun draped the day in gold, her nephew's wedding unfolded. An old mansion, once a sorority house, now a garden oasis. No church, but love charted its own course. The family assembled. Vows pledged among blooms.

Twilight embraced the reception, fairy lights, laughter, spirits. Her husband savored the evening. A photo shared: *Out on a date this evening.* The night wound down. Farewells exchanged. Her mother chose home over revelry.

In the quiet, Gabrielle packed. A heartfelt conversation bloomed, a daughter's yearning, a mother's wisdom. She tried to lure her mom to Florida's sunsets, but her roots held firm.

With dawn's rise, they began the journey back. Her husband's optimism shone. He invited her mom once more. She declined, gently. They bid farewell. Jeffrey's workplace faded into the distance. Gabrielle's heart stirred memories, unshed tears. They shared the wheel, navigated traffic's snarls, vowing to fly next time. The hotel's neon sign flickered welcome. Rest came.

Dawn traced the sky. They drove through quiet morning, returning home by early afternoon. A call to her mom confirmed their arrival. Her husband's voice carried warmth. Gabrielle turned to tasks: unpacking, laundry, restoring order.

With the house settled, she yielded to fatigue. Work loomed. She honored the commitment, not wishing to overstep Allen's grace. In the quiet before sleep, thoughts of Jeffrey surfaced. Where was he now on life's winding path?

As twilight descended, Gabrielle returned to her familiar workplace. The night audit loomed, but welcoming smiles met her at the threshold. "Your presence was sorely missed," they said, simple words that unfolded her heart.

As time meandered, the exhilaration of return faded. Leisure moments stretched. Gabrielle perched in the lobby, *The Bible in a Year* her companion. Yet guilt gnawed: she'd lapsed a week. Her husband's apathy during their truck journey echoed.

And then there was Jeffrey. His name sifted through memory's halls. Why did he hold such significance? Jeffrey had become her burning bush. But the heavens were hushed. Had they lost her coordinates?

Friday's first light whispered reprieve. After a tempestuous fortnight, Gabrielle longed for sanctuary. Fatigue draped her. Her husband welcomed the pause. His son, son's girlfriend, and eldest grandson were arriving, a maelstrom of mirth, storytelling, and feasts.

Their weekend unfurled with tender cadence. The world receded: Sunday Mass, a Subway lunch, and home's quiet embrace. RCIA had reached its denouement. No more lectures, no more doctrinal puzzles. Gabrielle basked in repose.

As evening kissed the horizon, Gabrielle felt a pull. The gas station's glow beckoned. A parched throat soothed by icy soda. Three $10 scratchoffs unfurled in her hand. Her fingers waltzed across metallic canvas.

Then, serendipity, a jubilant match: $500. Her pulse raced. The gas station lights stood sentinel for her joy. But an inner conflict stirred. Should she share the gain? Temptation danced. He was her companion, her ally. She whispered the secret. His eyes widened. She handed him the ticket, mutual elation sealed.

By morning, their household hummed with revelation. The ticket immortalized online. But prudence reigned. Her husband redeemed it swiftly; no clerk would steal their fortune.

Workdays shimmered with newfound sheen. Each night, Gabrielle visited the gas station. Wins and losses ebbed and flowed. Lottery tickets became her confidants. Her purse, an eager participant. Each ticket unveiled, she murmured, "Let the jingle fade; may the riches unfold."

On a sultry Friday, Gabrielle's workday ebbed. She crossed the threshold of home. Her husband stood beside her. Together, they set forth to gather the clan.

At the airport, his eldest grandson arrived. Their spirits ascended with the plane's descent. Cracker Barrel welcomed them—rustic charm, laughter, breakfast.

Later, his son and girlfriend arrived, delayed, but embraced. They journeyed home, resilience aglow.

The kids clamored for pizza. Aromas mingled with poolside chlorine. Dusk settled. Zest cascaded into the water—splashes, laughter, comedic plunges. Her husband joined the merriment. Gabrielle retreated to the bedroom. Weariness pressed. Sleep claimed her.

Saturday dawned radiant. The kids yearned for the seaside. Gabrielle and her husband answered the call, sunblock, towels, icy drinks in tow. The shore received them. Sandcastles rose. Seashells gathered. Time wove memories in brine and breeze.

As the sun descended, enchantment lingered. Miniature golf summoned them. The kids brandished clubs, eyes sparkling. Chuckles, wayward strokes, victorious cheers. Moments melded into a mosaic of joy.

As twilight brushed the heavens, they gathered for the evening's crescendo. The sea called them to a charming eatery by the water's edge. Aromas of seared seafood and buttery delights swirled around their toasts.

Then, the cinema, velvety seats, buttered popcorn, and silver screen magic. A saga of valor and laughter unfolded.

As the credits rolled, weariness tugged at Gabrielle. Her husband and the kids answered the call of a nocturnal swim. The pool became their playground. Gabrielle yielded to slumber's tender grasp, the distant splashes serenading her into dreams.

The next day, golden rays draped the Everglades. Gabrielle and her husband set out with the kids. Everglade City awaited. Their chariot: an airboat slicing through marshy maze. The engine roared. They skimmed the water, trailing ripples. Their guide spun tales of gators and birds. Suddenly, an alligator surfaced. Gasps filled the air. The kids cradled a baby gator, scales ancient and soft.

A rustic zoo followed, monkeys, birds, a panther in repose. Gabrielle captured each moment, photographs echoing the day's wonder. But discomfort crept in: a muffled world, a longing for clarity.

At home, she sought relief. Dawn brought no reprieve. Urgent care revealed the culprit: an inner ear infection. Medicine in hand, she surrendered to rest.

The kids remained undeterred, energy boundless. Gabrielle stayed behind; her husband returned with tales and empathy. "Rest," he urged. "It's for the best."

Hunger called them to a quaint pub. Gabrielle dined despite her ear's protest.

Then, a surprise: *Buzz Lightyear.* A cinematic escape chosen by the son's girlfriend. Medication wove its sleepy spell. Gabrielle drifted into dreams of interstellar flight.

Back home, the pool beckoned again. Her husband and the kids reveled under moonlight. Gabrielle, cradled by her bed, let laughter be her lullaby.

Morning arrived. The house would soon echo with absence. The kids' laughter marked their final day. Bob Evans hosted their farewell meal: pancakes, eggs, and reflective gazes.

Back home, luggage filled with memories. Rooms brimmed with banter. Gabrielle and her husband shared silent glances, their hearts heavy with goodbye.

The drive to the airport was quiet. Her husband's son and grandson departed in harmony. At the terminal, embraces lingered. Soft assurances exchanged. Security lines swallowed their presence.

Her husband's eyes shimmered, a canvas of pride and yearning. "They'll return," he whispered. Returning to a home now subdued, they moved through the quiet aftermath. The remnants of the visit were folded away.

Washing machines whirred, sorting joy into neat stacks. Then stillness settled, a void where footsteps once echoed. Her husband pierced the hush. "I miss them already," he said softly. "The silence will return." His eyes swept the empty spaces, the home holding its breath for the return of its heartbeat.

Gabrielle sought refuge in their bedroom. Weariness enveloped her. A nap beckoned, the bed cradling her in its quiet embrace.

She awoke to elongated shadows. Her ears, still tender from the airboat's roar, resisted the call to action. Yet the night audit awaited. Her husband offered a kiss of solace. "Rest," he whispered. "I'll keep our world turning." And with dusk cloaking the house, Gabrielle lay ensconced in quiet, the whispers of the day's emotions lulling her into peaceful repose.

Twilight draped the hotel lobby as Gabrielle stepped into her evening shift. Unbeknownst to her, the night would unravel into a tapestry of secrets and hushed exchanges.

At the front desk, Lisa was a bundle of nerves. Her eyes flicked toward the security cameras. Allen had sent a stern text, a directive to halt her socializing with bar patrons. Her charm, it seemed, had eclipsed her duties. Gabrielle, still contending with her ear's stubborn silence, found Lisa's turmoil a welcome distraction.

Lisa's purpose appeared clear: charm the male guests, perhaps secure a benefactor. Allen's watchful gaze brought a rare smile to Gabrielle's face. Justice, it seemed, had eyes in every corner.

Lisa confronted Gabrielle. "Does it irk you?" she asked, voice sharp.

"This constant surveillance?" Gabrielle shrugged. "Not in the slightest," she replied. "I'm here to work. If Allen wishes to watch, let him."

Lisa exhaled and clocked out.

Melissa, the bartender, soon approached, eyes gleaming with scandal. "Have you heard about Lisa?" she whispered. "She's made the bar her second home. Allen knows." Gabrielle nodded. Melissa herself was no stranger to flirtation. Gabrielle kept her distance. It wasn't her conflict to engage.

Days melded into monotony: fluorescent lights, subdued murmurs, and Allen's nightly texts.

At 8:00 p.m., Lisa's phone would buzz, a reminder to stay anchored at the desk. Gabrielle was spared by such intrusions; her shift began after the lobby had settled. Allen was likely asleep. Lisa bristled at Gabrielle's indifference. She had sought an ally. Gabrielle remained aloof coexistence, not camaraderie.

As Independence Day neared, Lisa's restlessness grew. She longed for freedom. Allen denied her request. Tenure dictated the holiday roster. Lisa threatened to feign illness. Allen remained unmoved.

Her 11:00 a.m. to 7:00 p.m. shift was no accident. Gabrielle approached, detached. "Anything pertinent for my shift?" she asked. Lisa's vexation ricocheted off her. "You're devoid of empathy."

Lisa snapped. "Can't you see my plight?" Gabrielle shrugged. "I don't make the schedule. If it's unbearable, seek employment elsewhere."

Lisa stormed out. Gabrielle remained unmoved. The squabbles were Lisa's to contend with.

Friday arrived with the promise of respite: garage sales, shared meals, and laughter with friends from Tampa.

Sunday brought Mass and a modest lunch. The weekend's joy left Gabrielle weary, yearning for rest before her nocturnal duties resumed.

In the lobby's twilight, Greg manned the desk. His eyes held secrets. "Lisa had a showdown with Allen," he whispered. "She asked for the Fourth off. He refused." Surveillance had tracked her every move. Allen's texts reminded her of her place. "Behind the desk," Greg said. "If she skips her shift, it's a resignation."

Gabrielle shrugged. "Her choice. Not my circus, not my monkeys." Greg nodded. Lisa's defiance, Allen's scrutiny, a tempest beyond Gabrielle's realm.

In the hotel's hushed corridors, Lisa's resignation echoed, a text sent on Independence Day. She chose kinship over the lobby's lifelessness.

Gabrielle, untroubled, saw an opening. Todd stood at the desk, eyes reflecting quiet authority. "Lisa is gone," Gabrielle said. "Could this mean a shift change for me?" He promised to confer with Allen. Hope flickered, daylight shifts, liberated weekends.

By Thursday, anticipation hung in the air. Todd confirmed: Allen agreed. A new auditor was coming. Gabrielle's spirits soared. Her husband smiled. "We'll adjust," he said. They nestled into domestic bliss.

Days stretched before them, a tapestry of tranquility and muted television melodies. Gratitude filled Gabrielle's heart. Lisa's exit had granted her a new cadence.

Dawn arrived. They ventured to the beach, stopped at a charming café for sweet confections.

Their backyard transformed into a sundrenched haven.

Sunday brought spiritual reflection. Stained glass cast kaleidoscopic promises. Dinner spun tales of faith and mystery.

At home, Gabrielle found solace in her armchair before the night summoned her to a silent vigil: spreadsheets and solitude.

At 10:00 p.m., Gabrielle stepped into the lobby. Heather, the candid bartender, was a beacon in the quiet. She spoke of vagabond adventures and scars etched in skin.

Her commentary on bodily functions left Gabrielle amused and bewildered. Heather categorized her moods: preperiod, period, postperiod. "Ever notice how the universe aligns with my cycle?" she mused.

"Preperiod, I'm a cosmic storm. During, I'm a serene goddess with Merlot." They sat on the worn couch, laughter punctuating the quiet.

Heather's phone buzzed with slot machine jingles. She played relentlessly. "Practice," she said, "for when I hit the real jackpot."

Melissa, the hurried bartender, would swoop in, counters wiped with tornado efficiency. She closed shop quickly, eager to join guests at the neighboring bar. Her motives were transparent: free food, a guest to foot the bill. "Networking," she declared. "All about connections, darling."

Melissa grated on Gabrielle's nerves. Feigning busyness, Gabrielle avoided prolonged interaction. Melissa chattered about conquests and latenight snacks. Her eyes gleamed with mercenary zeal.

Caught between Heather's cosmic tales and Melissa's calculated charm, Gabrielle became the silent arbiter of the night.

In the lobby's hush, their stories stitched a tapestry of laughter and exasperation.

Friday arrived. Gabrielle poised for respite. But Allen's urgent call disrupted her calm. Seth was ill. Gabrielle, nudged by duty and her husband, stepped in.

What began as a weekend cover spiraled into a monthlong marathon. Seth's promise proved empty. Days off became a mirage. Allen's loyalty to Seth puzzled her. Still, Gabrielle persevered.

Amidst the churn of hires and departures, Todd leaned against the front desk one evening, his eyes heavy with scheduling battles. "The girl Allen hired," he sighed, "she didn't last. The job chewed her up."

Gabrielle nodded. Todd's voice carried the weight of missed sleep and shared frustration. "But fear not," he said, "I waged a war of persuasion. Allen relented. A new night auditor is on the horizon, a beacon for our sleep deprived souls."

Meanwhile, Seth agreed to fill the gap. "Be patient," Allen implored. "The wheels of bureaucracy turn slowly."

Gabrielle trudged onward. Nights blurred into weeks.

August arrived, days off remained elusive. Allen's loyalty to Seth baffled her. Why cling to someone who rarely showed up?

Then came the new girl, freshfaced, stationed at the front desk. Gabrielle felt a mix of frustration and curiosity. Why hire for day shift while night audit remained untouched?

Todd shared her sentiments. The new girl had already quit, overwhelmed by the job's demands.

Finally, Allen agreed to hire another night auditor. Seth would cover Gabrielle's two days off while juggling his own shifts. His bank job loomed, but until then, he remained their reluctant savior.

Gabrielle wondered: *Would the elusive night auditor ever materialize? Or would Seth continue his dance between duty and disappearance?*

The week unfurled with Seth's refrain: "I can't make it tonight." Gabrielle filled the void again. Allen, undisturbed, introduced a new recruit to the day shift.

Cathy, the sales coordinator, reemerged from maternity leave. Her odd rhythm of early and regular shifts added to the carousel of faces.

The new girl vanished quickly. Cathy filled the gap, often late. Gabrielle's patience frayed. Her veiled jabs were mistaken for jest. Allen's favor held little sway. Gabrielle's allegiance teetered.

In the kitchen, another drama unfolded. A clash with a delivery driver, one less pair of hands in the culinary storm. Staff departures became routine. The day shift's punctuality struggles, a symphony of sighs and apologies.

When the chance arose to lend her talents to the kitchen, Gabrielle was ready to swap ledger for ladle. But before she could embrace the role, Allen introduced a whirlwind, a new chef whose appetite outpaced her skill. Her departure was swift. Gabrielle was beckoned once more to the kitchen. Night audit followed by morning prep.

Then, a quiet surprise: a $1 raise on her paycheck. Allen's silent nod to her unwavering dedication.

Amidst the whirlwind of responsibilities, a weekend reprieve shimmered on the horizon. Baseball beckoned: Dodgers vs. Marlins in Miami. Freeman and Betts danced across the field, heroes of Gabrielle's dreams, their grace a mesmerizing spectacle.

As the crowd roared, Gabrielle's thoughts wandered to Jeffrey. His absence echoed silently, a friendship just out of reach. She longed for connection, a shared understanding.

Between innings, she contemplated reaching out. Could words bridge the distance? She held onto hope that Jeffrey might see the truth in her message, the longing for camaraderie.

The weekend embraced them. Miami Beach shimmered. The sea vast, the ships grand. Their journey home was a nostalgic ride.

September arrived. Gabrielle's nights became a solitary ballet, figures and reports leading to her birthday's quiet joy. They found delight in simple pleasures: the beach's caress, the open road's freedom, dinner by candlelight.

Sunday morning, they stepped into the church's embrace. Father Michael spotted her husband, an unsuspecting soul ripe for service. "Usher," he declared, bestowing a name tag with priestly authority.

Her husband, now "Mr. Hospitality," wielded the collection plate with gravitas. Pews bowed before him as he dismissed them for communion. Gabrielle captured the moment, her social media post a playful nod to their priestly friendship.

Rachel approached, eyes sparkling. "The OCIA class awaits," she announced. Nine souls had signed up, hungry for knowledge. She promised a schedule, her email poised to infiltrate their inboxes. No room for protest. They were swept into the current, their fate sealed by her husband's gregarious nature.

"Blame him," Gabrielle muttered, halfjoking. "His conversations are breadcrumbs to volunteer tasks."

Her husband chuckled, unrepentant. "Tell Father Michael you're not keen on OCIA." But Gabrielle knew better. Father Michael's gaze held the weight of centuries. Refusal would crumble beneath it.

The Storm and the Stillness

"Then he arose and rebuked the winds and the sea, and there was a great calm."

—Matthew 8:26

Gabrielle arrived at her night shift to a hum of unease. The hurricane, once a distant swirl, had shifted course. Forecasts betrayed them: Category 4, winds screaming at 156 mph. The city braced. Shutters locked like sentinels.

Her husband sprang into action, securing windows and doors with a friend's help. Evacuation wasn't their plan; their inland home promised safety, bolstered by a whole house generator. He posted a photo: *We stand ready. Hurricane, do your worst.* Likes and prayers poured in.

At the hotel, Allen rallied his team. "All hands-on deck," he declared. Gabrielle passed the baton to Carol, whispering, "I'll confer with my husband."

Back home, they deliberated. His resolve was ironclad: Gabrielle would not return to the hotel. He called Allen. "She'll remain anchored here until the storm passes." Allen's reply crackled with reluctant understanding.

Night fell. The hurricane awoke, a behemoth born from a zephyr's breath. Winds howled. Dawn revealed its wrath. Darkness cloaked their home, shutters sealing them in.

At 1:00 p.m., the lights faltered. The generator surged, a lifeline against chaos. Internet vanished. The radio sputtered bulletins: rooftops torn, trees uprooted, power lines down.

Then came betrayal: water seeped into the spare bedroom. A smoke detector shrieked. They muted its cries, placed a bucket beneath the drip. Solar panels surrendered to the gale. The roof groaned. Walls quivered. They clung to each other in the closet's dim refuge.

Her husband, restless, patrolled the house. Outside, the storm relented. A haunting calm settled. "Daylight," he whispered. "At dawn, we'll survey the wreckage."

They waited. Gabrielle coaxed a local broadcast onto the screen. Images bore witness to endurance. They reclined together, hearts syncopated with anxiety. Slumber evaded them.

As the sun crept over the horizon, they emerged. Their haven bore the storm's scars, but the true devastation lay beyond.

The television revealed a somber tableau: Fort Myers Beach, once vibrant, now desolate. The pier was gone. Sanibel's causeway fractured. Matlacha's bridge shattered. Downtown submerged, silent witness to the surge's fury. The hurricane had been indiscriminate. First responders appeared, their purpose clear: seek, save, restore.

Gabrielle and her husband opened the garage door. The neighborhood was a canvas of havoc. Power lines drooped.

Neighbors appeared, faces etched with disbelief. Their generator hummed, a beacon of endurance. The mailbox had vanished. Solar panels lay tangled in the neighbor's foliage. Shingles littered the streets. Their pool heater had shifted; pipes once linked to the panels were gone. Her husband documented the damage, but calls to the insurance company were met with silence. Phones were casualties of the storm.

They walked the street, steps echoing in unnatural quiet. Neighbors gathered, somber but determined. A glimmer of hope: their solar panels lay in a vacant lot. Her husband retrieved them, leaning them against the garage, a symbol of resilience.

The front door remained sealed. With methodical care, he dismantled the protective shield, restoring another path to the world.

Later, they ventured out to check on friends. The roads were a labyrinth of risk, downed lines, toppled trees, broken signals. They pressed on. Relief greeted them: their friends were safe. A new roof had spared their home. Their generator purred. They welcomed others in need.

Yet imperfections lingered: lanai screens torn, water lines compromised. Running water, a memory. Her husband offered sanctuary. "Come to our house. Shower. Rest." But their friends had summoned a plumber. They would manage, though they might seek water for essentials.

Returning home, they cleared shingles from the lawn. Twilight approached. Fatigued but unyielding, they stood side-by-side, their home and spirits bearing Hurricane Ian's scars.

A new day broke. The gas company arrived, navigating debris to replenish propane, a promise of warmth and light.

They journeyed to the AT&T Store. Their phones latched onto a signal. He reassured Gabrielle's mother, broadcasted their tale of survival. The insurance company responded, a voice of assurance amid automation.

Seated in their truck, messages cascaded in. Gabrielle reached out to Allen. Work would wait. Survival came first.

Their yard remained strewn with debris. The lanai damaged. The pool, a murky reminder. The insurance adjuster arrived, efficient, promising swift repair.

With the hotel beckoning, Gabrielle prepared for her shift. Her husband drove her past the storm's scars, a quick stop for essentials, a quiet testament to their resilience.

The hotel's power outage meant stairs over elevators. The lobby became a hub of refuge and restless energy. Gabrielle's room, dim but welcome, offered brief respite.

After settling in and connecting with the front desk, she learned of the hotel's struggles. The generator, their lifeline. Her stairwell journeys mirrored her perseverance. Todd's weary presence and the silent cash register highlighted the night's challenges.

Allen's instructions were clear: "Count the drawer, drop the excess, let the night swallow the discrepancies."

Gabrielle huddled in the back office, cradling crumpled bills and jingling coins. The audit awaited, but the outage had disrupted its rhythm. Allen's voice echoed: "Keep running it until reality catches up."

Before diving into the ledger's abyss, Gabrielle embarked on a room by room pilgrimage. Charges demanded scrutiny.

As the night wore on, hotel denizens emerged from their sanctuaries. Smoke breaks became impromptu conversations. Camaraderie forged in adversity. "We are all guests in this tempest," someone said.

Her downtime evaporated. Emergency responders huddled over maps. Weary travelers sought solace. Gabrielle reconciled accounts, whispered reassurances, sipped lukewarm coffee.

At 7:00 a.m., Allen nodded. "You've weathered the chaos," he said. "Rest. Tomorrow brings new battles."

Gabrielle collapsed into a chair, fingers tracing the drawer's worn edges. The mess remained, but it was no longer hers to untangle.

In her room, weariness clung to her. She dialed her husband, craving the sound of his voice. They exchanged snippets of their day.

A soothing shower followed. Gabrielle cocooned herself in soft folds, surrendering to sleep. But before slumber claimed her, Jeffrey surfaced in her thoughts. Had he seen the hurricane photos? Did he care? Why hadn't he reached out? She still held hope that one day he'd accept her again, even just on social media. Why did he linger in her mind? Why did their brief friendship leave her longing for acceptance?

Night's interruption brought her back. She readied for the day ahead. One elevator was down, but fortune favored her: her room was a short distance away.

The front desk was a maelstrom. Greg weathered the storm of check-ins and cancellations. System quirks offered phantom rooms. Gabrielle, cocooned in her role, was insulated from chaos.

An emergency team arrived, adding peculiar energy to the night. Employees and guests shared moments of camaraderie. The outage's aftermath demanded balance. Allen's directives echoed. Gabrielle's night blurred with tasks. Carol's late arrival, a ripple in the tide.

At shift's end, Gabrielle ascended to her room. The phone tethered her to home. She reached out to her husband. Their conversation wove a tapestry of trials and triumphs. The generator's cry had ceased, a return to normalcy. Their neighbors summoned a public adjuster. Their roof became a canvasshrouded fortress.

Their own home lay exposed. Her husband acted, secured a tarp, prepared to challenge the insurance titans. Gabrielle, caught between duty and fatigue, offered quiet support. "Trust your instincts," she whispered. Cleansing herself of the day's residue, she surrendered to sleep's embrace.

Awakened by duty's call, Gabrielle resumed her post. The hotel's pulse beat steady under her watch. A full house greeted her, the digital *No Vacancy* sign a badge of resilience. A culinary misadventure disrupted the peace.

Todd issued a stern warning. Amid the fray, two young men stood out, their apology a quiet rebellion against the night's disorder. Gabrielle navigated the night's ebb and flow. As dawn approached, the chaos softened to a whisper. The young men's gratitude marked the night's end, a subtle nod to Gabrielle's understanding.

Todd, punctual as ever, arrived at 6:00 a.m. Gabrielle clocked out and retreated to her room.

Amid the storm's aftermath, a quiet milestone: their eighteenth wedding anniversary. Gabrielle called her husband at dawn. His voice was a balm.

At 1:00 p.m. they met, a Mexican restaurant their sanctuary. Laughter flowed, memories unfurled.

Post lunch, he whisked away her laundry and returned with fresh attire, a simple act, rich with care.

Alone, Gabrielle cocooned herself in blankets, seizing rest before duty called anew. Todd offered gentle reassurance: "Rest easy," he said. "The storm has passed. Tranquility reigns." He granted her a delayed entrance.

At 9:00 p.m., Gabrielle donned her uniform, stepped into her role with practiced ease. Behind the desk, the lobby's familiar cadence greeted her.

There they were, the nocturnal sojourners from yesternight, perched at the bar, faces lit with mischief. "Our nocturnal confidante!" they hailed, toasting her arrival. Camaraderie rekindled their banter a tapestry of mirth.

Two had been dismissed; their revelry had breached the bounds. "Worry not," they whispered. "Reinforcements have been beckoned."

As the clock waltzed toward midnight, their stories unfurled. Gabrielle, captivated, lost herself in the moment. Time blurred sweetly on the cusp of daybreak.

Meanwhile, Cathy, the sales coordinator and hotel resident, was conspicuously absent. Gabrielle was baffled, how could one not traverse the short journey from residence to workplace?

At 6:45 a.m., Gabrielle called. The phone rang. Cathy's voice, drowsy and indifferent, answered. No regret, only resignation. Domestic upheaval, a pull to northern roots. Her chapter at the hotel closed.

Gabrielle harbored a quiet hope that her successor might honor the clock. Irritation flared then faded. Gabrielle retreated to her sanctuary.

Later, as evening embraced her, Gabrielle recounted the day's events to her husband. His voice, steady as ever, asked about fallout. Gabrielle's reply mirrored his constancy: favored by Allen, shielded by integrity, she would stand firm against any turbulence.

As sunset painted the sky, her phone buzzed. Allen summoned her downstairs. Her first thought: Cathy had complained. But resolve settled in. Gabrielle had spoken her truth. It would be her compass. She descended to the lobby, ready to navigate office politics.

But Allen's request was simple: help in the kitchen. A cook had departed, leaving the staff shorthanded. Gabrielle agreed without hesitation. Already onsite, spared the commute, she stepped into the breach.

Curiously, Allen made no mention of Cathy. Had she kept their conversation to herself? Gabrielle remained nonchalant.

Allen shared his plans: interviews for a new night auditor. His intent: to free Gabrielle from nocturnal duty. She nodded, though déjà vu lingered. Todd had promised the same for months. Yet there she was, still ensnared.

Gabrielle retreated to her room, cocooned in silence, surrendering to sleep until duty called again.

Her evening shift began with Greg's revelation: "Guess what? Cathy complained about you."

Gabrielle raised an eyebrow. "Me? What did I do?"

Greg chuckled. "She didn't like your morning banter, the joke about her being late on purpose."

Gabrielle shrugged. "No skin off my nose. I'm pulling a double shift in the kitchen. If breakfast is late, she'll face Allen."

They chatted at the desk. Gabrielle glanced up, Cathy sat at the bar, flanked by husband and father. So that was the reason for her tardiness. Greg patted her back. "Good luck, my friend. You're in for an eventful night."

The hotel was fully booked. Smokers darted in and out. Gabrielle had no downtime. She hustled in the kitchen, preparing breakfast. Cathy's lateness weighed on her. She didn't want to leave the kitchen lady hanging.

When the kitchen lady arrived, Gabrielle greeted her with a weary smile. "I'm your sidekick today," she said. "But fair warning, Cathy's my relief."

The kitchen lady chuckled. "She's danced to her own clock for four years. Just come back when she graces us."

Dawn approached. Cathy arrived fifty minutes late. Gabrielle informed her Allen had been summoned. She could explain herself when he arrived. Without waiting for a reply, Gabrielle pivoted toward the kitchen.

Like clockwork, Allen appeared. Cathy, flustered and apologetic, spun a tale of oversleeping and alarm clock mischief. Her eyes darted toward Gabrielle, seeking validation. Gabrielle maintained her poker face.

Allen listened patiently, balancing discipline and compassion. "A couple more weeks," he murmured. His gaze met Gabrielle's. She nodded; the end was near for their chronically late colleague.

As morning wore on, Gabrielle toiled in the kitchen, fatigue mounting. When her shift ended, she stumbled to her room, called her husband, showered, and sank into sleep's embrace.

The night audit, mercifully, was not on her agenda. Yet weariness clung to her bones. At some ungodly hour, Gabrielle tiptoed to the laundry room, snatching towels with Seth as her silent ally.

Back in her room, she surrendered to the glow of the television. Snacks beckoned. Midnight blurred into oblivion. Gabrielle drifted into sleep, cocooned in anonymity.

At 5:00 a.m., she stirred. Warm water washed away the remnants of slumber. Dressed and ready, she descended to the lobby.

Seth, weary but determined, looked up. "I'm on kitchen duty," Gabrielle said gently. "Cathy will relieve you."

His face fell; Cathy's reputation preceded her. Gabrielle leaned in, conspiratorial. "Call her now. Tell her you're leaving at 6:00 a.m. No excuses."

He hesitated, then dialed. To his surprise, she answered. "Five minutes early," he announced, triumphant. "She cursed me out; said I woke her kids."

Gabrielle chuckled. "Desperate times call for desperate measures." He shrugged. "A little morning drama never hurt anyone."

As the sun climbed, Seth slipped out the back. Cathy, bleary eyed but punctual, took her place. Gabrielle admired the art of negotiation.

After the breakfast rush, she wiped down counters with a fellow worker. "Hungry?" she asked. "Lunch?"

Gabrielle nodded. "But first a shower."

She ascended to her room, the water washing away the kitchen's chaos. Refreshed, she met her downstairs.

They strolled to a nearby bar. Burgers sizzled, laughter mingled. Time slowed. For a moment, Gabrielle forgot the fluorescent lights and night shifts.

At 2:00 p.m., they slipped back through a side door, avoiding Cathy's gaze. Gabrielle retreated to her room, dialed her husband, and shared snippets of her day. The television murmured. She settled into bed.

Todd's urgent call shattered her rest. Seth had called in sick again. Gabrielle answered, already at the hotel, her temporary home. The night audit, her nocturnal companion.

In a few days, she would check out. Until then, she embraced the hours.

Past midnight, Gabrielle immersed herself in the audit's quiet hum. The lobby lay still, bathed in fluorescent glow. She reconciled accounts, the world outside fading away. Dawn crept in. Gabrielle transitioned to the kitchen. Amid sizzling and chopping, she found her rhythm.

After the morning's work, she retreated to her room. A knock, her husband, bearing clean clothes. He sought the hotel's WiFi, spoke of the public adjuster, a beacon of hope for their home repairs. They shared precious moments. Gabrielle rested, knowing restoration was near.

At 10:00 p.m., she entered the lobby. A new group of Spanish speaking guests awaited. With a translation app and help from a bilingual guest, the "Language Ambassador," she bridged the gap. His parting words lingered: "We are going to be friends."

Dawn brought unexpected punctuality. Carol, the front desk supervisor, arrived on time. Her warm presence infused the lobby with grace, a contrast to Cathy's indifference. Gabrielle's gentle reminders were met with sincere apologies. Improvement felt possible.

After a morning in the kitchen, a call to her husband grounded her. A hot shower washed away the day's fatigue. She succumbed to sleep, dreams transporting her far from duty.

Evening settled in as Gabrielle prepared for her shift. Greg leaned close, eyes scanning the lobby. "I've been looking for another job," he whispered.

Her curiosity stirred. "Why? What's wrong here?"

"No room to grow," he said. "My family needs better insurance."

Gabrielle nodded. "I get it. Sometimes we need to spread our wings."

"I have an interview tomorrow," he added. "Fingers crossed."

Gabrielle wished him luck, heart heavy with empathy. Greg was more than a colleague—he was a friend. "Keep it quiet," he said. "I haven't told Todd or Allen."

"Your secret's safe," Gabrielle assured him.

The night passed with thoughts of Greg's future and her own impending freedom. Carol breezed in. Gabrielle grinned. "Confetti," she joked, pointing to the empty desk. "We need confetti for this moment!"

Carol rolled her eyes, laughter dancing between them. Breakfast flowed with camaraderie and shared jokes.

By 11:00 a.m., Gabrielle stepped into the morning sun. Allen intercepted her. "Two more weeks," he said. "You're off kitchen duty."

Gabrielle raised an eyebrow. "You promise?"

"Interviews are underway," he chuckled. "You'll see."

She wanted to believe him, but skepticism clung tight. "Actions speak louder," she replied.

"Soon," he said. "And do you need to stay longer?"

"Two more days," Gabrielle said. "Then home."

At 9:00 p.m., the clock's glow nudged her awake. Dressing, her thoughts returned to Greg. Had his interview borne fruit? In the lobby, Greg's news awaited: a job offer, a raise, his two week notice already given. Allen's oversight had cost them. Gabrielle felt joy for Greg's new path and sorrow for the loss of shared moments.

Morning arrived. Carol surprised her again, early, two days in a row. Gabrielle scoffed. "A party in my honor seems fitting." They laughed, two souls navigating hotel life, finding solace in shared absurdities. The kitchen rush passed in a blur.

By 11:00 a.m., Gabrielle was free. A call with her husband brimmed with anticipation. She prepared her room for departure, settled into bed, embraced by the quiet promise of home.

At 8:00 p.m., she stirred, disoriented. The dusky glow signaled her final nocturnal task: packing up her life. She folded clothes, tucked away mementos, stripped the bed, bundled linens into a sack.

Downstairs, the laundry room hummed. This wasn't just about cleanliness: it was respect. The housekeepers deserved more than a haphazard goodbye.

Todd appeared at the desk, eyes gleaming. "He's quitting," he whispered. Greg had slipped his resignation under the door. Gabrielle feigned surprise. Secrets were currency in this twilight world.

"Oh, really?" she said, voice practiced.

Todd leaned closer. "You're next. Two weeks. You'll ascend from the night shift abyss."

Gabrielle raised a brow. "I'll believe it when I see it." Todd was resolute. "This time, it's real. A cosmic shift awaits."

His conviction was contagious. For a moment, Gabrielle dared to hope. Maybe the curtain would lift: a new act, a script rewritten in daylight hues. They left it there. No more words. Just the promise of change hanging between them.

The hotel lobby hummed with the soft glow of computer screens. Gabrielle, immersed in her solitary shift, reveled in the quiet.

At 5:00 a.m., just as expected, her husband appeared blearyeyed but warm, a gentle presence in the stillness.

"Cathy will be late," Gabrielle said, handing him her room key. "Use my laptop while you wait. I'll join you once she clocks in."

He nodded, settling into a plush armchair, the promise of breakfast and stolen time dancing in his eyes.

Minutes stretched. Gabrielle tapped rhythmically at the keyboard. Cathy's footsteps finally echoed down the corridor.

At 6:35 a.m., she sauntered in disheveled, halfawake. Her husband leveled a quiet gaze. His breakfast, courtesy of the kindhearted kitchen lady, had softened his mood, but Cathy's indifference grated. He said nothing, just sipped his coffee and watched her punch in.

As Gabrielle's shift ended, she retrieved a luggage cart. Her room awaited. Her husband thanked the kitchen staff. Their smiles mirrored the dawn's first light, a silent nod to shared moments in the wee hours.

On the drive home, he broke the silence. "Cathy is a testament to Allen's patience," he said. "If I were in charge, she'd be out the door."

Gabrielle chuckled. Her departure was imminent: she was moving out of state. "One week too long," he muttered.

Gabrielle shared her upcoming shift change: the 2:00 p.m. to 10:00 p.m. slot. Fridays and Saturdays would no longer be hers, but the hurricane had already blurred the boundaries of her days.

"At least you'll be home at night," he said, his hand finding hers. Gabrielle agreed. The promise of evenings together outweighed the loss of weekends.

As Gabrielle stepped over the threshold, the scent of home enveloped her. The house still bore the hurricane's scars, but relief bloomed in her chest. Her husband had spent his free hours restoring order.

The yard, once strewn with debris, now stood tamed. Neighbors, too, wrestled with broken branches and displaced memories. At each driveway's end, mounds of destruction waited for waste management's slow magic.

Amid the chaos, her husband unearthed fragments of their life. "Look," he grinned, "our little victories." The mailbox, a comical survivor, lay tethered to its post by rope. He dubbed it his "mail drop box." Gabrielle laughed, snapped a photo, and posted: *Poor people, rich in resilience.*

After the tour, Gabrielle stepped inside. A hot shower washed away the day's grit. Settling into bed, she marveled at the simple luxury of being home.

At 6:00 p.m., she stirred, disoriented. The television blared in the great room. Her husband lay sprawled on the couch, bathed in flickering light.

He blinked, then sat up, animated. "Guess what?" he whispered. "The internet is back! After three weeks we're reconnected!" His grin was infectious.

Gabrielle smiled, then gently chided, "The whole neighborhood can hear the TV." He turned it down, sheepish but unrepentant.

Dinner was modest. They nestled on the couch, cocooned in blankets, watching the local news, a grim carousel of destruction. Houses reduced to fragments. Lives irrevocably altered. Gratitude mingled with sorrow. They were among the fortunate.

Her husband leaned closer. "The church has been closed for weeks," he said. RCIA, now OCIA, had paused. "You haven't missed anything," he assured her.

Then came the tale: a classmate had sought solace at the church. Father Michael, it seemed, had deemed him a security risk. "I won't go back," the classmate declared. "It didn't sit right."

Gabrielle listened, torn between empathy and doubt. Had Father Michael honestly said that? Or was it miscommunication, a priest under pressure, wrestling with chaos?

"He's stressed," her husband mused. "I'll talk to Rachel. To Father Michael. We'll find the truth."

"Maybe it was just a misunderstanding," Gabrielle offered. "He wouldn't say that intentionally." Yet doubt lingered. She hadn't been there.

At 3:30 a.m., Gabrielle tiptoed to the great room. The television flickered, wreckage, resilience, stories etched into every fallen branch. Time blurred. Her husband stirred, hunger tugging at him. "Breakfast?" he murmured, eyes pleading.

Guilt tugged at Gabrielle. Two weeks at the hotel had left him hungry for food, for her presence. She flipped pancakes and brewed coffee. They sat side-by-side, the television their silent companion. The news looped. Their home, spared, stood as fragile sanctuary.

Her husband didn't press. He let her drift back into slumber, the couch cradling her weariness.

A text from Todd broke the stillness. Seth had faltered again. Gabrielle hesitated. Her husband's eyes met hers, gentle, pleading. "They've been good to you," he said. "A place to stay." His words tipped the scale. Gabrielle agreed, fingers tapping out a reluctant promise.

Back in bed, the day clung to her. The hotel waited. The night audit loomed.

At twilight, Gabrielle donned her uniform. Todd greeted her with a nod, a silent acknowledgment of her dedication.

But there was more. A new recruit had joined the ranks. Once an assistant GM on Sanibel Island, the hurricane had swept away that chapter. Now, he sought solace in the quiet hum of night audit.

Gabrielle pondered the pivot. Why trade grandeur for midnight solitude? Todd's answer was candid: the new hire had personal struggles. Life's tempest had left him adrift. The night shift offered refuge, a place to recalibrate beneath the soft glow of computer screens.

As the week unfolded, Gabrielle moved through her final graveyard shifts. The hotel pulsed with its usual rhythm, guests drifting in and out like tides.

Two young men approached the desk, their verdict on Seth blunt: "A dick." Gabrielle chuckled, understanding their frustration. But change was coming. A new night auditor would soon arrive, and Gabrielle was shifting to a new time slot. Their smiles widened, more of her, less of him.

Cathy took a morning off, leaving Gabrielle in Carol's hands. Carol breezed in five minutes late, mistaking Gabrielle for Seth. "You're late even when he's working!" Gabrielle teased, her laughter echoing through the lobby.

Clocking out, she offered a parting reminder: "I'll be back later. Tomorrow, I'm in the kitchen. Punctuality is the secret sauce." Carol's vague promise to "try her best" lingered.

At home, Gabrielle tiptoed into the kitchen. The aroma of bacon and coffee greeted her. Her husband's sleepy smile said it all: *Welcome home.*

They shared breakfast in golden morning light, curtains casting stripes across the table. Afterward, Gabrielle showered, washing away the residue of night shifts and hotel intrigues.

That night, a twelve hour marathon awaited. She surrendered to sleep, sleeping pills whispering promises of oblivion.

When the alarm jolted her awake, Gabrielle blinked at the clock. The pills had worked. She'd slept deep and long.

Twilight painted the hotel lobby. Todd stood at the desk, concern etched into his face. A guest group had stirred complaints. Allen summoned their supervisor: "Tread carefully or face eviction." Todd leaned in. "Keep your eyes peeled. Report any shenanigans."

Gabrielle nodded. But truth be told, the group had been courteous. Their laughter echoed softly, their footsteps light.

As Todd retreated, Gabrielle prepped for breakfast. Carol arrived on time, her efficiency a welcome sight.

By 11:00 a.m., the kitchen lay still. Her exit loomed.

But that day held a twist. Travis, the new night auditor, had arrived. Allen introduced them: a handshake, a nod. His eyes held secrets.

Todd had warned her: Travis had once been an assistant GM on Sanibel Island. The hurricane had swept away that chapter. Now, he sought refuge in the quiet hum of night audit. Gabrielle wondered: *Why trade grandeur for midnight solitude?*

Todd's answer was candid: Travis had personal struggles. The night shift offered a place to recalibrate.

Later, Gabrielle shared the news with her husband. "Sketchy," she murmured. Her intuition prickled. "But let's give him a chance."

That evening, Gabrielle met a guest who left an indelible mark, a fragile woman in her seventies, eyes reflecting weariness and distress. The hurricane had ravaged her home. Now she sought refuge. Her car, laden with belongings, parked at the curb. She implored Gabrielle for help. Without hesitation, Gabrielle retrieved a luggage cart, loaded her possessions, escorted her to her room, a temporary sanctuary.

Then came the second request: "Could you park my car?" Gabrielle agreed, the weight of her vulnerability settling on her shoulders. Greg, ever the cynic, laughed. "Full service hotel, huh?"

Gabrielle didn't let it slide. "This woman could be your own kin," she said quietly. Greg's expression shifted. He glimpsed the world through her eyes.

When Gabrielle returned with the parked car, Greg's tone softened. "Nice what you did," he said. "Didn't mean to upset you."

"I wasn't upset," Gabrielle replied, just a silent advocate for empathy.

Other guests lingered in the lobby. Greg, despite quitting, still bore the weight of his shift. He nodded, apology hanging between them, then vanished, fearing Gabrielle's lecture. But she held no sermon, only gratitude that he'd reconsidered.

The hotel lobby buzzed with unusual energy. No one rushed to their rooms. The camaraderie of adversity held them close. On the couch by the front desk sat a couple, their dog curled at their feet, eyes closed in peaceful slumber. They had seen Gabrielle's earlier kindness. Gratitude spilled forth.

They began to talk, a trio bound by circumstance. Their home, once a sanctuary, lay in ruins. Photos revealed the devastation. Memories reduced to rubble. Yet amid the wreckage, they clung to gratitude. Insurance softened the blow, but survival humbled them.

Their dog, arthritic and loyal, had navigated five flights of stairs. The lobby became their refuge, a makeshift living room where stories flowed. They laughed, lamented, counted blessings that survived the storm.

At 1:00 a.m., they rose. The dog stretched, eyes half closed. "Time to call it an evening." Gabrielle watched them retreat, their footsteps echoing down the hall. She didn't begrudge the hours spent with them, their resilience seeped into her bones, their gratitude a balm for her weariness.

The lobby emptied. Gabrielle played catchup until dawn tiptoed in. She shared their story with Carol that morning. "The dog at their feet," she said. Carol nodded. "They linger," she replied. "In the lobby, they find solace."

But Gabrielle's duties beckoned. Her last day in the kitchen had arrived. Relief washed over her. The long shifts had taken their toll.

By 11:00 a.m., the kitchen lay still. Allen approached with news: Greg had given his notice. Her path shifted again, two more-night audits, then the 2:00 p.m. to 10:00 p.m. shift would be hers. A new rhythm.

Gabrielle shared the update with her husband. His smile mirrored her relief. "Two days," he said. "Then the dawn of change."

That evening, the lobby hummed with anticipation. Todd stood at the desk. Travis, the new night auditor, would join her. Gabrielle had expected this. Allen's morning briefing, the passing of the torch.

Travis arrived fifteen minutes late. Relief washed over them. He clocked in, settled at the desk, a talkative soul eager to impress. Hotels unfolded before Gabrielle, his past exploits, his systems mastered. Confidence bordered on arrogance. Gabrielle remained unmoved.

Todd's words echoed: she was the mentor now. Night audit procedures. Breakfast setup. Travis nodded, a willing apprentice. Todd retreated, leaving them to their nocturnal dance.

They began with the checklist. His chatter flowed, a river of anecdotes, a testament to his journey. But Gabrielle sensed the undercurrent, the unspoken challenge. Tomorrow, he would stand alone. The night audit, his canvas. She was not intimidated. He understood, a silent agreement forged in the quiet hours.

As the lobby settled, Gabrielle watched him. Their paths converged, mentor and novice navigating the night shift. She guided him through breakfast setup, the art of anticipation, and the rhythm of presentation.

As he disappeared into the kitchen, Gabrielle lingered at the desk, ears attuned to the lobby's murmurs. Travis emerged an hour later, the kitchen's secrets wrapped in foil and parchment. His chatter resumed, a torrent of ideas, alternative methods, critiques.

Gabrielle, seasoned and steady, remained impartial. His ways were different, perhaps efficient, perhaps chaotic. But she clung to tradition, the checklist, the tried and true. He unveiled his observations: the hotel's shortcomings, missed beats. Gabrielle listened, patience tested. But she had no stake in the game.

She was the night owl, the silent observer. Her résumé, a tapestry of twenty-four years, hung between them like a quiet banner. Titles mattered less than duty fulfilled. Gabrielle spoke: Allen and Todd held the reins. If Travis sought change, he'd find them. She would execute, adapt, and move on.

The night flowed, a river of numbers, a bridge between shifts. Dawn tiptoed in. Clash or concord, it mattered little.

The next night, Travis's comparisons spilled forth: "At other hotels. . ."

Gabrielle listened, patience stretched thin. She held her ground, their way, the hotel's way, etched in memory.

Breakfast setup followed. He snapped pictures, documenting the ritual. Tomorrow, he would stand alone.

At 6:00 a.m., Carol arrived. Travis vanished, promising to return. "How'd it go?" Carol asked. Gabrielle hesitated then shared her truth, his credentials, his repetition.

Carol nodded. A shared experience. Allen's approval lingered. "An asset," he said. Gabrielle hoped he was right.

At home, her husband reminded her she was not an evaluator. His laughter teased gently. Travis remained a puzzle. But Gabrielle acquiesced. Her night audit awaited. Her 2:00 p.m. to 10:00 p.m. shift beckoned. She surrendered to sleep, to the enigma of Travis.

Twilight settled over the hotel. Gabrielle resolved to face the night with equanimity. Her Bible accompanied her. "You're on your own tonight," she told Travis. "I'll be on the couch if you need me."

His response: "Do whatever you want. You can even go home." But duty held her. Allen's directive echoed: "Be there if he needs you."

Gabrielle settled on the couch. The *Bible in a Year* podcast whispered verses. Guilt tugged: should she be more engaged? But she stayed, fingers tracing well worn pages.

At 6:00 a.m., relief washed over her, the final night audit shift. Travis would be her relief on the 2:00 p.m. to 10:00 p.m. shift.

Cathy arrived late as usual. Travis offered to wait, an unexpected courtesy.

At home, Gabrielle shared her quiet vigil. Her husband's laughter reminded her—her role was defined. The night audit was behind her.

Two days off followed, a fleeting breath. The first day slipped away in sleep. The second dawned with breakfast among friends. They laughed, lingered.

Their house, repaired swiftly, stood in contrast to Gabrielle's own, still tarped, still waiting. Neighbors rallied, hands mending what nature had torn. Their friends bypassed insurance, opted for personal solutions.

Gabrielle's path diverged. Her home, a canvas of destruction. Repairs stalled. Her husband's patience waned. He called the public adjuster. "Be patient," came the counsel. But patience was scarce. Gabrielle knew it was their only ally.

Her first 2:00 p.m. to 10:00 p.m. shift began as the sun dipped low. The air buzzed with transition. Greg, the soon to depart veteran, stood beside her, a bridge from past to future. Their glances held unspoken understanding.

Allen had split Greg's final shifts, foreseeing a premature exit, a strategic move. The hotel's heartbeat would not skip.

Cathy's departure marked Gabrielle's days off. A party had been thrown. Gabrielle pondered the sincerity of office farewells. Curious, she turned to Greg. "Was it a good riddance party?" she asked, half joking His laughter echoed, but he remained tightlipped.

At 4:00 p.m., Allen lingered. He approached Gabrielle, eyes crinkling with warmth. "Good to see you in the daylight," he said. Gabrielle smiled. "And it's good to be seen."

His cryptic words hung in the air, a whisper of hidden currents beneath hotel politics. Just before Allen left, Heather breezed in, the lively bartender, all sparkle and sass. "You're on this shift now?" she asked, eyes dancing. Gabrielle nodded. Heather clapped her shoulder, grinning.

"Don't get too comfortable," Allen interjected, his tone enigmatic. Plans were afoot, but their details remained shrouded.

Later, Greg shared whispered secrets. Carol was destined for greater things; the sales coordinator's throne awaited her. And Gabrielle? Poised to step into her morning shoes. She pondered her place in the dance.

At 8:00 p.m., Greg bid adieu, leaving behind a void soon filled with fresh faces. A group of travelers arrived, their chatter a blend of languages, a symphony of arrivals and departures. Among them stood the Language Ambassador, a familiar face from checkin. He stepped forward, offering help.

English eluded most, but his multilingual grace eased the process. Passports, room keys, travel weariness, all navigated with ease. Gabrielle thanked him. "Why the early shift?" he asked, eyes crinkling. "You're a night owl."

Gabrielle leaned on the counter. "Evenings now," she said. "You'll be seeing more of me."

His response was unexpected: a compliment wrapped in candor. "You're a pleasant sight," he said, gaze lingering. Flattery danced on the edge of flirtation. Gabrielle blushed, caught off-guard. His workers pulled him away, a wink sealing the unspoken pact.

Heather had witnessed it all. She sidled over, eyes gleaming. "Sugar daddy hunting, huh?" she teased. Gabrielle laughed, deflecting the jab.

The night flowed. Travis arrived, tardy but forgiven. As her shift wound down, Gabrielle clocked out, bidding Heather farewell. The hotel's pulse softened.

Gabrielle stepped into the cool night. Her husband's voice accompanied her home, a silent guardian, waiting up.

She slipped into the shower, water washing away the day's residue. His rhythmic breathing echoed through the house as Gabrielle tiptoed to the great room. The television murmured, a lullaby for a weary traveler.

At 5:55 a.m., the veil between dreams and waking blurred. Gabrielle jolted awake, sweat and chills mingling. Jeffrey had appeared in her dream, standing resolute in a church. His message echoed: *Here, my dear, you shall uncover your answers.* His face haunted her. Gabrielle longed to speak to him, to apologize, to mend the rift. But he remained elusive.

Morning light filtered through the curtains. Her husband had let her sleep in, knowing she'd burned the midnight oil.

He returned from the gym as she stirred. They exchanged pleasantries, voices weaving through the quiet. The day beckoned. Gabrielle prepared for her shift, the 2:00 p.m. to 10:00 p.m. rhythm now her cadence.

At the hotel, Greg greeted her. That day, he wore the mantle of the day shift, ready to bid farewell to twilight hours. His path diverged; hers stretched ahead. Carol would soon fill the void. Greg's presence had become a mere echo in the symphony of hotel life.

Alone at the desk, Gabrielle navigated checkins, inquiries, the ebb and flow of transient souls. Allen appeared with purpose. Seth, the weekend night auditor, grappling with personal matters, had requested leave.

Allen's solution: Gabrielle would take the 2:00 p.m. to 10:00 p.m. shift six days a week. Todd would manage the nights.

Gabrielle pledged her commitment, echoing Allen's gratitude. The hotel hummed with activity, schedules interlocking. Gabrielle recalled her GM days juggling personnel, the delicate dance of staffing. Different businesses, same challenges: turnover and adaptation.

As twilight settled over the hotel, it was just Heather and Gabrielle, two sentinels guarding the front desk and bar. The 2:00 p.m. to 10:00 p.m. shift unfurled its challenges: towels, plungers, endless requests echoing through the lobby. Gabrielle juggled phone calls, room keys, and the delicate art of patience.

Why, she wondered, *was this shift entrusted to a solitary soul?* Guests multiplied, relentless in their demands.

Heather leaned across the counter, eyes were weary. "The hotel doesn't pay enough for this," she murmured.

Gabrielle nodded, fingers dancing across the keyboard. "But think of it as a symphony," she said. "Each guest, a note. Together, they compose time." Her laughter softened the edges of exhaustion.

Travis, punctual for once, swept in. Gabrielle glimpsed freedom, the elusive 10:00 p.m. escape. Clocking out felt like victory.

She dialed her husband, the road home stretching ahead. His voice accompanied her through the dark.

She recounted her conversation with Allen, the six days a week pact. Her husband's caution echoed: "Don't let them exploit your goodwill." Gabrielle vowed to tread carefully, to balance compassion with selfpreservation.

Back home, the television flickered, a quiet companion in the late hours.

Days blurred into weeks, a relentless cycle of shifts and midnight vigils. Sleep became a luxury. Her nights stretched until 3:00 a.m. Two days off were reduced to none.

October unfolded. Their house still bore scars, storm damage, insurance battles. The public adjuster's verdict was clear: not all repairs would be covered.

So, Gabrielle toiled. Her footsteps echoed through hotel corridors. Guests became companions: towels, plungers, late night queries.

Yet silver linings appeared. A $1 raise graced her paycheck. Allen bestowed a new title: front desk supervisor. A grand name for a solo act. Her name tag gleamed. Business cards adorned the desk, a testament to her role in this hotel theater.

At night, moonlight spilled through the curtains. Jeffrey's face surfaced, a distant star, fading but not forgotten. Gabrielle whispered her wishes to the dark. Maybe he sat somewhere, pondering the same choices. She vowed to hope for a future where his name no longer ached.

Then came Greg's final act. Their schedules aligned, the 2:00 p.m. to 10:00 p.m. shift, shared one last time. Gabrielle wondered why she hadn't taken the day off. But Allen had doubts. Greg might vanish midshift, leaving the desk adrift.

As the clock ticked toward his departure, Greg unveiled a surprise. His guitar appeared. The lobby was transformed into a concert hall.

Susan, the new bartender, cheered him on. "Play on," she said, dismissing the mundane tasks that waited. Guests glanced up, bemused. Greg strummed, lost in his own world. The front desk hummed with unanswered calls.

By 9:45 p.m., the strings fell silent. Greg approached, his ride waiting. "Clocking out," he said. "I'll miss you." Gabrielle echoed the sentiment. But truth be told, relief washed over her. Greg's effort had waned since his notice. Allen needed him. Greg knew it. His bare minimum had become a silent pact.

As he stepped into the night, guitar slung over his shoulder, Gabrielle watched him go.

November unfolded. The 2:00 p.m. to 10:00 p.m. shift, a familiar refrain. Only four days off punctuated the month. But the rhythm suited her. The hotel's regulars paraded through the lobby, their names etched in memory.

Allen marveled at the camaraderie. Guests paused to exchange pleasantries before retreating to their rooms. "You've become the face of the hotel," he mused. Gabrielle nodded. Working every day had its benefits, she had become a living directory of names and stories.

Allen's strategic hires aimed to ease Gabrielle's burden. One recruit for the night audit, another for the front desk. Daylight beckoned and Gabrielle stepped into the role of mentor, guiding newcomers through the labyrinth of checkins, calls, and guest requests.

Elissa struggled. Cameron, seasoned by prior hotel experience, adapted more swiftly. But neither seemed built for the long haul.

Cameron and Susan, the bartender, found camaraderie in shared immaturity. They performed their duties—no more, no less.

Weeks passed. Cameron embarked on a nocturnal adventure. Travis, sage of hotel lore, took him under his wing. Together, they unraveled spreadsheets, reconciled accounts, explored the mysteries of the night audit.

But secrets surfaced. Travis's mentorship had quirks. He'd leave Cameron to fend for himself, sneaking off for clandestine naps in his car.

Cameron confided in Gabrielle. Travis's advice: "Call me if anything comes up." A hotel superhero on standby.

Gabrielle urged Cameron to escalate, to inform Todd and Allen. But she stayed a silent observer. She hadn't seen the naps firsthand. The hotel's nocturnal rhythm continued, its secrets tucked in shadows.

Then came a seismic shift. Carol, once destined for the sales coordinator role, dropped her bombshell. She was quitting right before Thanksgiving. Her eyes welled with tears. Financial woes had pushed her to the brink. Wages garnished, bills mounting. Allen's promise had evaporated.

She didn't want to leave, but necessity drove her toward an insurance company. Gabrielle nodded, understanding. Carol's resignation echoed through the corridors; a ripple of change swept the team.

For Gabrielle, it meant relentless shifts, six to seven days a week until Allen found a replacement. Cameron, now trained, stood on his own. Elissa, still struggling, faced a different fate. Allen's confidence in her waned. Each morning, Elissa stepped into the lobby, uncertainty clinging to her.

Todd, back from an erratic schedule, became her mentor. Together, they unraveled the front desk's rhythm. By Carol's farewell, Elissa was ready to fly solo, a bittersweet transition.

On her last day, Carol sent Gabrielle an email, a digital promise to stay connected. They stayed a team in flux: Gabrielle, the seasoned anchor; two new recruits finding their footing; Travis, the silent sage; Todd, orchestrating it all.

December loomed, a month of hope. Maybe two days off would finally return to Gabrielle. But optimism was premature.

On December 2nd, Allen and Todd delivered the news: Travis faced a family emergency. Whisked away to Ohio. The plan seemed simple: Cameron on night audit, Gabrielle on 2:00 p.m. to 10:00 p.m., Elissa on 6:00 a.m. to 2:00 p.m. Seven days of seamless coverage.

But life had other ideas. Elissa, her belly a quiet harbinger, approached Allen. Pregnancy demanded two days off weekly. Todd stepped in to cover. Cameron, juggling college and work, agreed to the seven day marathon.

But after one week, he surrendered. Travis's absence left them off balance. Todd adjusted the score: two days of day shift, two days of night audit, one day of 2:00 p.m. to 10:00 p.m. Gabrielle's lifeline to sanity.

But Cameron's discontent brewed. Travis stayed an enigma. The team drifted. And so, Cameron walked away. A note of discord in the hotel's ever revolving symphony.

The Light That Waits

"The Lord is my light and my salvation—whom shall I fear?"

—Psalm 27:1

Amid workplace turmoil, a phone call shattered Gabrielle's husband's world. On December 11th, his youngest son delivered the news: his eldest was battling cancer and the outlook was bleak. Urgency reverberated through the line. "Come home for Christmas," the son pleaded. "See him, maybe for the last time."

Thanksgiving had passed uneventfully. But in two short weeks, everything had changed. His mother confirmed it: cancer had taken hold. Time was running out.

Her husband stood speechless, tears welling as he vowed to be there. He promised to call his eldest son.

Then he turned to Gabrielle, eyes pleading, seeking permission to leave, to be by his son's side.

Gabrielle reassured him. "Go," she whispered. "No hesitation."

He dialed his eldest son. But the conversation was strange, without mention of illness, just mundane chatter. A dissonance that gnawed at him.

Gabrielle pondered the silence. Perhaps the truth demanded presence, a face to face revelation.

He called his youngest again. They agreed: the eldest would not speak of his illness until they were together.

With resolve, her husband called Gabrielle's mother. Could he stay for the holidays? She welcomed him with open arms.

Flights were booked. Schedules rearranged. Christmas Day would carry him toward uncertainty. A one-way ticket. Gabrielle remained in Florida, her job anchoring her. They forged a pact: to be there for each other, across miles and through uncertainty.

Amid her afternoon and evening shifts, Gabrielle carried a secret. The news of her husband's son pressed heavily, but she chose silence. She would protect her colleagues until clarity appeared. Allen reconfigured schedules. Todd stepped in seven days a week. Elissa found her rhythm in daylight. Their impromptu symphony held the fragile balance. Gabrielle persevered.

Her husband's youngest son became a beacon, transmitting slivers of reality. The illness had spread. Hope waned. His mother spoke of grim prognosis. But was she a harbinger of truth or a weaver of melodrama?

Gabrielle clung to prayer. Maybe the darkness was less consuming than they feared. Treatment options dwindled.

Her husband persisted. Gabrielle danced between work and worry. Her prayers whispered into the void, for solace, clarity, and a glimmer of hope.

Then the hotel shimmered with yuletide spirit. Allen curated a celebration. Gift cards were distributed, passports to sister hotels. Gabrielle's reward: a night in Nashville. The feast thrummed with unity. Colleagues exchanged tales, shared laughter. Allen offered another surprise, a $100 gift card.

Then came the final gift: "A fresh face at the front desk," Allen announced. Charlie, a veteran from a sister hotel, stepped forward. Minimal training needed. He would blend in seamlessly.

Gabrielle and Charlie worked the bustling 2:00 p.m. to 10:00 p.m. shifts. Soon, he would take the night audit.

Travis, on sabbatical, would eventually return. But for now, Charlie stood as the steadfast guardian.

Gabrielle's shift ended, and she stepped into the nocturnal embrace, her heart brimming with the thrill of Christmas Eve. Stars gleamed with celestial brilliance. Church bells wove a sacred melody through the frost-laced air.

At the chapel's entrance, her husband's silhouette stood framed by stained glass. Their eyes met. Life's maelstrom had swept them from hallowed ground, but that night, they reclaimed their spiritual bond.

Midnight Mass began. Father Michael spoke of renewed hope, of the divine infant cradling the cosmos.

Her husband's gaze lingered on the Nativity, his thoughts reaching toward his distant son, locked in a battle beyond comprehension. Beneath the soaring arches, they sought comfort, redemption.

After the service, they stepped into the night. Her husband captured the moment, a photo against the chapel's glow, a silent declaration of love and prayer.

Back home, they exchanged heartfelt gifts, aware that the next day he would leave. His son waited. Gabrielle's wish was simple: that love would guide him through the storm.

Christmas morning unfolded in quiet solemnity. Gabrielle prepared breakfast. Her husband moved through the house, eyes clouded, voice full of instructions. His nervous energy crackled. Gabrielle listened, half attentive, her mind tethered to his son's distant struggle. She prayed the truth was less dire.

She drove him to the airport. Their hands clasped, a silent promise. "I love you," she whispered. He echoed it, eyes holding hers. The terminal swallowed him. She knew he would call a lifeline across the miles.

Back at the hotel, Gabrielle resumed her role at the front desk. Her husband, somewhere above the clouds, navigated security lines and checkins. As the sun dipped, Gabrielle whispered a prayer for healing, clarity, strength.

Christmas at the hotel was subdued. Allen granted shortened shifts for family time. Gabrielle let Elissa leave early. Only Tammy, the executive housekeeper, remained. Gabrielle confided in her, her husband's absence, his son's illness. Tammy's empathy wrapped around her, a promise of prayers.

Heather, expecting a slow day, sought early release. Allen agreed. Gabrielle's phone buzzed, her husband had arrived safely and was on the way to the hospital.

Later that night, he confirmed the harsh reality: stage four cancer. The prognosis, no room for hope. Gabrielle offered to join him. He insisted she stay. He would call when the time came.

In the quiet lobby, Heather and Gabrielle sat together, two souls seeking solace. Gabrielle unraveled her heart, the illness, the distance, the weight of waiting. Heather listened. Overwhelmed, she left early. The bar stood empty. Gabrielle remained the lone sentinel at the desk.

Her thoughts wove a tapestry of love, worry, and quiet resilience. Twilight painted the sky. Her phone buzzed again. Her husband had reached her mother's house. He spoke of his son, once vibrant, now fading. All the youngest son had said was true.

The hospital would release him. Hospice would guide him toward the end. Her husband's voice wavered, tears blurring the distance between them. The doctor's words echoed with clinical finality: less than a month to live.

The weight of truth pressed hard, threatening to break the dam of emotion. "I love you," Gabrielle whispered. "Do you want me to come?"

He reassured her. Her mother, his youngest son, would be there. He would call if he needed her. Gabrielle promised to hold the fort, to tend their home while he faced the storm.

She stepped into the quiet house. Its walls echoed with absence. They hadn't been apart since moving to Florida, except for her brief hotel stay after the hurricane.

The television flickered, its glow chasing shadows. But sleep eluded her. Gabrielle prayed for her husband's peace, for his son's comfort, for strength to endure the separation. She whispered her own promise: *I'll be here when you call.*

The next morning, her phone stirred her from sleep. Her husband had timed it perfectly, wanting to talk before her hotel shift. He was at her mother's house. They stayed up late watching Christmas movies. Gabrielle felt relief. He asked for small tasks around the house. Gabrielle moved with purpose, checking each item off his list.

Then came his next move: he was leaving for his ex-wife's home. His oldest son, released from the hospital, awaited him there. The visit didn't excite him, but she extended an invitation. "Behave yourself," Gabrielle teased. "She's probably just as overwhelmed as you." He promised he would. His voice held both resolve and vulnerability.

That afternoon, her phone buzzed again. He stood at his ex-wife's house. People flowed in and out. Her husband recounted each visitor, their names, their stories. Then a revelation: his estranged son, absent for four years, had crossed the threshold.

They talked. Lunch plans were made. Conversations promised. Relief colored her husband's voice. Maybe reconciliation was within reach. Gabrielle listened, her heart echoing his journey. She assured him: "Call anytime. Day or night."

At the hotel, Gabrielle's thoughts lingered. The quiet before checkins wrapped around her. Allen stood nearby, attentive. Gabrielle confided in him, her husband's son's illness, the impending need to leave. The date remained elusive. Her husband would decide when. Allen's response was gentle: "Go," he said. "Just let me know. We'll manage." He offered condolences, promised prayers, and gave her a silent hug.

Her shift unfolded gently. Charlie worked beside her, eager and capable. His transition to night audit neared. Heather, the bartender, shared stories, and laughter. Gabrielle let Charlie take the lead.

Todd arrived to relieve them. Gabrielle approached him, voice tinged with apology: "At some point, I'll need to leave to be with my husband." Todd was reassuring. They would manage.

The days blurred—a phone call at dawn, another during her commute, one more as the sun dipped low. Her husband's voice wove grief and love. He stood by his son's side, witnessing the slow unraveling. Gabrielle offered pep talks, feeble words against mortality. "Stay strong," she urged. "Spend time with him. Let him know he's loved."

But the truth hung heavy. Her husband grappled with emotions that threatened to consume him. They prayed for peace, for reconciliation, for moments of grace. Phone calls bridged the distance. Her mother kept him company. Gabrielle lay in their quiet house, whispering her own prayer for strength, healing, and love.

Then, one fateful night, after their conversation had ended, her phone stirred. Her husband's voice reached out. The weight of reality had settled. His son's days were numbered.

His ex-wife, too, had accepted the truth. She turned to their youngest son, the bearer of unimaginable burdens, to begin funeral arrangements. The task weighed heavily on the young man's heart.

Her husband's voice trembled as he recounted the scene. Gabrielle urged him to step up, to guide his youngest through the storm. His strength, tested by life's tempests, could be a beacon.

After their call, Gabrielle prayed for peace, for guidance, for resilience to fill his heart.

Later that morning, his voice carried a different timbre, relief and resolution. He had spoken to Jeffrey. Jeffrey's words reassured him: if their youngest son chose Jeffrey's services, he would be in capable hands. Trust had been extended.

But the name stirred something in Gabrielle. Months of silence, blocked communication. Would he acknowledge her? Would she be ready to face him? As her husband hung up, relief and trepidation settled in Gabrielle's chest.

She prayed for strength for herself, for her husband, for the delicate dance ahead. And she wondered: was Jeffrey the answer to the prayers she'd whispered for her husband's peace?

On New Year's Eve, as midnight approached, her phone buzzed. Her husband's voice, a blend of nostalgia and longing, reached across the miles.

For two decades, they'd welcomed the New Year together. This time, he stood elsewhere, by his son's side, where love demanded he be. No revelry, no champagne. Just quiet reflection. The stillness suited him. At midnight, they exchanged wishes, a virtual kiss across the miles.

On New Year's Day, her phone stirred her from sleep. He had risen early, driven to see his son before the house filled with visitors. Gabrielle agreed, the quiet moments held sacred weight.

Throughout the day, his calls punctuated her routine. His voice accompanied her commute. He promised to wait until evening to call again, knowing she needed rest. And true to his word, he reached out as she drove home.

They talked as the road stretched before her. He shared stories, visitors, his son's fading strength. When he hung up, Gabrielle knew he was safe at her mother's house. His exhaustion made her ache.

That night, Gabrielle lay in their quiet home, whispering her prayer for strength, for healing, for the fragile threads of love that bound them all.

Then, in the quiet hours before dawn, her phone rang. Her husband's voice, raw and trembling, pierced the stillness. "Come," he pleaded. "Come now. I need you."

The urgency hung heavy, a fog of grief and desperation. "See him alive," the message whispered. Gabrielle urged caution, her heart pounding as she imagined her husband hurling through the night.

The ex-wife's house, shrouded in mist, beckoned. Distance blurred. Time warped. In fifteen minutes, he bridged the chasm, speed limits forgotten, love and fear propelling him forward.

Outside the house, a somber congregation stood. Their murmurs echoed the truth. *Too late*, they seemed to say. *He is gone.* Her husband's voice cracked over the phone. "My son," he choked, "gone." Five minutes separated life from eternity. "Come," he implored.

Gabrielle promised. "I love you," she whispered, her fingers trembling as she hung up.

In the den, the computer glowed. Flights were booked. She would fly out the next day. Her husband sat vigil beside his son's still form. Gabrielle imagined their whispered conversations, the weight of unspoken words.

Her mother called. "He spent yesterday with him," she said. "They talked, laughed. His boy was ready." Gabrielle clung to those words. The flight loomed, a journey toward grief, toward farewell. Her husband had missed the final breath, but he had touched the veil.

At sunrise, Gabrielle called their nearby friends. "His son," she whispered, "gone." They agreed to drive her to the airport.

In the quiet, Gabrielle packed. Her siblings called. She shared what little she knew, the frantic call, the foggy drive, the missed moment. "Tomorrow," she promised, "I will be there." Their love wrapped around her.

She messaged Allen and Todd: "His son passed away." Her fingers faltered. "I'll work today," she wrote, "but tomorrow I leave. How long is uncertain."

The drive to work blurred. Her husband's voice reached across the miles. "I stayed," he said. "The funeral home will come soon." His ex-wife had made the arrangements. "Jeffrey," he added, "I spoke with him this morning." His son would rest in capable hands.

Gabrielle listened, heart aching. "Tomorrow," she said, "I will fly." Her husband's voice held relief. "Good. We have a meeting planned." Gabrielle would stand beside him, a silent witness to the rituals of loss.

But Jeffrey, Gabrielle hesitated. Their history was tangled. Yet how could she refuse? Her husband's grief was a tempest; her own, a quiet storm. She agreed: if her flight were on time, she would go. He signed off, returning to her mother's house. "I love you," Gabrielle whispered. Tomorrow, she would be there.

At work, Allen greeted her with open arms. "I'm sorry," he murmured. "Take all the time you need." Gabrielle nodded, her voice a fragile echo. Her shift blurred with worry. The ex-wife loomed. Jeffrey stood at the crossroads of memory. Gabrielle considered calling her husband, confessing her fear, her desire to retreat. But love held her fast. In her heart, she whispered: *Be with me. Make everything all right.*

That evening, her husband called. "I slept," he said. Her mother had cooked dinner. "Tomorrow, breakfast with my sons, then I'll pick you up. Three o'clock meeting with Jeffrey."

Gabrielle nodded, heart fluttering. But anxiety gnawed. She wished for a flight delay, a cosmic pause. Yet love demanded presence. So, she prayed again: *Make everything alright.*

Her husband's list arrived. "Bring these," he said. Her suitcase bulged, half hers, half his.

At 3:00 a.m., Gabrielle packed. Sleep eluded her. The moon watched as she wrestled with anticipation.

The alarm sounded. Her friends arrived. They whisked her to the airport, guardians of their home while she journeyed into grief. "Call us," she promised, "when we know our way back." The one-way ticket in her hand symbolized uncertainty.

Checked in, her flight awaited. Three and a half hours to her destination. At noon, her husband would be there. But the ex-wife and Jeffrey, their presence weighed heavy. Gabrielle closed her eyes, seeking sleep, bracing for what lay ahead.

Mid flight, the pilot's voice crackled, "Emergency diversion." A clogged toilet had disrupted their course. The irony was not lost on Gabrielle: a shitty situation indeed. Charlotte airport. Passengers suspended in limbo. Mechanics worked. Fate intervened.

They disembarked. Gabrielle called her husband. "Flight change," she said. "I'll still make it." At the counter, an agent rearranged her journey. She called again. "Landing around 1:00 p.m."

"Jeffrey at 3:00 p.m.," he replied.

Gabrielle braced herself, the meeting she dreaded but could not avoid. As the plane ascended, she nestled into her seat, eyes heavy with fatigue.

The plane touched down earlier than expected. A call to her husband, he waited in the cell phone lot, a beacon of familiarity. "Lunch," he said, "before Jeffrey." Gabrielle nodded, heart fluttering. Resilience took flight.

Over lunch, her husband's voice, heavy with weariness, wove a tapestry of grief and frustration. Jeffrey loomed large. "She took charge," her husband said. "But it's her deal. I'm not responsible."

The youngest son had been enlisted, but the ex-wife's whims shifted. Now she orchestrated the farewell, a discordant composition. "Cremation," her husband said, his voice edged with sadness. His son's wish clashed with her decree: a showing. "Let her," he concluded. "No fight."

As they left the restaurant, the afternoon sun cast long shadows. Jeffrey awaited. Gabrielle clung to her husband's hand.

At the funeral home, the scent of polished wood and fresh flowers enveloped her, a poignant reminder of past visits, of fragile conversations with Jeffrey.

Inside, hushed voices. Her husband's son and ex-wife stood together, a tableau of blended family dynamics. His son met them in the parking lot. "Everyone is waiting," he whispered. They entered the meeting room. Jeffrey had not yet arrived.

Then the ex-wife spoke, her voice brittle yet oddly conciliatory. "I'm glad you're here," she said. Gabrielle nodded politely. No scene, no discord. Pleasantries exchanged, Gabrielle settled into her seat, eyes fixed on the door.

And then, Jeffrey. A handshake and hug for her husband. A sideways hug for Gabrielle. She remained seated, rooted. Her husband leaned toward him. "Our mutual friend, have you spoken to him?"

Jeffrey nodded. "Just recently."

Then, as if choreographed by fate, Jeffrey excused himself. "I've forgotten something," he murmured. He returned, handing her husband his phone. "Someone wants to speak to you." Her husband stepped away. Gabrielle sat alone at the head of the table. Jeffrey settled beside her. His presence, comforting and disconcerting.

They had shared many conversations in that room, navigating grief and practicality. Now, he turned to the ex-wife, guiding her through the terrain of arrangements. "Clothing?" he asked. Her youngest son retrieved the garments.

Then came the revelation: her son had wanted no services. But she insisted on a showing. "Cremation," she said firmly. "He wasn't religious." Jeffrey nodded, pen poised. "Four days from now," he declared.

Then he turned to her. "What kind of service?" By now, Gabrielle's husband had returned, gratitude etched on his face. Jeffrey filled him in a four hour showing: favorite music, no sermons, no prayers. Just quiet goodbyes.

Jeffrey's demeanor softened. He offered a prayer card book, weathered and wellloved. She accepted it, fingers tracing the edges. But she hesitated. "I'm not good at this," she whispered. Jeffrey nodded, understanding.

Then, as if guided by grace, she slid the book toward Gabrielle.

Their eyes met. Gabrielle knew without opening it. "Perhaps the Irish Blessing?" she offered. Her son, a free spirit, would appreciate its lyrical cadence, open roads, windkissed journeys, the eternal embrace of the heavens. It resonated. The same verse had graced her husband's parents' farewell, a thread connecting generations.

Jeffrey gave Gabrielle a knowing look, a half smile of quiet agreement. He would recite it during the showing. He promised to embellish the memorial card, a nod to her son's love of motorcycles. A silhouette of a rider, a whisper of chrome and leather.

Then came the grand finale: a video tribute. Six songs, snapshots of laughter, a canvas of remembrance. But practicalities intruded. The ex-wife voiced concern. Would this farewell require a mortgage? Jeffrey promised clarity. He excused himself, disappearing into the hallway.

As they waited, Gabrielle wondered: was Jeffrey a guardian of souls, or a magician of solace? His return would reveal the sum of compassion, the currency of farewell.

In Jeffrey's absence, the room exhaled. Then, amidst the hush, his ex-wife leaned toward Gabrielle. "An urn," she murmured, eyes seeking solace.

Gabrielle nodded. She and her husband had already decided they would shoulder that burden. "I'll find something," Gabrielle assured her. "Something that speaks motorcycles, of his spirit."

While Jeffrey calculated the ledger of grief, Gabrielle delved into the digital labyrinth, showing images, each pixel a tribute.

Jeffrey returned, settling into his chair. His eyes scanned the bill, line by line. He whispered explanations: embalming, flowers, the quiet dignity of service. Then came the revelation: a family discount. Almost half-off. Friendship softened the cost.

Her husband absorbed the news. The ex-wife's laughter rippled unexpectedly. "No mortgage," she quipped. The tension eased, but her husband's face flickered with hurt. He had borne the weight of loss. Casual jest stung. She promised payment. Pictures of her son would soon arrive. A pact was forged.

As the meeting ended, Jeffrey ushered them toward the exit. Her husband excused himself, seeking solace in the restroom. Gabrielle stood alone with Jeffrey. The hallway stretched, its walls bearing silent witness.

Jeffrey, perceptive as ever, broke the silence. "Tell me about your husband's son," he said gently. Gabrielle hesitated. She still harbored thoughts of his unanswered texts, still blocked on social media. But this wasn't the time.

"He had cancer," she said softly. "A secret he carried like a stone in his chest . . . And a heart attack," she added. "A silent battle fought alone."

Jeffrey leaned against the wall. "I had my own heart attack," he revealed. "Ninety percent blockage. September." His fingers traced an invisible scar. "Life changes."

"Are you better now?" Gabrielle asked. He smiled, cryptic, resilient, vulnerable.

Then, the urn. Gabrielle broached the topic, her voice tentative. Could they order smaller urns? Jeffrey disappeared, returned with a worn book. Pictures spilled across its pages. He promised to explore options, urged her to look online as well.

Her husband returned, gratitude etched on his face. Jeffrey's discount had softened the edges of loss. But disappointment lingered; the ex-wife hadn't thanked him directly. Jeffrey brushed it aside. "Not necessary," he said.

Florida came up, the hurricane, their damaged home. Then laughter, a fragile bridge across hardship. Gabrielle's husband recounted her chaotic morning flight. Jeffrey found humor in their human follies.

They talked about life, loss, the fragile dance of existence. Twenty minutes, a lifetime compressed. Jeffrey sensed the finale. Another client awaited. He stood, extended his hand to her husband, a handshake, a hug.

Then to Gabrielle, a hug unexpected, warm. "Call me," he said. "Anytime." His hand rested on her shoulder.

As they stepped into the fading light, Gabrielle felt lighter. Jeffrey had woven compassion into their sorrow. The gesture whispered: *You are not alone.* And for that fleeting moment, Gabrielle believed it.

In the car, her husband vented. His ex-wife loomed large. Jeffrey's funeral home had been a stage for strained interactions. Gabrielle listened. The road stretched ahead, a ribbon leading back to her mother's house. She understood his frustration. Gratitude should have flown freely.

At her mom's house, Gabrielle retrieved her suitcase. Her mom welcomed her. Her husband recounted the funeral home episode, his voice a tempest.

Then her sister arrived. The showing loomed, a canvas waiting for their family's touch. She proposed a wreath, a tribute woven from memories.

Gabrielle hesitated. The day had been long. But she conceded. "Tomorrow," she said. "Hobby Lobby." Gabrielle succumbed to sleep. Her husband found comfort in quiet conversation with her mother. The night held a silent acknowledgment of their collective journey through sorrow.

The next morning unfolded with purpose. Gabrielle's sister arrived. Together, they embarked on a pilgrimage. First stop: breakfast at Cracker Barrel. Her husband and mom joined them. Over scrambled eggs and coffee, Gabrielle pursued urn options. She chose one, placed the order. A quick message to Jeffrey. His reassuring reply confirmed the path.

Next: Hobby Lobby. Her mom and sister gathered flowers. Her husband wandered the aisles, lost in thought. Gabrielle juggled conversations, texted friends, arranged a lunch reunion.

Back at her mom's house, the wreath took shape. Her sister's fingers arranged blooms. Gabrielle assisted, her mind flitting between urns and plans.

Her husband's phone buzzed, a symphony of condolences and logistics. Her sister departed, leaving the wreath behind. Tomorrow, she would deliver it to the funeral home.

Dinner arrived via DoorDash. Her husband retreated to the shower, seeking solace in warm water and silence. Then, Gabrielle's secret, a surprise for her husband. Six miniature motorcycle urns, each personalized with his son's name and dates. A tribute to his passion. She ordered them for his other sons and even his ex-wife, a gesture of shared grief.

Morning tiptoed in. Her husband embarked on a mission of comfort: donuts from their favorite bakery.

Her sister arrived, arms cradling two canvases. Portraits of her husband's son, brushstrokes woven with memory. "For you," she said gently. "To carry with you."

The funeral home awaited: the wreath, the pictures, a symphony of love. Her husband's gratitude spilled forth, but practicality loomed. How would they transport the canvases to Florida? "Jeffrey will know," Gabrielle reassured him.

The sun hung low as her sister bid farewell. Gabrielle and her husband followed suit, stepping into the crisp afternoon air.

Their paths diverged, Gabrielle off to meet friends for lunch, her husband to reconnect with old neighbors.

At the meeting spot, Gabrielle spotted her friends waiting. Their smiles were warm, their condolences genuine. Over sandwiches and iced tea, Gabrielle shared her husband's son's story, the brave battle, the finality of loss.

Then, one friend leaned in. Her daughter, lost in a car accident, had become a legacy. She spoke of the foundation they'd built, the annual ride, the awareness campaigns. Her eyes lit with purpose. "Carbon monoxide poisoning," she said. "Silent and deadly. We bring people together."

Gabrielle noticed the others exchanging glances. They were used to her, this friend who steered every conversation toward her daughter's memory. She veered into financial territory, a stock market whiz, a Lamborghini. They listened politely, but their minds wandered.

One friend, patience waning, excused herself. She had to pick up her son. Gabrielle silently urged her to wait; her husband would arrive soon. And he did. He'd only caught up with one old friend. The rest were busy or absent. He joined them with a grateful smile. "Sweet tea," he asked. Gabrielle fetched it.

Farewells followed, hugs, promises to attend the showing. One friend would be there. The other pledged prayers.

As the two departed, the remaining friend resumed her narrative. Her husband listened, patient but weary. Finally, he feigned urgency. They stood to leave. She hugged them both, her presence promised at the showing.

In the car, the engine hummed beneath lingering echoes. Her husband glanced at Gabrielle. "Did she talk about her daughter the entire time? And those people, how much they've made?"

Gabrielle nodded, weariness palpable. "Yes, every sentence carried her daughter's name."

She reminded him, this friend hadn't been available for a farewell party when they moved to Florida. She'd been too busy. The other two had slipped away, their patience fraying. Her husband didn't press further. Instead, he shifted gears, steering them back to her mom's house.

As they drove, Gabrielle's phone buzzed. The motorcycles and urn had arrived at the funeral home. Jeffrey was out but promised to check upon return.

Two hours later, his message came: the items now rested within the hallowed walls. And then the question: should they be displayed at the showing?

Her husband handed her his phone, eyes searching hers. Gabrielle typed: "Ask the ex-wife. It's her show, not ours."

Jeffrey obliged, sending pictures. The urn stoic and sacred. The motorcycles sleek and defiant.

"They look badass," Gabrielle whispered. "Your wife did a good job." She wondered if they held the same power in person.

Jeffrey's reply: "Yes." Gabrielle thanked him, though his silence lingered.

Her husband leaned over, reading the exchange. His eyes softened. He squeezed her hand. "You took care of it," he murmured.

Back at her mom's house, quietude cloaked the storm brewing. His youngest son called. Gabrielle and her mom listened as grief spilled through the phone. His mother, the ex-wife, had thrust him into emotional chaos. Estate duties weighed heavy, selling off belongings, cleaning up remnants of a life cut short.

But the revelation stung: she'd liquidated most of it while his brother still breathed. Her rationale: debts owed, bills paid. His voice trembled. "I can't take it anymore," he confessed. "After the showing, I'm leaving. I can't bear her any longer."

Her husband listened. "Get through tomorrow," he advised. "Without losing your composure. Then go home." His calm masked inner turmoil.

When the call ended, restraint snapped. He vented, words aimed squarely at his ex-wife. Gabrielle had expected it. She sat back, a silent witness, letting him release the pressure valve.

Her mom tried to reason. "She's been kind lately," she offered. "Letting you see your son." But his anger was wildfire. Reason couldn't contain it.

Just then, her sister and brother-in-law arrived in the charged atmosphere. Her husband recounted the drama, each word a brushstroke on their shared canvas. Her sister's husband, sensing tension, steered the conversation to safer shores. They spoke of mundane things, of memories, of anything but the ex-wife.

Her sister leaned in, whispering her secret mission: she'd delivered the pictures and wreath to the funeral home. The lady there promised to mark them for Gabrielle and her husband after the showing, a small kindness in a sea of chaos.

Hours slipped by. Plans were made. Her mom would ride with her sister and brother-in-law. Gabrielle and her husband would arrive earlier. They called it a night, hearts heavy with anticipation.

Morning arrived. Gabrielle and her husband stirred, sleepy smiles exchanged. In the kitchen, the unspoken routine: breakfast at a cozy diner down the street.

"Mom," Gabrielle called. "We're heading out. Want to join us?" Her response was gentle but firm. "No, dear. Bring me something back." Her husband nodded. "Of course. What would you like?"

At the diner, her husband leaned in, serious. "I've been thinking," he said. "About Florida." He had planned to stay, to help. But something had shifted. "She wants to manage it, the details, the messiness. It's what she always wanted."

Gabrielle listened, heart heavy. There were items he'd hoped to retrieve, but he knew they were likely gone. Sold, discarded, lost in the currents of distance.

"And the money," he added. "He owed me. Years of it. She'll keep everything. I won't fight her."

Gabrielle reached across the table, fingers brushing his. "You're doing the right thing," she said softly. "Letting go is brave. It's not about dollars, it's about peace."

He nodded, gratitude in his eyes. "I'm proud of you," Gabrielle whispered. "For not arguing. For choosing peace."

Back at her mom's house, the weight of the morning hung heavy. Gabrielle settled into a chair. The laptop blinked to life, flights back to Florida, a search for escape and return. Her husband stood by the window, exhaustion etched into his face.

Gabrielle turned to her mom. "This whole situation . . ." she began, words tangled in emotion. Her mom understood. She reached out, squeezed Gabrielle's hand. "Your husband is strong," she said softly. "I'm proud of him."

Then came one of her classic pep talks. Her husband listened, jaw set, as she offered wisdom for the showing ahead. "Be civil," she advised. "You don't have to engage unless necessary. Keep the peace for your sake and your son's."

As if on cue, Gabrielle's phone buzzed. Jeffrey. *Crucifix above your son's head?* he asked. Cryptic. Tense.

Her husband's reply was swift and firm: *No. My son wasn't Catholic, and his mother doesn't want it. But thank you.*

Jeffrey persisted. *She'll arrive at noon,* he typed. *She wants time alone.*

Her husband's response was resolute. *I'm not coming that early. She can have her time. I'll be there around 1:00 p.m.* Then silence.

They gathered and left, the clock inching past noon. The funeral home awaited. But first coffee. Then St. Michael's Church. He surveyed the renovations, seeking solace in familiar pews. They would attend Mass the next day.

Then the call came. Gabrielle's friend, voice trembling. She couldn't make it to the showing, illness and work. Gabrielle reassured her. But then came the request: "Can you ask Jeffrey to place ashes in my bracelet?"

Gabrielle snapped. "Not today," she blurted. "This isn't about your daughter. You live down the street, ask him yourself." Her tone, sharp and unkind, surprised even her. But she couldn't bear another layer of grief.

Gabrielle hung up, heart racing. Why did it upset her so? On this day, Gabrielle craved simplicity. She yearned for quiet, not the weight of someone else's sorrow.

They arrived at the funeral home at 12:45 p.m. The car's engine hummed. Her husband gripped the steering wheel, knuckles pale. He took a deep breath, eyes fixed on the entrance.

Then his youngest son appeared, eyes mirroring his father's sorrow and relief. He stepped forward, arms outstretched. "Dad, I'm over it," he said. Her husband rested his hand on his shoulder.

"Stay calm," he whispered. "We'll get through this. Then you can go home." Gabrielle stood witness to the fragile exchange. Pride swelled within her, his love for his son, a quiet tapestry of healing.

Inside, his son leaned close. "They're all in the break area," he murmured. "Waiting." Her husband's footsteps echoed down the corridor. His son stayed by Gabrielle's side. Together, they entered the room. Floral tributes surrounded his brother. Gabrielle studied the blooms. His son spoke softly, sharing stories behind each arrangement.

Then Jeffrey appeared. His eyes held questions. "Is your husband with you?" he asked.

"Yes," Gabrielle replied. "He's here."

Jeffrey nodded, a flicker of something passing across his face. "I'll go say hello," he said, and retreated. His footsteps faded into silence.

Then the ex-wife entered. Her embrace surprised Gabrielle. "I'm glad you're here," she whispered. "Is your family coming?" Her vulnerability caught Gabrielle off-guard. Hadn't they once been adversaries?

"Yes," Gabrielle replied. "They'll arrive soon."

She smiled. "Your family has been good to my son. He spoke highly of them."

Gabrielle nodded. "He was part of our family too." As other mourners arrived, Gabrielle stepped away, leaving behind the ghosts of old wounds.

The funeral home buzzed with whispered conversations, tears and memories weaving through the dim corridors. Gabrielle glimpsed her husband, his laughter mingling with theirs, a quiet symphony of reconciliation.

When her mom and sister arrived, Gabrielle helped her mom with her coat. Together, they stepped into the room where her husband's son lay in repose. The boys greeted her warmly. Hugs exchanged, words spoken in hushed tones.

Gabrielle slipped away, her footsteps echoing down the hallway. At the entrance, a man stood, a sentinel of compassion. His face unfamiliar, a puzzle piece added since their move to Florida. His eyes held kindness. "Let me assist you," he said, guiding Gabrielle to the coat rack. "If you need anything, don't hesitate." Gratitude swelled. Gabrielle thanked him.

Back in the room, her sister approached, eyes alight with mischief. "Guess what?" she whispered. "Your husband's ex-wife just hugged me like we're long lost friends."

Gabrielle chuckled, but a stern look silenced her. "Behave," she warned. "We're here to keep the peace."

Her sister grinned. "As long as you and your husband do too." Then, conspiratorial: "Have you seen the urn?" Gabrielle shook her head. "Not yet. Let's find Jeffrey."

There he was, the man who'd helped with her mom's coat, now deep in conversation with Jeffrey. Gabrielle and her sister approached. "Jeffrey," Gabrielle began, "about the urn and the motorcycles . . ."

He led them to the arrangement room. On the table sat the urn, its polished surface reflecting their emotions. Jeffrey hesitated. "I haven't displayed it," he confessed. "Wasn't sure if it was appropriate."

Gabrielle met her sister's eyes. "It's not our decision," she said softly. "We're witnesses to this farewell. If she wants it displayed, she'll let you know."

Jeffrey nodded. Understanding passed between them.

As he left, Gabrielle and her sister lingered—the urn, a vessel for memory; the motorcycles, sentinels of spirit.

They returned to her mom. Gabrielle sat beside her. The room buzzed with sorrow. Faces blurred by grief. Gabrielle felt like an outsider, a stranger to her husband's son's friends, to his ex-wife's family.

But familiar faces appeared, former colleagues, remnants of a life before Florida. And then, her lunchtime confidante, the friend who had promised to come. They found a quiet corner.

"You won't believe what happened," Gabrielle confided. She told her about the other friend's call, the ashes, the bracelet, the sharp exchange.

Her friend's eyes widened. "Why would she do that?"

Gabrielle interrupted, "I asked myself the same thing."

They exchanged icy glances. Gabrielle doubted they'd be swapping pleasantries again.

Then her mom signaled it was time. Three hours of absorbing collective grief had taken its toll. She stood fragile yet resolute. "I need to go home," she murmured.

Gabrielle found her husband and his sons. Their eyes softened. They gathered around her mom, hugs a silent promise. "We'll visit soon," they assured her.

Gabrielle led her toward the exit. There stood Jeffrey. His gaze followed her, questions unspoken. Her mom's coat hung on the rack. Gabrielle helped her with it, the fabric a cocoon of memory. Her brother-in-law trailed behind. "Always the sarcastic one," he teased.

Gabrielle smiled. "It's a gift," she shot back.

The man who'd helped her earlier held the door open. Her mom settled into the car. Gabrielle lingered, waiting for her sister. When she appeared, Gabrielle hugged her mom once more. "We'll be back," she promised. "And don't worry about dinner. We'll figure it out."

Her mom smiled. "I'm not worried. We'll eat on the way home."

Gabrielle stepped back inside. The air hung heavy, sorrow and anticipation mingling. The showing neared its end. Guests settled into their seats, grief palpable. Her husband chose the back row, avoiding the front where his ex-wife and sons sat, a deliberate choice.

The room hummed with soft melodies, a playlist curated from his son's favorite songs. Each note echoed the ache in their hearts.

Then Jeffrey appeared from the shadows. He stood at the front, quoting the Irish Blessing, his voice steady, threaded with empathy. "May the road rise up to meet you," he intoned, and it felt as though he spoke directly to her husband.

When Jeffrey beckoned everyone forward, they hesitated. But the ushers dismissed them first, granting a private moment with the casket. Her husband leaned in, tears streaming down his face, kissing his son's forehead. "Goodbye," he whispered. "I love you." The weight of loss etched in every syllable.

As they stepped away, Jeffrey enveloped her husband in a bear hug. Grief transcended words. "It doesn't make sense," Jeffrey murmured, "but God will see you through this." A tissue. Another hug.

Around them, mourners shuffled, offering condolences. Gabrielle urged her husband to sit, fearing he might collapse beneath sorrow. But he stood, resolute, waiting for his other sons. He hugged them tightly, with love and pain mingling. Even his ex-wife received a hug.

Then came the unexpected turn. She asked about the flowers. Her husband mentioned only those brought by Gabrielle's sister.

Gabrielle approached Jeffrey, heart pounding. "Could you mail those items to us?" She offered her credit card.

Jeffrey's reply was gentle. "I'll take care of it. I'll send a bill, no need for payment now." Then a hug—warm, unexpected. Gabrielle whispered her gratitude. "You're welcome," he murmured.

They lingered, caught between vulnerability and propriety. Gabrielle half joked about the bill. Jeffrey's laughter danced in the air, a fleeting connection before he retreated.

Back with her husband, Jeffrey reappeared almost orchestrated. He stood behind Gabrielle as her husband thanked him again. Invitations spilled forth: Mass at St. Michael's, followed by brunch. Jeffrey's kids weren't Catholic, but breakfast was a different story.

Her husband mentioned 8:00 a.m. Mass. Jeffrey smiled. "Join us at 10:00 a.m. for breakfast. Mass will be over by then." They agreed. Gabrielle marveled at Jeffrey's unexpected willingness. Her thoughts remained tucked away.

After bidding farewell to the funeral home, Gabrielle and her husband sought solace in a quiet dinner. The weight of the day clung to them: memories, faces, shared grief. It was a moment to catch their breath before returning to her mom's house.

As they settled into their seats, her husband extended an invitation to his sons. The youngest declined, eager to escape post funeral traffic. Home beckoned, a sanctuary for solitude and processing. A promise to call hung in the air. The other son had duties, a child to retrieve from his ex-wife's care. Her husband nodded, understanding.

The restaurant hummed around them. Her husband's surprise spilled forth: "So many people came," he said, eyes wide. His son had woven a vast web of connections. Friends, acquaintances, distant relatives all converged to honor his memory. Even his ex-wife sought moments of connection.

Her husband remained guarded, offering curt replies when necessary. He understood why his youngest son sought distance, a choice born of survival.

Then, a twist of fate: Gabrielle's encounter with his ex-wife. She embraced Gabrielle, treated her sister like an old friend.

Gabrielle relayed this to her husband. Laughter bubbled between them. "Your sister didn't cause a scene?" he asked.

Gabrielle shook her head. "I gave her a pep talk," she said, smiling. "Behave," she'd warned, half in jest. And she did, surprising them both.

As the meal wound down, they returned to her mom's house. She sat in her favorite armchair. They visited, sharing memories and quiet laughter. The weight of loss lingered. And when sleep finally claimed them, Gabrielle wondered about Jeffrey. Would he join them for breakfast as promised? The early bird Mass awaited. Her husband's invitation lingered.

Morning dawned with quiet purpose. Gabrielle and her husband made their way to 8:00 a.m. Mass at St. Michael's. Gabrielle missed that place, its hallowed halls resonating with devotion. They settled into their usual front pew.

Her husband slipped away to greet familiar faces. Gabrielle remained alone. Prayer enveloped her. She whispered gratitude for Jeffrey's presence, for shared laughter, for quiet understanding. She prayed for Jeffrey, for her husband, for the fragile threads that connected them all.

Mid prayer, Father James appeared. "Good to see you again," he said warmly. He asked about Florida, and Gabrielle shared their journey, her husband's son, lost to cancer, a grief that hung in the air.

Father James promised prayers. "Is your husband here?" he asked. Gabrielle nodded. He set off to find him. Their meeting was brief but significant, a priest's blessing, a whispered hope.

When her husband returned, his eyes held a mix of emotions. "I caught up with some old friends," he said. Father James's words had offered comfort. Together they had stood, a grieving father and a priest shouldering the weight of loss.

The Eucharist, the communal prayers, bridged the gap between heaven and earth. And in that sacred hour, Gabrielle believed that somehow, things would be okay between Jeffrey and her.

After Mass, they drove to meet Jeffrey for breakfast. Gabrielle's nerves churned. This was uncharted territory, their first joint venture with Jeffrey. Her husband's invitation had paved the way, but Gabrielle wondered if Jeffrey even registered her presence.

The car ride was a tempest of what ifs. Her stomach churned. Her husband noticed. "Are you alright?" he asked gently. Gabrielle brushed it off.

At the restaurant, Jeffrey waited. His handshake was firm, his hug a bridge between strangers. He acknowledged Gabrielle. For a fleeting moment, she wondered if he sensed her unease.

"How was Mass?" he asked. His voice carried the resonance of faith. Her husband and Jeffrey delved into familiar territory: Father James, shared pews, the ebb and flow of liturgy. Jeffrey, a fellow Catholic, found solace in St. Michael's, the same sanctuary that had cradled Gabrielle's prayers.

Breakfast unfolded, a tapestry of conversation woven by two men. They traversed landscapes: the showing, vintage cars, mutual acquaintances, even politics.

Gabrielle sat on the periphery, an observer. Occasionally, she dipped in, a sarcastic quip, a quiet nod. But mostly, she marveled at their camaraderie. Old friends, reunited. Their laughter echoed, a bridge across time.

Gabrielle watched Jeffrey's eyes crinkle as her husband recounted stories. Their laughter warmed the room. As breakfast waned, Jeffrey insisted on covering the bill. Gabrielle and her husband protested, but Jeffrey's resolve held. Her husband relented, a silent agreement between men.

He excused himself to the restroom, leaving Gabrielle and Jeffrey at the table. The air cracked with possibility. Gabrielle wanted to ask him why he had avoided her. Why wouldn't he accept her friend request? Her mind swirled. How could she convey the tangle of emotions, gratitude, longing, unspoken connection?

Then Jeffrey spoke. "The man with your mom yesterday," he asked. "Was that your father?"

Gabrielle laughed. "No," she replied. "My father passed in 2006. That was my brother-in-law."

Her husband returned, ready to leave. They rose from the table. Jeffrey's hug enveloped Gabrielle, a mirror of the one at the funeral home. She clung to the moment, reluctant to let go. But propriety pressed in. She patted his back, a silent plea: *That's enough.*

Her husband requested a photo. Gabrielle snapped the shot, capturing their camaraderie. Jeffrey asked for the picture.

Then business resumed: the items from the showing, a bill to be sent. Her husband shook Jeffrey's hand, sealing a pact for future connection. "Next time we're in town," he said, "We'll reach out."

Jeffrey agreed. "We'll talk again," he assured. As they said goodbye, Jeffrey headed to the counter to settle the bill.

The drive back to her mom's house wrapped them in silence. Her husband broke it, voice tinged with gratitude. "I'm glad Jeffrey joined us for breakfast," he said.

The photo beckoned. Gabrielle hesitated; Jeffrey's contact info eluded her. His privacy, a boundary she dared not breach.

Her husband urged her to retrieve the number from his phone. "Send him the picture," he insisted. So, Gabrielle did, a digital token of their shared morning.

Jeffrey's reply came swiftly: *Thanks!* Simple, warm.

Gabrielle responded: *You're welcome.* But his silence afterward puzzled her. Had she over stepped?

Her husband, unaware of her inner unease, had other plans. "Post the photo," he said, a public nod to unlikely camaraderie. Gabrielle obliged, tagging herself and Jeffrey. Likes poured in. But Jeffrey remained silent. Maybe he preferred anonymity. Maybe he hadn't seen it.

Back at her mom's house, Gabrielle wondered: *Would he remember their laughter, their fragile hug?*

Later that evening, the Olive Garden welcomed their motley crew: her husband, her mom, Gabrielle, and his ex-daughters-in-law. Women who once orbited his life, no longer wives yet not quite exes. Grandkids swirled around them, their laughter a counterpoint to the weight of the gathering.

The women shared stories, secrets, things the ex-wife had done before his son's passing. Hurtful things that lingered. Her husband listened, stoic. His youngest son had hinted at some of it, but these revelations cut deeper. He didn't confront them, not in front of the grandkids. But Gabrielle knew the tempest brewing.

After dinner, they posed for photos. The grandkids giggled, unaware. Her husband turned to them: "You need to visit us in Florida." They agreed, youthful promises hanging in the air.

On the drive back, emotions simmered. Her husband vented, frustration, grief, betrayal. Her mom sat quietly in the back seat, a witness to the storm. She offered a gentle reminder: "You still have your youngest son."

But her husband's resolve was firm. "I'm done with her," he said. "I hope I never have to talk to her again." His youngest son had left right after the showing, seeking refuge from the chaos.

Back at her mom's house, Gabrielle packed for the early flight. Her husband showered and collapsed into bed. Sleep calmed him.

But Gabrielle and her mom lingered, their voices hushed in the dim living room. She worried about him and his anger. "He needed to vent," Gabrielle reassured her.

And in the quiet hour past midnight, they lost track of time, their whispers weaving a bridge between past and present.

At dawn, they stirred. Goodbyes were bittersweet. Warm hugs whispered wishes. The airport waited. Her husband furrowed his brow. The rental car loomed in his mind. "Will the paperwork align?"

Gabrielle reassured him. "They have records. It'll be fine." But anxiety clung to him as they navigated the winding roads.

At the airport, relief washed over him. The car was accepted. Paperwork in order. Still, he fidgeted. Two hours early, he was ready to leave. Security was a ritual of belts, shoes, and Xrays. They emerged on the other side. The gate beckoned.

Then the announcement: flight delayed. An hour's wait for tardy attendants. His nerves ignited. He paced; phone pressed to his ear. Friends couldn't pick them up. Another airport, another delay. Panic etched his face.

Gabrielle listened, then acted. *"Leave it to me,"* she said. Fingers flew across her screen. A car rental near home, secured with reward points. $25, peace of mind. She shared the plan. His shoulders eased.

Thirty minutes later, flight attendants arrived. They boarded, delayed but undeterred. As the plane taxied, Gabrielle glanced at her husband. His grip relaxed. Florida awaited. The cabin hummed. Her husband surrendered to sleep. His breaths synchronized with the plane's rhythm.

As they descended, the world came into focus. Blue tarps clung to rooftops. Scars of hurricane winds. Their own home shared this fate.

Her husband stirred. "The next day," he vowed, "I'll make the calls. Assessments, estimates, repairs." Gabrielle nodded. She knew the weight he carried.

The wheels touched down. Reality returned. They retrieved the rental car. The engine purred. Her husband's stomach grumbled. "Home," he muttered.

But Gabrielle knew better. She coaxed him. Just a quick stop. He protested, but she steered them to a roadside diner. The bell chimed. Comfort food wrapped around them. He ordered reluctantly. Gabrielle smiled. Partnerships were built on such compromises.

Lunch consumed, they resumed their journey. The car, laden with suitcases, carried them home.

Their street appeared. The blue tarp flapped in greeting. They unpacked. Her husband's restlessness persisted. "The rental car," he said. "Let's return it now." Gabrielle argued for delay. He insisted.

They retraced their route. The attendant accepted the keys. Paperwork a routine. Her husband exhaled. Relief washed over him. "The loop is closed," he said. "Back to normal." As if the mundane held solace.

The Restoration and the Rise

> *"Those who hope in the Lord will renew their strength. They will rise on wings like eagles."*
>
> —Isaiah 40:31

As dusk draped the horizon, Gabrielle and her husband crossed the threshold of home. The journey had been long, but the familiar walls embraced them. Gabrielle unpacked, laundry tumbling into the washer's rhythmic hum. Her husband retreated to the den, fingers dancing across the keyboard, emails, bills, bursts of laughter punctuating the silence.

Friends called, keepers of their spare key, and soon laughter spilled into the living room. Stories of grief and resilience wove through the air.

An invitation for breakfast followed; Gabrielle declined, work awaited. Her husband accepted with gusto.

Later, the house settled into quiet. Gabrielle sank into the couch, exhaustion pressing down. A gentle shake stirred her. "Come to bed," her husband whispered. She protested, laundry unfinished. "I took care of it," he said softly. "You were sleeping soundly."

Morning light filtered through the curtains. Her husband returned from breakfast; nostalgia etched in his voice. "It would've been my mother's birthday," he said. He asked Gabrielle to honor her memory online. She crafted a tribute, images of laughter and love, a prayer for her boys.

Then, an unexpected ping: an email from Jeffrey. Not a bill but a plea: *Proofread the death certificate*. Gabrielle corrected the errors, her fingers steady.

Her husband entered, gratitude spilling forth. "You were the right person," he murmured. "Jeffrey knew it too."

At the hotel, Allen greeted her warmly. “Welcome back. We missed you.” His concern was genuine. He spoke of family, of balance, of the fragile harmony they both sought.

Todd hovered nearby, steady as ever. Fresh faces staffed the desk, filling the void Gabrielle had left.

But one name lingered in absence: Travis. “Hoping he’ll return soon,” Allen sighed. Until then, Gabrielle’s rhythm resumed, 2:00 p.m. to 10:00 p.m., seven days a week. Allen’s parting words carried weight: “Until further notice.”

She checked her phone, a whisper from Jeffrey, gratitude for the death certificate corrections. He promised to send the revised version once the state gave its approval. Her husband would have his copy.

Gabrielle replied, a brief note brimming with warmth. “Great,” she typed, followed by a heartfelt thank-you. The words felt small, but they carried the weight of shared sorrow.

Hours passed. Then her phone buzzed again, her husband’s name flashing on the screen. The package had arrived, the one requested from Jeffrey. A cardboard box, heavy with memory.

Inside, the wreath, its petals bruised, its ribbon frayed. Her husband’s voice held disappointment, a quiet plea for restoration. Gabrielle promised to mend it. “When you have time,” he said, gratitude threading through the words. “You always know how to fix things.” His faith in her warmed her heart.

Six days after her return, Gabrielle found herself scrolling. Indeed, a habit never quite abandoned. Job alerts still fluttered into her inbox. And then, a luminous listing: general manager at her very own hotel. Her pulse quickened. How could this be?

She stepped into the lobby, answers tucked within the walls. Tammy, the executive housekeeper, was her confidante. Gabrielle approached her, heart fluttering.

Tammy’s eyes met hers. “Is it true?” Gabrielle asked. “Is Allen really leaving?”

Tammy nodded. “He confided in me, Todd, and a few others. Allen is stepping down.”

Gabrielle absorbed the gravity.

“Keep this close,” Tammy cautioned. “The team doesn’t know yet.” Gabrielle vowed to be the silent sentinel.

That evening, she shared the news with her husband, a quiet exchange of sorrow and acceptance. He, too, had sensed the winds of change.

The next morning, Gabrielle stepped through the revolving doors. Allen's office beckoned. With a gentle tap, she entered.

His eyes met hers. "I apologize," he began, "for the abrupt unveiling." Gabrielle nodded.

"Sadness and joy waltz within me," she confessed. "Your retirement is both a lament and a celebration."

He leaned back. "Sixteen days," he murmured. "The month's end will be my curtain call."

Surprise pirouetted through her thoughts. "So soon?" But she masked it with well wishes. "May your days of leisure be painted in hues of contentment," she declared. "You've earned this encore."

But Allen had more to reveal. "Other matters linger," he said. "In a few days," he promised, "we'll harmonize once more."

They chuckled. "You know where to find me," Gabrielle quipped. "Amidst the lobby's ebb and flow." His laughter echoed as she retreated.

Todd would inherit the rhythm, two weeks of apprenticeship, a symposium of knowledge transfer. The desk would not falter. The new recruit would dance across seven days, a rhythm Gabrielle knew well.

Then a request: "Could you be our matinee muse?" Elissa needed respite. "Two days a week," Allen proposed.

"An early overture at 11:00 a.m.?" Gabrielle assented, a commitment to harmony.

And then, a pivotal day. Gabrielle stepped through the familiar doors. Allen and Todd awaited her, their expressions solemn. Allen invited her to his office. Todd flanked him. Gabrielle took her seat, the weight of the moment settled.

Allen began to unfold a narrative that would chart a new course for her career. He revealed that the regional director had visited for his quarterly evaluation. During the visit, Gabrielle's name surfaced, a rising thread in the hotel's tapestry.

With quiet gravity, Allen extended an offer: director of sales and marketing. He also mentioned the assistant GM role, but Gabrielle declined with grace. She had worn that mantle before in the food industry. Her aspirations reached higher. The director role aligned with her vision.

Allen detailed the responsibilities, the expectations, the compensation: a $5 hourly increase, 8:00 a.m. to 4:00 p.m., Monday through Friday, with occasional front desk shifts. Training would precede the transition. Hourly pay during the course, then salaried status upon completion.

Allen suggested she consult her husband. But Gabrielle's voice held conviction. "No need," she said. Her decision was made.

Allen, surprised by her resolve, seemed to waver, but Gabrielle stood firm. "Formalize the offer," she requested. "I'll sign without hesitation."

He agreed, asking for a brief interlude to draft the letter. Gabrielle exited his office, heart brimming with possibility.

Less than an hour later, Todd approached with the document. "Review it," he said. "If it meets your approval, sign." The offer would begin on Saturday, aligned with the pay cycle. She signed but requested a keepsake. Todd provided a copy. The original returned to Allen. One chapter closed. Another awaited.

Alone, Gabrielle called her husband. His voice, brimming with pride, promised celebration. And he kept his word, greeting her despite the late hour, his joy magnifying her own. He regarded the offer letter as a symbol of their united dreams. His congratulations wrapped her in warmth. Plans for a celebratory lunch were laid with care. Gabrielle tempered his enthusiasm, training still loomed. But his spirits remained high, buoyed by the pay raise.

At dawn, he championed a festive luncheon. Gabrielle chose Carrabba's Italian Grill. He captured their joy in a photo, broadcasting it to the world: *Celebrating my wife's promotion with a lunch date! She is transitioning but has already become director of sales. Overflowing with pride and love. Congratulations!*

After the feast, Gabrielle returned to the hotel. Her thoughts teemed with promise. Allen greeted her with news: Travis's return was imminent. Her full assumption of duties was within reach.

But the search for a new front desk colleague persisted. Amid interviews and Allen's looming departure, an unexpected bond formed. Todd connected Gabrielle to the corporate director of sales. The call was cordial yet disconcerting. The director's voice, sweet but layered, left Gabrielle questioning sincerity.

A frank talk with Todd unveiled past tensions between Allen and the corporate director. A shadow flickered across Gabrielle's path. Yet Todd's laughter, his affirmations, became a beacon. His vow of support illuminated her way.

The next morning, as Gabrielle prepared for work, her husband asked about Jeffrey. He was awaiting his son's death certificate, several thank you notes, and a copy of the video tribute. He preferred not to involve his ex-wife. Gabrielle promised to manage it.

That evening, she found a quiet moment to compose an email to Jeffrey at the funeral home:

Subject: Outstanding Request and Final Arrangements

Dear Jeffrey,

I hope this email finds you well. I am writing to follow up on a few outstanding items:

- *Death Certificate: Could you please provide an estimated time of arrival for my husband's copy of his son's death certificate?*
- *Fingerprint Information: We require the PIN number to access my stepson's fingerprint data on your website.*
- *Memorial Video and Thankyou Notes: My husband wishes to have a copy of the memorial video played during the visitation, along with approximately ten thank you notes from the funeral home.*
- *Final Bill: We are also awaiting the invoice detailing the costs for the motorcycle arrangements and the shipment of items to our residence postservice.*

We understand the demands of your profession and appreciate your dedication to all your clients. However, we are eager to bring closure to these matters as swiftly as possible. My work schedule has been exceedingly demanding, leaving little time or energy to mediate between my husband and his ex-wife. While I strive to keep harmony, the ongoing communication has become overwhelming. The sooner we can resolve these final details, the more peace we can restore to our lives.

Thank you for your prompt attention to these requests. Your aid is greatly appreciated during this challenging time.

Warm Regards, Gabrielle

A few hours later, Jeffrey's reply arrived, succinct and unadorned:

Hello Gabrielle, All the requested information is ready and will be dispatched via mail tomorrow.

Gabrielle chose not to respond. It was time, she decided, for Jeffrey to experience the silence he so often afforded others.

As dawn painted the sky, the rhythmic dance of hammers and the steady cadence of footsteps resonated within their home. 118 days post-hurricane, the roofing company stood at their doorstep poised to heal the wounds left by Ian.

The preceding days had been a maelstrom of anxiety. Their public adjuster brought tidings of relief, but with urgency: the insurance check needed to be cashed at once. The company had filed for insolvency. Her husband rushed to the bank. The check cleared. Their spirits lifted.

They watched as the blue tarp was peeled away. The workers laid down the underlay for the shingles. A crossroads appeared: metal roof or shingles? The allure of metal beckoned, but practicality prevailed. They chose shingles, a shade that whispered harmony with their home's palette.

Gabrielle captured the scene: roofers perched like artisans of recovery. She shared the snapshot on social media, a declaration: after 118 days, the journey of rebuilding had begun.

That afternoon at work, Gabrielle checked her email. Jeffrey had written. He had shipped everything she asked. Snow had delayed him, but the skies had cleared. Gabrielle couldn't help herself. She replied:

Thank you! I was beginning to question the definition of tomorrow ☺ I forgot what a little bit of snow in the area does. . . Do you know what they call snowmen in Florida? Puddles ☺ *Enjoy your day!*

Response? Of course not.

The waning days of January found Gabrielle immersed in a relentless tide of work, a marathon of shifts without respite.

Amid the whirlwind, a new chapter began: Nancy arrived at the front desk. Allen, buoyed by optimism, entrusted Gabrielle with her training.

Nancy's résumé spoke of experience, and Allen's enthusiasm was palpable. Yet beneath the surface, Gabrielle sensed an undercurrent of disquiet. Nancy's demeanor hinted at storms yet to come.

Elissa, too, confided in her reservations. A silent pact was forged between them, to tread carefully and let time reveal the truth.

The hotel's nightly rhythm welcomed Travis back, returning from sabbatical. Charlie, once his standin, now split his time between day and twilight. Gabrielle, reluctant and wary, confided in Todd. Travis's long absence, the decision to hold his position, unsettled her.

Todd mirrored her concerns, but pointed to Travis's skill, his rapport with guests. Still, Gabrielle urged vigilance. "Keep an eye on his nocturnal realm," she said.

Allen's departure marked the end of an era. His presence had been a constant beacon in the ebb and flow of hotel life. Though he wished for a quiet exit, the team's affection inspired a modest tribute, a silent acknowledgment of his impact.

Gabrielle's arrival coincided with his farewell. In that brief intersection, he offered a warm embrace, mutual respect, a promise that his guidance would linger a little longer. Gratitude filled her response. She wished him a future as rewarding as the legacy he left behind.

After a grueling twenty-three day stretch, Todd granted Gabrielle a day of rest, a gift of rejuvenation. The announcement was music to her and her husband's ears, heralding not just repose but the promise of sun-drenched shifts ahead.

The week that followed was a whirlwind, mentorship, and transition. Gabrielle juggled dual roles: training Nancy and stepping into her new position. The key to her office was handed to her. With it, the freedom to infuse the space with her essence.

Over two afternoons, her office became a canvas. Her desk found new homes, not once but thrice, as she sought harmony of form and function. Colleagues teased her about the ever revolving landscape. But Gabrielle stood firm, armed with Todd's blessing to craft a sanctuary from the sterile corporate world.

She hung up pictures of her family to make it feel like home. And one photo stood apart: Jeffrey. A screenshot from the night he turned her down. The night their friendship ended. The night he declared her out of his social media realm.

A realm Gabrielle still longed to reenter. The photo would serve as a reminder of him, of her silent wish for renewal. A reminder that he was still part of her life, even if only in a photograph, even if only in her heart.

Her 11:00 a.m. to 7:00 p.m. shift unfolded with Todd guiding her through the intricate dance of deposits and direct bill accounts. His revelation: Gabrielle would serve as his right hand, in addition to her sales directorship. She met it with pride, ready to rise to the challenge.

As dawn broke over her first two early shifts, Gabrielle navigated new waters. She signed up for the training class, despite its distant start date in May.

Todd's disappointment was palpable, but they accepted the waiting game. A virtual meeting with the corporate Director of Sales offered Gabrielle a glimpse into the digital tools that would soon become her companions.

Her enthusiasm left her yearning for the solace of home. Todd's laughter at her candid admission was a gentle endnote to the day's symphony, his chuckle granting her leave with warmth and understanding.

Returning home in daylight was a novel joy, a rare gift shared with her husband, who was equally unaccustomed to such early reunion.

Their evening plans were simple: dinner out, ahead of the crowds, at the familiar comfort of Applebee's. But the night had more in store. A car show next door beckoned with its gleaming display of automotive history. Chrome and curves, engines, and echoes of eras past.

They wandered among the classics, hand in hand, losing track of time until the night sky gently reminded them of home.

The next day, Gabrielle and her husband spent time together around the house. The long awaited package from Jeffrey had arrived: everything her husband had requested.

Relief and gratitude filled him. "I want to do something nice for Jeffrey," he said. Gabrielle promised to produce something meaningful, to send alongside the check for shipping and motorcycle costs.

That evening before Mass, Gabrielle composed a letter to Jeffrey on hotel letterhead, now bearing her new title. It was a symphony of gratitude for his compassion, his staff's care, their "Spirit to Serve." She enclosed gift cards, free night certificates, and a VIP invitation to the upcoming car auction.

Her husband read it slowly, tears tracing his cheeks. "It's beautiful," he whispered. They mailed it before Mass, sealing closure with kindness.

Then, the 4:00 p.m. Mass. For weeks, work had kept Gabrielle from the familiar wooden pews. But that Saturday, the sun shone brighter; the air held anticipation. It was time to return. Her husband had been faithfully attending OCIA classes. His commitment inspired her. Her new schedule allowed her to join him once more.

Father Michael greeted them with warmth. His understanding during her absence had touched Gabrielle deeply. No judgment, only welcome.

Her husband shared the news of her promotion. Father Michael's congratulations felt like a blessing.

They settled into the front pew. As hymns filled the air, Gabrielle bowed her head in prayer. But her thoughts drifted to Jeffrey. To the letter. To the hope that it might rekindle their friendship, even if only on social media. They had connected again during the showing, though the past remained unspoken.

Amid sacred verses, Gabrielle whispered a silent plea for reconciliation.

After Mass, they stepped into the fading daylight. The church bells echoed behind them. Dinner at Bob Evans felt like a celebration: faith, friendship, and the quiet joy of being seen.

The sun peeked through the stained glass windows. It was a new day, a day of reconnection and rediscovery.

Gabrielle and her husband stepped into the church for early morning Mass. The hymns swirled around her, wrapping her in a comforting embrace.

After the dismissal, they made their way to the OCIA class. As the door swung open, Gabrielle was met with a chorus of smiles. The class gathered around her.

Each person offered a heart felt hug, eyes shining with genuine joy. "Welcome back! We missed you!" they said. "Your husband held down the fort, but it wasn't the same without you."

Gabrielle felt a mixture of emotions, gratitude, relief, and a touch of guilt. She had missed many classes during her hectic work schedule. The syllabus had moved forward, leaving her a little behind. But Gabrielle was no stranger to the material; she had walked this path before. Still, she hadn't taken notes. She was winging it, relying on memory and intuition.

As they settled into their seats, the whiteboard beckoned. The lesson unfolded. Gabrielle listened intently, catching up as best she could. The camaraderie of the group buoyed her, shared laughter, whispered explanations, and the collective pursuit of faith. It was good to be back, surrounded by these faithful hearts.

Days later, Jeffrey replied, not with brevity, but with heart: "Wow! What do I say? I'm not good with accolades. I hope what I do pleases God. Your generosity was overwhelming. The letter was heartfelt; I'd like to place it in an album I'll take with me when I retire. Thank you for your trust. Except your friendship, I value that the most."

Her husband handed her the message. "Respond," he urged. Gabrielle did, warm, playful, promising future invitations.

Jeffrey's final reply was brief, yet kind: "Maybe next time. Take care." Gabrielle sent Jeffrey a friend request on social media, her hope flickering like a candle in Lent's quiet.

In the latter part of February, her work days became a whirlwind, two days from 2:00 p.m. to 10:00 p.m. shift, one day from 11:00 a.m. to 7:00 p.m., two more of 6:00 a.m. to 2:00 p.m.

A juggling act. Sales responsibilities, front-desk support, short-staffed and stretched thin. The desk clung to her. Gabrielle yearned for reprieve but hesitated to pressure Todd. He was in a precarious position, awaiting word on the GM role.

A month of anticipation, the title dangling just out of reach. His mood mirrored the weather: overcast, with bouts of gloom. Gabrielle played the role of reassuring friend. "Don't fret," she told him. "You've got this. The promotion is practically yours." But the powers that be had their own script. They made him dance on the edge, testing his mettle. If he had faltered, the regional director would have appeared.

But to Gabrielle's relief, they stayed distant. She knew the stakes. If the GM mantle eluded him, Todd would likely walk away. The suspense stretched taut until the final days of February.

Then, the regional director stepped into the spotlight. With a flourish, Todd's promotion was announced. Effective immediately. The room erupted in applause, save for a few begrudging souls.

Gabrielle was genuinely thrilled. He had earned it. He had toiled diligently throughout her tenure. Relief washed over her. He was staying. The hotel was in capable hands.

As the days melted into weeks, Gabrielle settled comfortably into her new role. The rhythm of day shifts became her familiar tune.

Evenings unfolded gently, homecomings sweeter, her cozy abode a balm for her weary soul. But two days still lurked in the shadows: the 2:00 p.m. to 10:00 p.m. shift.

Cunningly, Gabrielle scheduled them early in the week, a strategic maneuver to reclaim her weekends.

Sundays became sacred, reserved for church. Saturdays were for her husband, their escape from the mundane. They ventured to the beach, the shoreline that had eluded her since the hurricane's tempestuous dance.

Top down, sunlight on their shoulders, the beach beckoned. Gabrielle shared the moment on social media: *145 days posthurricane, and I finally made it back to the beach, my happy place.*

The day after their beach escapade, they cocooned at home. The pool cage remained unrepaired, the roof still a work in progress, awaiting its crowning glory, shingles. So, they surrendered to the cozy confines of their living room, the television casting its glow.

Gabrielle, phone in hand, scrolled through her digital universe. And then, Jeffrey. She navigated the labyrinth of privacy settings, heart fluttering. Had he unblocked her? Deleted her? Spammed her into oblivion? The verdict: no blockage, no deletion, but no friendship either. His page, veiled in secrecy, revealed nothing.

Gabrielle wrestled with disappointment. How could she convey her desire for connection? Wasn't their recent encounter enough to show she had changed? She lingered in the in between, yearning for acceptance, for the elusive click of "*friend added.*" Jeffrey hovered on the precipice of her virtual world tantalizingly close, maddeningly distant.

Fueled by frustration and ache, Gabrielle took to her social media stage. Her post echoed across the digital expanse: *How can a faceless friend offer more warmth than someone who claims to value my friendship?* Her keystrokes were heavy with longing. A picture accompanied her lament: *If you're not good enough to be a social media friend, make sure to never bless them with your presence again.* Jeffrey remained a cipher, wrapped in privacy settings. Gabrielle lingered in twilight, caught between longing and resolve.

The following day was Ash Wednesday. Gabrielle playfully dubbed it "hardcore Catholic day," a term that always brought a wry smile.

She worked the day shift, but by evening, she and her husband found themselves in the quiet embrace of Mass. The scent of incense hung in the air, mingling with hushed whispers.

Father Michael marked their foreheads with the ashen cross, a reminder of mortality and penance.

Her husband had decided to give up Pepsi for Lent. A small sacrifice, but meaningful. He turned to Gabrielle. "What about you?" he asked. Gabrielle hesitated.

The truth welled up, raw and unfiltered. "People," she replied softly. "I'm giving up on people, those I've longed to be friends with, but who never reciprocated. Those who didn't love me enough to truly be my friend."

His brow furrowed. "That's deep," he said. "But why carry that burden? Why worry about those who don't want to be your friend? You have enough friends already."

His words struck a chord. Did he sense the hidden ache? The unspoken name? Gabrielle kept it vague. Her heart a locked chest. "You're right," she murmured. "Maybe I do."

A few days later, the roofers returned. Shingles lay in readiness. As the sun ascended, casting long shadows, Gabrielle watched their peculiar method. They scaled the heights with intent, each bundle nestled in their arms. But there was no cacophony of hammers, just hushed placement, a mute tribute to the deities of domicile.

"Why?" she pondered, immortalizing the scene. The shingles arrayed like a tessellated coverlet, borders interlocking in quiet solidarity. Amused, Gabrielle posted the image: *They proclaimed new shingling was imminent. I lack the roofer's craft, but surely this isn't the customary method?* Replies cascaded in. Her contacts, equally mystified, offered hypotheses. Were the roofers contemporary druids, summoning the essence of an impervious abode?

Days passed. Weeks stretched. Gabrielle half-expected to awaken to shingles transformed into a noble wyvern, a sentinel against the storm. But reality reclaimed its dominion. The roof persisted in stasis, no beasts, no chants. Just shingles, abiding in anticipation for the moment their fate would be unveiled.

The Reckoning and the Release

"You will know the truth, and the truth will set you free."

—John 8:32

Later that day, her husband received an unexpected call. The voice on the other end belonged to his friend's wife. She spoke with urgency: her husband was taking an unanticipated hiatus from social media. Curiosity piqued, he probed further. His friend had become elusive, evading calls and messages. Concerned, he reached out to the wife.

According to her, another acquaintance had whispered dark secrets into her husband's ear. The accusation: she and Gabrielle had engaged in hushed discussions about his infidelity. Gabrielle hadn't seen their friends since the hurricane. Her days blurred into nights, seven day work weeks at the hotel.

Her husband's fury ignited. He knew the truth. He had seen Gabrielle's unwavering dedication, her absence from social gatherings. His resolve solidified: Gabrielle would call his friend's wife and confront the whispers headon.

Gabrielle dialed. Silence greeted her; she left a message urging a return call. Minutes later, Gabrielle's phone lit up. She answered, activating speakerphone to include her husband. She unraveled her side of the story. Their mutual friend remained unresponsive. Another acquaintance had dropped the bombshell: they were the culprits, weaving tales of infidelity.

Gabrielle protested, incredulous. Her name? Entangled in this intrigue? She was a worker bee buzzing between shifts and sleep. Marital dramas held no allure. She had no desire to defend herself against baseless accusations.

The call ended, leaving echoes of quivering voices and unanswered questions. Her husband leaned in. "Did you hear it?" he asked. "The tremor in her voice?"

Gabrielle nodded. "There's more to this tale," she whispered.

He looked at her, confused and angry. "Why your name? How did you get entangled in this web?"

Gabrielle shrugged, her resolve unwavering. "They're using me as a scapegoat. A convenient coverup for their own tangled affairs. But I refuse to be their pawn."

Their mutual friends from Tampa had become distant memories. Her husband's anger simmered, fueled by loyalty and disbelief. "We're better off without them," Gabrielle declared. "Their drinking and drama, what purpose does it serve? They gather like vultures, tearing apart reputations, weaving tales."

He nodded, jaw clenched. "But I won't let it go," he vowed. "The truth will surface."

That weekend, Gabrielle and her husband joined their OCIA class for a momentous occasion at the grand cathedral, the Rite of Acceptance ceremony. Father Michael drove himself, explaining he had a meeting afterward. Dinner plans were off the table; the class had swelled in numbers, too large for any restaurant. Disappointing but heartening.

As they entered the cathedral, her husband reprised his role as banner boy, proudly carrying the church's emblem during the opening procession. His joy radiated through the sacred space.

After the service, they settled into their pew, awaiting their turn to capture a moment with the bishop. Gabrielle snapped selfies with her husband. Father Michael, seated behind them, injected humor into the solemnity, photobombing their picture with a mischievous grin.

Gabrielle shared the moment on social media: *When you're at church taking pictures and your favorite priest decides to photobomb.*

The following day, Gabrielle returned home from work to find her husband distressed. His friend had suffered a fall, now hospitalized. His wife had contacted Gabrielle's husband, prompting a visit. But during the visit, his friend remained distant, barely acknowledging him.

It puzzled her husband. Neither of them had done anything to call for such coldness. As Gabrielle pondered the situation, theory began to take shape. It seemed likely that the friend had been gossiping about their mutual acquaintance and had been called out. Rather than owning his actions, he shifted blame onto them, leaving her husband caught in the crossfire.

This would explain the frosty behavior. Perhaps he sought a break, hoping tempers would cool down, knowing her husband had every right to be angry. Her husband conceded Gabrielle's analysis made sense. Yet the whole affair still troubled him.

A few days passed. His frustration lingered. The silence, the desire for distance, weighed heavily. Then a text arrived from the friend's wife: the hospital stay would be extended to a few more days.

Her husband, who was loyal, visited again. But his friend remained distant, barely acknowledging him. Frustrated, her husband laid it bare. "If you want to talk, the ball is in your court. Just call."

To his wife, he expressed reluctance to continue visiting unless explicitly invited. Gabrielle urged him not to lose sleep over it. His friend's aloofness stemmed from guilt, a gnawing awareness of his own wrongdoing.

As Gabrielle headed to work, his discontent still simmered. She knew him well; he wouldn't let it go easily.

On the chilly last day of February, a glimmer of hope peeked through the clouds that had hung over their home for far too long. 153 days since the hurricane had battered their neighborhood, and finally, progress. Brand new shingles crowned their weather worn roof.

Gabrielle stood watching as the crew worked diligently. The rhythmic hammering echoed the promise of restoration. She snapped a photo, shared it on social media, captioned with quiet triumph: *Resilience in the face of adversity.*

The catalyst? The final insurance check. Her husband had navigated the paperwork, ensuring the funds were deposited and cleared. With the check in hand, they moved forward, determined to mend what nature had torn asunder.

Their public adjuster had fought valiantly. Yet the coffers fell short of their grand vision. Then the contractor stepped in. Somehow, they calculated the funds would suffice for essential repairs. Skepticism gnawed at Gabrielle. It felt too convenient, too orchestrated.

"Is it not curious?" she mused. "Before, they clamored for more money. Now, with less, they assure us it's enough. It feels like a wellrehearsed play." Her husband nodded, relief and weariness in his eyes. "Sketchy, indeed."

In early March, Gabrielle began exerting gentle pressure on Todd. She had been stationed at the front desk for far too long. Her expanding responsibilities demanded a shift.

Finally, Todd relented. He hired Karly, a vivacious young woman with prior hotel experience. From the outset, they were charmed by her friendly demeanor. She held promise, a potential future assistant GM.

The prospect of stepping away from the desk filled Gabrielle with excitement. She knew Karly's learning curve would be swift. Soon, Gabrielle could focus entirely on her sales role.

Yet amidst the whirlwind of work and household responsibilities, an unexpected thought persisted: Jeffrey. Why did he occupy her mind daily? Why, despite their lack of friendship, even on social media?

A few days later, her sister's call shattered the mundane rhythm of Gabrielle's life. Her voice trembled. Gabrielle's stepsister had been diagnosed with cancer. The prognosis was grim.

Gabrielle hadn't seen her in years. Their relationship was a fragile thread, frayed by time and divergent paths.

Nine years her senior, she had left their childhood home at eighteen, a distant figure whose life unfolded in shadows and vices: drugs, cigarettes, alcohol.

Growing up, Gabrielle harbored resentment. She had done their parents dirty, or so Gabrielle believed. She rarely attended family gatherings, holidays, birthdays, anniversaries. Her absence left an ache, a void of missed opportunities and unspoken words.

Gabrielle wondered why she had chosen that path, why she had distanced herself from the warmth of their family hearth.

Now, faced with mortality, Gabrielle's emotions swirled: sadness, compassion, guilt. She told her sister she couldn't make it home but asked to be kept informed.

When she hung up, Gabrielle turned to her husband. His eyes held understanding. He had met her stepsister only twice: once at her father's funeral, once at her grandmother's. Her presence had been fleeting, a shadow cast upon grief.

"I was never close to her," Gabrielle admitted. "But if she passes, I'll have to make the trip for my mom. She'll guilt me into it, or worse, I'll guilt myself."

His hand found hers. "We'll deal with it when the time comes," he said.

At the hotel's front desk, things hummed along, at least on the surface. The team was fully staffed. Gabrielle reveled in the sense of order. But beneath it, a curious enigma stirred: Nancy, hand picked by Allen. "A great asset," he proclaimed.

Yet Nancy had a knack for chaos, misplaced reservations, misdirected calls, and her favorite refrain: "I wasn't properly trained." It became her mantra.

In the market area, her true colors appeared. The cash register was her nemesis. She fumbled with prices, rang up items haphazardly, left a trail of discrepancies. Gabrielle's morning deposits consistently revealed more money than expected.

The puzzle led straight to Nancy. "Nancy isn't ringing up her market items," Gabrielle told Todd. "We need to address this." Todd agreed.

Nancy was summoned. The interrogation began: How did she ring up items? Why the consistent errors? Nancy's responses were a tapestry of excuses. "I wasn't trained properly," she insisted.

Todd pressed further. "How do you know the price?"

Caught in contradiction, Nancy stammered ignorance, then certainty, a tangled dance of half truths. Gabrielle watched, a chilling thought creeping in: *Was Nancy pilfering from the till?* Perhaps she lacked the cunning to cover her tracks. Trust evaporated. Suspicion stayed.

Todd gave her the benefit of the doubt and marched her to the desk to show the proper method.

Later, Gabrielle cornered him. "She's stealing," she said, urgent and low. "We must cut our losses."

But Todd shook his head. "You're overreacting. She genuinely doesn't know how."

Despite Gabrielle's protests, Todd chose mentorship over accusation. Gabrielle remained unconvinced. Her instincts whispered: this was only the overture to a longer saga.

Mid March brought an unexpected thrill. Their hotel hosted a flight crew for a unique airshow at the nearby airport. As director of sales, Gabrielle received a special invitation. The prospect of touring historic planes and even taking a ride piqued her interest, but someone else would appreciate it even more: her husband.

With anticipation, they set off that sunny afternoon. The tarmac buzzed, mechanics checking engines, pilots in flight suits, the scent of aviation fuel in the air.

Their first stop: the B24 bomber, a majestic beast with a massive wingspan. The crew welcomed them aboard. Gabrielle marveled at the cramped quarters where brave pilots once flew perilous missions.

But the highlight awaited her husband. He climbed into the cockpit of a T34 Mentor, a nimble trainer aircraft. The pilot briefed him. The engine roared. They taxied down the runway. Gabrielle watched them ascend into the boundless sky.

After the flight, her husband returned with a grin stretching ear to ear. A reporter had interviewed him. The segment would air that evening.

Their living room became a makeshift studio. They huddled around the television, waiting for his moment of fame.

There he was, sharing his airborne adventure, eyes shining with joy. Gabrielle felt a surge of pride. Her husband the star of the evening.

Later, he posted about the escapade. Their phones buzzed with congratulatory messages. Gabrielle reveled in the knowledge that she had orchestrated this delightful afternoon for him.

Sometimes, as a busy professional, she forgot to prioritize moments of pure enjoyment. But that day, watching her husband's excitement, Gabrielle realized they all needed a break. She earned some "wife points" that afternoon, a day well spent.

A few days later, the contractors arrived. Their mission: restore the house to its former glory. Painters transformed faded walls into a canvas of renewal. Her husband couldn't hold his excitement, pacing the hallway, peeking out the window. Each brushstroke was a step toward reclaiming their sanctuary.

As the week unfolded, the symphony of hammers and drills played a harmonious tune. The lanai cage, once a twisted mess, now stood tall and proud, its mesh glistening in the sunlight. They could almost hear the pool water beckoning. Her husband's grin widened with each passing day, mirroring the progress outside.

Then came the moment of revelation: the exterior color. They deliberated. The shingles whispered their preference. They settled on a deep, dignified hue, a shade that harmonized with the landscape.

Armed with his smartphone, her husband captured the transformation, before and after, a weather worn dwelling reborn. He shared the visual tale on social media, inviting friends and family to see their journey of resilience.

187 days after the hurricane's wrath, they stood in their driveway, surveying the complete repairs. The once battered house now stood tall. The lanai cage framed the pool. Their hearts swelled with pride.

As the sun dipped below the horizon, her husband squeezed Gabrielle's hand. "We did it," he whispered.

A few days later at work, Todd summoned Nancy into the office again. Gabrielle stood outside the door, a silent witness. Nancy had made a costly blunder, a direct bill account mishandled. Guests were double-charged.

As she listened to Todd's stern voice, Gabrielle couldn't help but wonder: was there a pattern? Nancy's excuses were always the same: "I wasn't properly trained," "I'm still learning."

Gabrielle's frustration bubbled over. She cornered Todd. "How much longer are we going to tolerate this?" she demanded. "Nancy's been here for weeks. She keeps making the same mistakes. It's affecting our team's efficiency!"

Todd raised an eyebrow. "Easy there," he cautioned. "She's still a newbie. We can't expect perfection right away."

"But she's managing direct bill accounts," Gabrielle protested. "That's not rocket science. Her excuses are wearing thin."

Todd sighed. "Look, I get it. But maybe she does need more training. Here's the plan: I'll pair her with someone experienced, a mentor."

Gabrielle leaned in. "Who?"

"Karly," he said, a glint of mischief in his eyes. "She's got her act together, eyeing the assistant GM role. Good practice for both."

And just like that, the stage was set: Nancy, the newcomer with a penchant for mishaps, and Karly, the ambitious mentor.

In the bustling world of hospitality, where personalities collide and responsibilities intertwine, Nancy found herself caught in a web of conflicting expectations. She yearned for more training, believing mastery would empower her. But her path was fraught with challenges.

Todd's well intentioned plan took an unexpected turn. The chemistry between Nancy and Karly was far from harmonious. Personalities clashed. Cooperation remained elusive.

Nancy, confident in her abilities, rebuffed Karly's help. She insisted she knew the ropes, didn't need hand holding. Her independence strained the relationship.

Todd intervened, his tone more resolute. He reminded Nancy that her lack of training was precisely why he'd paired her with Karly.

Nancy remained steadfast. "She's just bossing me around," she said. "She's not really training me."

Todd faced a dilemma. He couldn't risk Nancy running a shift solo. He presented two options: transition to the day shift for more training or consider quitting. Working the evening shift alone was not an option.

Nancy mulled it over during her days off. The day shift clashed with her preferences. But it was her only avenue for the training she craved. Todd's watchful eye, Karly's overbearing attitude weighed heavily.

The following day, Karly shared the saga with fellow staff. Rumors spread: the clash of personalities, Todd's tough stance, Nancy's reluctance to adapt. The hotel's corridors buzzed with speculation. Nancy found herself at the center of it all.

As the clock ticked, Todd's patience wore thin. Two days had slipped by since their last conversation. Nancy remained silent. Why she chose silence, he would never know. Defiance? Contemplation? Either way, Todd sensed something hung in the balance.

Against his better judgment, he reached for his phone. Gabrielle suggested letting the silence speak. But Todd needed closure. He composed a message: *Have you decided?*

Nancy's reply arrived swiftly. She couldn't work the day shift; it clashed with her life outside the hotel. But her alternative proposal intrigued Todd: she was willing to embrace the night audit, partnering with Travis.

In her eyes, he was the sole beacon of competence amidst a sea of uncertainty. Todd's temper flared. Nancy's audacity struck a nerve. He had laid out the options: day shift or nothing. Yet here she was, defying him.

Todd's reply grew stern. The day shift was her sole path to training. Nancy, unyielding, declared she would not bend. Todd's patience waned. "Your only option," he said, "is the day shift." No compromise. The hotel's machinery required welloiled cogs, not rebels.

Nancy's resolve remained unshaken. "I will not work the day shift," she texted. Her pride, her stubbornness, all hung in the balance. Todd sighed. He had given her the ultimatum. She returned it with her own: quit or conform. Nancy's decision rippled through the ranks.

In the end, she quit, leaving them short staffed once again.

Then, a delicate dance of fate unfolded. One of the kitchen staff abruptly quit—a family emergency, a motorcycle accident involving a close relative. Todd faced another hiring challenge.

Amidst the chaos, Karly stepped forward. She volunteered for double duty: mornings in the kitchen, afternoons at the front desk. Her reasons were two fold: financial necessity and a looming eviction. Hurricane damage had made her apartment uninhabitable. Her insurance covered hotel stay was about to expire.

Todd, recognizing her determination, granted permission. She juggled aprons and key cards, her footsteps echoing through the corridors.

Days turned into weeks. Karly became a fixture, a whirlwind of multitasking fueled by desperation and resilience. Todd found himself drawn into her story. She confided in him: impending homelessness, uncertainty. His heart softened.

He reached out to corporate, seeking an exception. Permission granted, three months of respite or until she found a permanent solution.

She moved into the hotel, a room of her own, a sanctuary amidst chaos. For now, she was safe.

Gabrielle sighed with relief. Karly's extra hours allowed Gabrielle to focus on her role. The hotel's machinery hummed smoothly thanks to Karly's sacrifice.

April arrived with a rare treat: Easter weekend off, the first holiday Gabrielle had fully enjoyed since joining the hotel. She and her husband embraced the season, attending the Easter Vigil at church.

The occasion was doubly special: they witnessed the OCIA class baptisms. The week leading up to the Vigil had been a whirlwind of masses and activities. Despite her sporadic attendance, Gabrielle was present when it truly mattered.

The Vigil unfolded beautifully, and this time, they exited the church much earlier than the year before. Divine intervention, perhaps granting them extra time for what came next.

Easter Sunday dawned. They decided to head to Sanibel Island, a place Gabrielle hadn't visited since the hurricane.

As they arrived, Gabrielle's heart sank. The damage remained visible, scars etched into the landscape. Guilt weighed heavily as they strolled the shoreline. They captured moments, sunlight casting a golden glow, waves lapping at their feet. Gabrielle shared them on social media: *I'm at the beach with my favorite peep.*

Amidst the sand and sea, Gabrielle confided in her husband. The OCIA class loomed again in the fall, but this time, Gabrielle hesitated. The guilt of missed classes gnawed at her. She had left him to shoulder the journey alone, and it weighed on her conscience.

His response surprised her. He understood. The OCIA path was a significant commitment. If Gabrielle chose not to continue, he wouldn't either.

Together, they resolved to explore other ways to serve their church community. They informed Rachel and Father Michael that their path would diverge.

A few weeks later, her husband's youngest son arrived for a visit. Work had taken him to Tampa, and after wrapping up business, he came to reconnect.

Gabrielle joined her husband on the trip to pick him up. On the way home, they stopped at a waterside restaurant near her hotel. The sun was setting. The three of them sat together, sharing stories and laughter. Conversations flowed effortlessly, punctuated by the gentle lapping of water against the dock.

Though work kept Gabrielle busy, she cherished the time they spent together. It wasn't about her, it was about family, the bond between father and son.

Each day, her husband and his son explored the city: historic streets, local markets, even a baseball game. Their laughter echoed in narrow alleys, memories stitched into the fabric of their connection.

In the evenings, they returned home, tired but content, plunging into the pool. The water embraced them, washing away the day's fatigue. Father and son, silhouetted against the twilight sky.

As the visit ended, her husband wore a mix of exhaustion and fulfillment. His son's departure left an emptiness, bittersweet but full of meaning.

A few weeks passed. Then came the call. Gabrielle's sister delivered the news: her stepsister had passed away. The gravity of the moment hung heavy. Her sister's voice trembled. She promised to keep Gabrielle informed about the funeral arrangements. Then came the question: would Gabrielle be coming home?

Gabrielle hesitated only briefly. She knew her mother would be disappointed if she didn't attend. Despite the short notice, Gabrielle assured her sister she had already planned to be there. It would be a swift trip: fly in, pay respects, fly out. But family mattered. She couldn't bear to miss the chance to say goodbye.

She shared the news with her husband. He surprised her: he would go with her. His unwavering support eased the burden of grief. Together, they prepared for the journey.

Later that evening, Gabrielle's mom called. Her voice wavered as she spoke about her stepsister's daughter, who was planning the funeral. The upcoming weekend was marked for the somber occasion.

Gabrielle adjusted her flight plans, ensuring she'd arrive in time to honor her stepsister's memory. "Quick in and out," she told her mom. Work commitments loomed. Her team was stretched thin. But her mom understood. "Thank you for coming," she said. "It means the world to us."

The next day at work, Gabrielle approached Todd. She explained the situation. Todd rearranged the schedule. They were short staffed in the kitchen, but a new hire had just stepped in. The timing was fortuitous. They would manage without her.

On their flight, her husband started a solemn conversation. His words carried weight, settling into the cabin air. He expressed his desire to prearrange their end of life services. He didn't want Gabrielle or his sons to bear the burden during a time of grief.

The catalyst: the loss of his oldest son, a wound that had never fully healed. He couldn't bear the thought of his youngest son facing similar stress when the time came. As they touched down, he resolved to act.

In town, he made a decisive call to Jeffrey. Their conversation was pragmatic but poignant. Her husband requested an appointment to discuss his final wishes, a prelude to the inevitable. Jeffrey understood. They would meet the following morning.

As the sun dipped below the horizon, her husband's determination stood as a testament to love and foresight. They would face the future with a plan, instructions etched in stone, ensuring that when the time came, their hearts could grieve without the added weight of logistical concerns. The morning appointment with Jeffrey would be a step toward peace.

During their stay in town, Gabrielle refrained from making plans with friends. The weight of impending events, the showing, the funeral, left little room for casual gatherings. Her husband understood. His focus was singular: to address the practical matters surrounding his own mortality.

As twilight settled over her mom's house, Gabrielle broached a delicate topic: the financial aspect of his prearranged funeral plan. His resolve extended beyond emotion. He wanted logistics in place. But how would they fund this solemn preparation?

Gabrielle proposed a solution: a home equity loan. Not just for the funeral plan but to breathe new life into their home. The exterior stood pristine, a testament to their care. But the interior remained untouched since move in day. It was time for transformation.

In her mind's eye, Gabrielle envisioned fresh closet inserts, a rejuvenated guest bathroom, and a canvas of new paint embracing every wall. Her husband agreed. But he added a layer of foresight: a cushion of extra cash, a safety net for the unforeseen. His directive was clear: investigate the loan. Gabrielle dove into research, navigating interest rates, terms, and possibilities.

The following morning, they rose early, sharing a quiet breakfast before their appointment with Jeffrey. The weight of their purpose hung in the air: to prearrange final affairs, to face the inevitable with practicality and grace. Her husband had suggested that Gabrielle consider a preplan too. But her response was firm: her work place life insurance would suffice.

As they stepped into the funeral home, Jeffrey awaited them, a blend of professionalism and warmth. His handshake conveyed sympathy and resolve. His quick hug bridged formality and familiarity. The meeting room welcomed them again.

Before the formalities began, her husband excused himself to the restroom. Gabrielle and Jeffrey sat in silence. The room seemed to hold its breath. Gabrielle grappled with her emotions. Jeffrey had yet to accept her friend request. Bitterness flickered. She wanted to address it, but this was about her husband's peace of mind. She sat quietly, her phone a refuge.

Jeffrey, sensing her unease, inquired about her husband's well being. Gabrielle defected, waiting for his return. When he returned, Gabrielle pocketed her phone, ready to engage. Jeffrey's curiosity lingered. "Why the change of heart?"

Her husband's answer was succinct: "peace of mind." Jeffrey's gaze shifted to Gabrielle, a silent query. Why hadn't she shared this earlier? Gabrielle shrugged, unwilling to delve into personal dynamics.

Her husband's revelation surprised Jeffrey. Why hadn't he invited him for breakfast to discuss the plan? The oversight was acknowledged. They agreed it could've been a valuable conversation.

Their purpose for being in town, her stepsister's passing, was explained. Jeffrey offered condolences, bridging the gap between duty and empathy.

The conversation turned to specifics. Her husband expressed his desire to complete and pay for arrangements. Gabrielle's life insurance was considered sufficient. In the unlikely event of simultaneous loss, her husband's wishes would guide her path.

Jeffrey excused himself, returning with paperwork. Notes were taken. Prices calculated, a dance of practicality amidst echoes of mortality. Jeffrey laid out the logistics, costs, coordination between states. He would collaborate with a Florida funeral home to ensure a seamless transition. He emphasized that when the time came, Gabrielle would need to contact him. He would manage the transfer but cautioned about potential cost fluctuations. Her husband nodded, understanding the gravity.

As the conversation closed, Jeffrey presented the final bill. Her husband promised to mail a check once they returned to Florida. Jeffrey assured them upon receipt, everything would be documented, policies written, sealed, and mailed. "This has given me some peace of mind," her husband confessed.

After the arrangements, Jeffrey and her husband slipped into conversation, a reunion between old friends. Church, OCIA, familiar faces. A longing lingered. St. Michael held a special place in their hearts. Distance had severed ties. Jeffrey smiled. St. Michael's was now his parish too. The threads of coincidence pulled tight.

The conversation shifted. Their home, once a canvas of repairs, now stood complete. Jeffrey admired the colors, hues of renewal and resilience.

Then, an unexpected twist: Jeffrey's upcoming trip to Florida. He promised to visit. Her husband's eyes sparkled. Gabrielle felt a flicker of surprise. Was it genuine or polite fiction? She chuckled inwardly. Promises made in passing often dissolve.

Twenty minutes of small talk. Jeffrey excused himself. His day off had been sacrificed for their peace of mind. Her husband apologized. Jeffrey waved it away.

At the front door, under framed memories, Jeffrey clasped her husband's hand, a handshake of shared purpose. A half hearted hug for Gabrielle, a bridge between acquaintances. His parting words promised future conversations.

As the door closed, Gabrielle wondered: would the visit materialize or remain a whispered hope?

On the drive back to her mom's house, the weight of the conversation lingered. Gabrielle turned to her husband, curiosity tugging. She had researched online. Mortgage companies clamored.

Amid the cacophony, one voice stood out: the lady from Rocket Mortgage. Her warmth and efficiency convinced them. She gathered their details, promising to weave them into a financial tapestry. Credit checks, calculations, and the machinery of paperwork hummed to life.

During lunch, their phones buzzed once more. The lady's voice crackled through the line, a low rate, a lifeline to their plans. They expressed interest, but there was a caveat: they wouldn't be home until week's end. Undeterred, she assured them everything would be ready when they returned to Florida.

Her husband's emotions danced with excitement and reluctance. Mortgaging their home wasn't his preference, but the sum was modest, the payments manageable.

And then, a pragmatic twist: a little extra cash, tucked away for emergencies. His satisfaction settled over the decision, a bridge between practicality and peace of mind.

The remaining days of their visit were cloaked in somber purpose, a tapestry woven from grief and shared memories. Gabrielle's side of the family gathered, drawn together by the rhythm of a showing and funeral for her stepsister. The hours stretched long, yet Gabrielle felt quiet gratitude for being present during those poignant moments.

Amidst the sea of familiar faces, one stood out, the high school boyfriend her stepsister had once loved. He had been Gabrielle's favorite among her many suitors, a beacon of kindness and stability. As Gabrielle observed him, she couldn't help but wonder: *What if she had chosen differently? What if she had stayed with him, married him?*

His unwavering goodness still radiated, a testament to paths untaken. Gabrielle discovered he still maintained a connection with her mom, inquiring about her stepsister, a thread linking their shared history.

And in those moments, Gabrielle glimpsed an alternative reality, a life where she walked alongside this steadfast man, perhaps finding fulfillment and joy.

But life had other plans. Her first husband, a shadowy figure from childhood, met a tragic end: suicide. The reasons remained shrouded, lost in the fog of youth. Her mom hinted at legal troubles, impending imprisonment. Her stepsister had left him, but the "why" remained elusive.

A second marriage followed, a tumultuous union with a drunkard and druggy. His presence at the showing and funeral felt like a discordant note, a dissonance in the symphony of grief. Yet people cope in their own ways. Gabrielle steered clear, focusing instead on her children. Their faces held traces of her spirit. In their eyes, Gabrielle glimpsed resilience.

After the farewell, Gabrielle and her husband boarded a plane bound for Florida. Before leaving, her husband had a candid conversation with her mom. The truth hung heavy: the holiday might pass without their return. Two funerals in a single year had etched sorrow into their calendar, leaving little room for festive reunions. Her mom, though disappointed, offered understanding.

As the wheels touched down on familiar soil, Gabrielle transitioned from grief to routine. Work awaited, its demands unyielding. Vacation time had been cashed out earlier in the year, a practical decision by Allen.

Her husband's voice echoed in her mind: "Missing work is a luxury we can't afford." So, without pause, Gabrielle stepped off the plane and into the rhythm of responsibilities, a testament to resilience, a quiet nod to life's unwavering march.

The Claim and the Canvas

"Enlarge the place of your tent. . . stretch your tent curtains wide."

—Isaiah 54:2

Stability tiptoed back into Gabrielle's hotel, but the front desk remained a revolving door. She oscillated between paperwork and guest greetings, a dance she knew too well.

Todd promised reinforcements. "Soon," he said, but weeks passed. A new kitchen hire quit after a week. Gabrielle and Karly moonlighted as culinary understudies.

Then Elissa departed on maternity leave, leaving Gabrielle the lone daylight sentinel. Todd pitched in for three days, a gesture of solidarity. May arrived with a fragile semblance of normalcy, but the strain lingered.

At home, a parallel drama unfolded. Gabrielle's home equity loan hit a snag: a contractor's lien lurked like a shadow. Her husband's fury ignited. Calls flew, voices clashed. Florida's lien laws offered little solace.

Days later, the lien vanished. The loan process resumed, unlocking dreams of transformation: fresh paint, closet inserts, and king sized comfort for the guest rooms.

But friction flared. Her husband balked at her plans. Gabrielle's patience snapped. "I work tirelessly," she declared. "Now it's my turn." She stormed out, returned calmer, and by dawn, a truce was forged.

Furniture vanished online, making way for Gabrielle's vision. She painted walls in serene hues, curated gray and blue accents, and summoned her husband for assembly duty. His grumbles faded into grudging admiration: "It looks nice." A compromise emerged: the second guest room would remain untouched. But Gabrielle's ambition persisted. She transformed it into a baseball haven, a shrine to the Yankees, all under $200. Her husband softened.

Then came the big leap: a guest bathroom remodel for her mom's mobility needs. The tub bowed out; a walkin shower took center stage. Simultaneously, Gabrielle gifted her husband a garage floor makeover, a nod to his love for polished concrete.

June became a symphony of drills and paint brushes. By month's end, their home stood reborn. "We have a brand new house," her husband marveled, pride eclipsing past protests. Gabrielle chuckled. For all his grumbling and griping, he wore his contentment like a badge of honor.

Back at work, Todd hired Emma for night audit. Within three weeks, anxiety unraveled her resolve. She quit, leaving Gabrielle tethered to the 2:00 p.m. to 10:00 p.m. shift.

Relief arrived in July: Elissa returned post maternity, Charlie post-surgery. The front desk exhaled.

But whispers of a new resort rippled through the ranks. Its GM, a shadowy figure who had lingered for years during construction, poached staff with promises of greener pastures.

Elissa succumbed, despite Todd's counter offer of a raise and Sundays off. Gabrielle bore the brunt, covering weekends, simmering with quiet discontent.

Todd was incensed. He cornered Gabrielle, his frustration palpable. "We can't let this happen," he declared. "That resort manager is poaching our staff like a hungry fox in a hen house."

Gabrielle nodded. "Kicking him out would create a scandal," she cautioned. "Bad for business." Todd grumbled but agreed.

Meanwhile, Gabrielle waged her own battle. She reminded Todd that Elissa's departure would leave them short staffed again. "We need another front desk person," she urged. "Proactive hiring, remember?"

He nodded, promising to work his magic. But Gabrielle knew better. His efforts would be half hearted. Week after week, she pestered him.

One tranquil evening, in the sanctuary of her home, a restlessness enveloped Gabrielle. With no agenda to occupy her, she reached for her social media feed. It had been ages since she indulged in the virtual dance of updates and anecdotes.

As she scrolled, she reconnected with the tapestry of lives that continued to weave in her absence. Amidst the casual perusal, a thought of

Jeffrey fluttered in. Their recent encounters had been amicable, yet he stayed absent from her circle of online companions.

Driven by curiosity, Gabrielle glanced through her husband's account—he was a social media friend of Jeffrey. And there it was: Jeffrey's declaration of newfound love. His heart now intertwined with a colleague.

A tempest of sorrow surged. Tears burgeoned, threatening to breach their dams. The man who once professed a life too full for Gabrielle, an ex-wife, children, a business, now paraded his affection for another. *Why?* The word escaped her lips, a fragile murmur lost in the silence. The query haunted her as tears cascaded freely.

Gabrielle closed the portal of her husband's social media, her heart fracturing with the realization: Jeffrey's desire for solitude was a cloak. His heart's chambers closed only to her. She knew then he would never accept her friend request, not now, not with a new found love.

In the sanctity of solitude, Gabrielle chose not to unveil this wound. The words remained prisoners to her grief.

That night, she turned her gaze heavenward. In whispered prayers, she sought understanding from the Divine. Why did he not want her, not even as a friend? Why was she not good enough?

Back at the hotel, the office hummed with peculiar energy. The new resort had become the talk of the water cooler. Employees huddled in corners, sharing secrets.

At the heart of it all stood the resort's general manager, a shadowy figure moving through their ranks. He lured staff with promises. They whispered of job offers, of greener pastures. Gabrielle, too, had heard the siren song. But she harbored no illusions.

One afternoon, she donned her armor of honesty and embarked on a mission to dispel the myth. Each employee who approached her received the unvarnished truth. "The grass," Gabrielle declared, "is not greener—it's merely wider."

The resort was a behemoth compared to their cozy hotel. Most of her colleagues, accustomed to gentle rhythms, would flounder there. Attendance and punctuality issues, once overlooked by lenient Todd, would now be counted against them.

Gabrielle delivered her message individually. "Choose your path," she advised, "but spare me the resort's tales. My loyalty lies here, within these walls."

Gabrielle became the oracle of the office, her desk a confessional booth. Colleagues came seeking clarity, and she offered it without illusion, without agenda.

The resort's GM, a man Gabrielle had come to know during her 2:00 p.m. to 10:00 p.m. shifts, watched their interactions with keen interest. They exchanged pleasantries, discussed the resort's progress, and navigated the stormy seas of hospitality.

Covid19 and hurricanes had conspired against the resort's grand opening. Gabrielle knew their names, their positions. The resort's hierarchy unfolded before her. The GM had taken note of her ascent within their hotel. Her promotion earlier in the year had not escaped his attention.

Then came the inevitable conversation, the one Gabrielle had predicted. As twilight painted the sky, he cornered her. "You," he said, "are an enigma. Your honesty, your rapport with guests commendable."

Gabrielle nodded, her shield raised. "But," he continued, "I will not pitch you a position at the resort. Not now, not ever."

His words surprised her. "Why?" she asked.

"Because," he confessed, "I respect your loyalty. You are a rare breed, loyal to your post. Others," he gestured vaguely, "are free to choose their path. But you, you are a keeper. I will not insult you with an offer."

They left it at that, an unspoken truce hanging in the air. Gabrielle returned to her desk, the whispers of the resort fading. The battle for loyalty raged on, but Gabrielle stood firm, a sentinel guarding the hotel's heart.

At the close of July, the lobby buzzed with anticipation. Todd had been quietly considering promoting Karly to assistant GM. But there was a catch: Karla needed to untangle her personal affairs and move out of the hotel. It was nonnegotiable.

As the days ticked away, Karly sorted her finances, packed her belongings, and bid farewell to the room that had been both residence and refuge. Todd's stipulation had been met. She was ready to ascend.

Yet a curious shift occurred. Her once-abundant hours began to dwindle. The kitchen ran smoothly. Her front desk shifts were well managed. She now had two days off each week. But discontent simmered. Rather than approach Todd directly, Karly sought solace in colleagues, late night conversations, hushed tones in the breakroom.

It was during one such exchange that Travis, a seasoned veteran who had once held the assistant GM title elsewhere, offered advice: "Put it in writing." Todd's open door policy was legendary. Anyone could stride into his office unannounced.

Yet Karly hesitated. She feared her concerns would be dismissed if spoken aloud. Instead, she chose the digital route, an extensive email dissecting every nuance of her experience.

Todd poured over the missive, seeking Gabrielle's opinion as the unofficial second in command. Her grievances spilled forth: she felt burdened, a lone sentinel at the front desk while her peers shirked their duties.

Her 2:00 p.m. to 10:00 p.m. shift revolved around checkins, stocking the market, tending to guests.

In the quiet of the market's storage area, she had wept, overwhelmed by the relentless demands. Attempts to rally her colleagues were ignored. They saw her as an equal, bound by the same nondescript title. Their indifference stung.

Gabrielle couldn't help but find the email amusing. It felt theatrical, Travis's influence unmistakable. Todd saw the humor too but recognized the issue. If Karly couldn't approach him directly, how could she navigate the complexities of leadership?

Todd summoned her to his office. Gabrielle sat as a silent witness. "Why an email?" he asked. Her response echoed vulnerability: she doubted her words would carry weight face to face.

Todd challenged her: "What about when you hold the title? Will it be different then?" She hesitated, realizing titles alone wouldn't bridge the communication gap. His verdict was clear: titles mattered less than open dialogue. His door remained ajar, a gateway to understanding. She agreed: no more emails. If issues arose, she would speak.

Todd leaned back, the email displayed on his screen. "Let's address this," he said. He outlined the 2:00 p.m. to 10:00 p.m. shift, Karly's domain. A delicate dance: checkins, guest needs, market upkeep. Other shifts bore different responsibilities, subtle variations shaping the hotel's rhythm. Karly nodded, acknowledging the nuances.

Yet her frustration simmered. Her peers, in her eyes, were lackadaisical. They flitted through duties, leaving her to pick up the slack. She yearned to correct them, to rally them toward excellence.

But there lay the crux: titles. She shared the same nondescript title, rendering her pleas impotent. Todd sought specifics. "What are they not doing?" he asked. If warranted, he promised to address it. Her response was lament: "They're lazy. They don't work as hard as I do."

The words hung in the air. His verdict was swift: the assistant GM position would remain elusive until the New Year. No one at the front desk had tenure except Gabrielle, the seasoned observer, keeper of rhythm and memory.

Todd's plan unfolded: two front desk supervisors would appear, and from their ranks, the assistant GM would rise. October would be the crucible, the moment of reckoning. "But," he added, leaning forward, "do not fixate on their shortcomings. Their work, or lack thereof, is their reflection, not yours."

Wisdom wrapped in practicality. Karly's gaze shifted to the book on his desk, its cover a beacon of hospitality philosophy: "Yes is the answer." A manifesto of solutions, a roadmap through the labyrinth of guest requests. No more "no," only possibilities.

As the meeting drew to a close, Todd turned to Gabrielle. "Anything to add?" Gabrielle echoed his sentiment. Their doors stood open. Issues were not burdens to bear alone. They were a triad now: Todd, Karly, and Gabrielle, woven together by shared purpose and the promise of growth.

After Karly left, Todd invited Gabrielle to step outside, where conversation could unfurl without prying ears. His furrowed brow betrayed the gravity. Gabrielle couldn't resist. "You know," she began, "You should've slipped her a different kind of manual. *How to Win Friends and Influence People.*"

Her tone was wry. Karly's email manifesto hadn't quite cut it. Todd chuckled, but his eyes held concern. "More than meets the eye," he murmured. In her years navigating hotel corridors, Gabrielle had met the whisperers, those who spun tales in shadowed corners. She, too, had likely been the subject of whispered discontent.

"She's using this place as more than a paycheck," Gabrielle confided. "It's a refuge, a temporary haven. But now that she's flown the hotel's nest, her hunger has shifted. It's not about sustenance anymore; it's about titles and zeroes."

Once, she'd been an eager recruit, fueled by zeal and the desire to prove herself. Now, her eyes held a different hunger. "She won't wait," Gabrielle predicted. "Not for the New Year. Not for October. She wants it now: title, authority, the whole shebang."

She had hesitated to walk into Todd's office, opting for the safety of an email. But secrets have a way of seeping through cracks. "Confidentiality?" Gabrielle mused. "She'll spill it all: secrets, strategies. She's a loose thread in the fabric of trust."

Todd's jaw tightened. He knew the stakes. "Can we salvage her?" he asked.

Gabrielle met his gaze, unyielding. "She's a tempest," she replied. "A whirlwind of drama and discontent. You don't need that headache."

His disappointment was palpable. But truth has its own gravity. Some souls are worth saving. Others are best left to drift. Todd squared his shoulders, resolved. Karly's fate hung in the balance.

The office clock ticked past closing time. Todd's footsteps echoed down the corridor, leaving behind a trail of decisions. Karly sought Gabrielle out. The bartender had yet to arrive.

It was just the two of them, the remnants of the day's hustle. She didn't mince words. "October," she spat, frustration palpable. "And then the first of the year? It's a lifetime away."

Todd's timeline had ignited a fire. But Gabrielle leaned back, gaze steady. "His hotel," she reminded her. "His rules." Her grievances flowed. The front desk's apathy gnawed at her. "Lazy," she muttered. "They don't care like I do."

Elissa's impending departure loomed. Gabrielle listened, but she knew better. It wasn't about them. It was about her, the resort's hours aligning with her needs.

Then the revelation: the resort's gravitational pull. Charlie, fresh from surgery. Travis. They would all be swept away. Their ranks would be thin. Short staffed once more. "Your chance," Gabrielle offered, "to climb the ladder. Time in position is the invisible currency."

But Karly's retort was sharp: "Not training anyone new without more money and a title." Gabrielle raised an eyebrow. "Guess training's off the menu," she quipped. "Assuming they're not quitting."

Her metamorphosis weighed on Gabrielle, the girl who once embraced the hotel's pulse, now a creature of discontent. "Remember who you were," Gabrielle urged. "Before moving out of the hotel."

Her eyes flickered, a memory of zeal, of purpose. But now? The job was a means to an end. A roof. A paycheck. Todd's support, or lack thereof, gnawed at her. "Correct them," she pleaded. "They're lazy."

She painted vivid portraits of desk transgressions: night auditors dozing off, market neglect. Gabrielle leaned forward, voice low. "Your shift," she emphasized. "Your responsibility." Todd would discern the truth. Disciplinary action, if called for, would follow.

"Not your job," Gabrielle added, "to fix them." Karly sighed, defeated. Gabrielle's refusal to echo her complaints had sealed her fate.

As the bartender arrived, she shifted her focus, leaving Gabrielle to her thoughts. Karly would either rise or fade into the hotel's tapestry.

A few days later, Todd's office bore witness to Karly's latest gambit: a note, neatly typed, sealed in an envelope. Todd recognized her handwriting. He beckoned Gabrielle to his sanctum. The envelope lay unopened, its secrets suspended in time. "Did I not tell her?" he muttered.

Gabrielle tore the seal, revealing her plea: stability, days off etched in stone, a lifeline to pay her bills. The hotel's wages, it seemed, fell short of life demands.

But Gabrielle knew her game, the chessboard of promotion, the currency of discontent. Her note was a challenge, a gauntlet thrown at Todd's feet. He chuckled, amused yet unimpressed. "Failed attempt," he declared. "Pissed me off."

His verdict was swift: Gabrielle would address her needs, weave her schedule as she desired. Promotions? More money? Not on the horizon. And no more notes, only face to face conversations. His anger still smoldered. He had spared her the confrontation.

Gabrielle beckoned Karly to her office, eyes wary. "Your schedule," Gabrielle began. "Let's make it work." Mondays and Tuesdays off, 2:00 p.m. to 10:00 p.m. the rest.

Her interviews loomed, a lifeline beyond the hotel's walls. Mondays and Tuesdays, the hotel's crescendo. Checkins surged, guests bustling through the lobby.

She thought she was slick. Gabrielle played along. "We'll manage," she assured. "No worries." Her annoyance prickled. Gabrielle's indifference, a thorn. But Gabrielle had no qualms. Her path was hers to tread.

Then came the refrain: "More money," Karly murmured. "Promotion." Gabrielle met her gaze, unyielding. "Talk to Todd," she urged. "In person." Her discomfort surfaced, a fear of not being taken seriously.

Gabrielle posed the question: "Assistant GM, emails and notes, or face to face? Karly's silence spoke volumes. "Trust," Gabrielle murmured. "Confidentiality." Todd needed an assistant GM who could navigate the labyrinth of decisions not through notes but through heart to heart conversations.

Gabrielle leaned across her desk, voice low. "Sit down with him," she urged. "Unfiltered."

Karly's discomfort deepened. "He makes me feel incompetent," she confessed. Gabrielle nodded. Todd's stern demeanor could be daunting.

But this was her crucible. "Make a list," Gabrielle advised. "Only about you. Your grievances, your dreams, etched in ink."

"Adult workplace," Gabrielle emphasized. "Communication matters." Karly's eyes widened. "Threats won't work," Gabrielle continued. "He won't yield. Todd is no pawn in your game."

Karly sighed, defeated. She echoed, "Resolve our differences."

Gabrielle nodded. "Only you," she reminded her. "Not the others." The hotel's fate rested on her ability to bridge the gap. "I don't want you to quit," Gabrielle said. "But you must find your voice."

The next day dawned, laden with unspoken tension. Gabrielle had relayed their conversation to Todd, a prelude to Karly's arrival. But when Karly swept through the lobby, her gaze averted, she bypassed his office. No hello. No acknowledgment. Just a blur of purpose.

Todd stepped forward. "Schedule," he broached. "Did it work out?"

She nodded, curt. Bills loomed, their shadows stretching across her path. "Second job," she murmured. "Necessary."

His patience waned. "In person," he insisted. "No more notes." Todd's door was a threshold, an invitation to dialogue. But she hesitated. Her fear palpable. "Intimidated," she confessed.

"Heart-to-heart," Gabrielle had advised. "Only about you."

But she faltered. Her voice a whisper. "Fine," she replied. "Everything is fine." As Todd retreated, his anger simmered. Gabrielle approached her. "Why?" she asked. "Why not talk to him?"

Her eyes held uncertainty. "Nerve," she admitted. "Fear." Gabrielle sighed, her patience thinning. "Your choice," she said. "Promotion or silence."

Two weeks slipped by. Karly would glide into the hotel, steps purposeful, head straight for the front desk. Todd would appear. Their conversations clipped, arrivals, information, and little else.

But she craved dialogue, sought solace in whispers. The corridors buzzed with her grievances. Everyone had advice. "Talk to Todd," they chorused. "He holds the keys."

But when she realized that her allies were few, she retreated. The front desk staff faded. Only Travis stayed. One on one," he urged. "With Todd." She hesitated. Her fear of inadequacy, a chasm. Todd, too, grew weary, a puppet master tired of petty games.

Then came the schedule, a delicate dance of days off. The hotel's pulse slowed. The quietest season. Todd rotated the days, granting three instead of two. But her fury simmered.

She stormed into his office, demanding answers. "Next week," he explained. "Someone else." Her rage echoed through the halls. The hotel across the street, a tantalizing escape. She whispered about her plans, her voice a tempest.

But fate played its hand. The job fell through. Instead, the power company beckoned, a company vehicle, door to door surveys, up to $30 an hour. Four days a week, perhaps six, with overtime. Todd, unaware, continued his duties, the hotel's guardian, blind to her shifting allegiances.

The corridors whispered secrets. Karly's hasty exit, a crescendo of frustration and ambition. Gabrielle had congratulated her, wished her luck. But uncertainty lingered. The drug test, a hurdle she hoped to clear. Her admission: pot smoker. It confirmed Gabrielle's suspicions. Gabrielle offered a nod, her well wishes trailing.

The next day, Karly approached Todd, a sealed notice in hand. Her two weeks' notice, a formal declaration of independence. Todd accepted it. "Commit," he urged. "Work your scheduled shifts."

But Gabrielle knew better. Her resolve was brittle. The hotel's rhythm shifted. Her days were numbered. And then, the unraveling, a midweek departure. She left her uniforms, her frustration palpable.

Travis, a witness to her exit, received her final words. "Done," she declared. "No more."

Todd, blindsided, received the news via text, confirmation of Gabrielle's foresight. "You were right," he admitted. "Should have listened." The 2:00 p.m. to 10:00 p.m. shift became Gabrielle's burden once more.

After quitting, Karly entered the hotel's message system, a platform accessible to all. She composed an extensive note, candid and raw. Her feelings spilled forth: frustration, regret, and a claim that her departure was not entirely voluntary.

She recounted instances where she felt overlooked, unfairly judged. The crux of her complaint: Todd. She accused him of neglecting responsibilities, creating a less than ideal work environment. She did not hold back specific incidents, pointed examples. Her words resonated with colleagues who had felt similarly.

Then, a bold step: she posted her message on the hotel's internal board. Visible to all night shift, morning arrivals. As dawn broke, employees huddled around screens, reading her impassioned plea for fairness and accountability. Swift action followed.

Todd, alerted, removed the post and revoked her access credentials. Gabrielle missed the initial commotion. She was working the middle shift. But coworkers shared screenshots. Phones buzzed with fragments of Karly's message.

As Gabrielle read, a suspicion gnawed at her. Could she have had help crafting such a detailed, eloquent note? Her mind settled on Travis, an astute observer, likely witness to the same managerial lapses. Yet without proof, Gabrielle chose not to pursue it.

Instead, she discreetly informed Todd of her lingering doubts, leaving the rest to the hotel's internal dynamics. Karly's note had ignited a spark. Whether it would fizzle or ignite a larger flame remained uncertain.

August arrived. Gabrielle found herself ensconced once again in the familiar rhythm of the 2:00 p.m. to 10:00 p.m. shift. Todd embarked on a quest to find a replacement.

After diligent search, he unearthed a candidate, a seasoned professional from another property in the company. She hailed from New Jersey. Her arrival was eagerly anticipated. But there was a catch: she couldn't begin until after Labor Day.

Gabrielle's reaction: acceptance, tinged with mild discontent. She understood the gap, but reservations lingered. The front desk had been perpetually under staffed for her entire year and a half. The revolving door of personnel had become a disconcerting norm. Gabrielle yearned for stability.

Yet, as days unfolded, she discovered a silver lining in her twilight hours. The 2:00 p.m. to 10:00 p.m. shift bestowed a unique vantage point, an opportunity to interact with the hotel's regular guests.

Familiar faces, their stories etched into the fabric of the establishment, graced the lobby each afternoon. Gabrielle reveled in the art of welcome, a rhythm of recognition and warmth.

Then there was Charlie. Returned from knee surgery, his presence a quiet testament to resilience. Initially, Gabrielle had harbored doubts.

But as weeks passed, her skepticism waned. He navigated the front desk with newfound precision, managing inquiries, overseeing administrative tasks with calm competence. His reliability was unwavering. No sick calls. Only absences during recovery.

What surprised her most was the shift in perception. Beneath professional camaraderie, Gabrielle found herself appreciating his work ethic. His diligence transcended duty, a quiet commitment to the team, a thread that bound them into the transient world of hospitality.

It was the end of August, and the air buzzed with the tension of an impending hurricane. Unlike the ferocious gale that had besieged them the previous September, this one promised a deluge rather than devastation. Yet caution draped the city.

On the eve of the expected maelstrom, Gabrielle savored a day of reprieve when her phone chimed with a message from Todd. He urged her to seek refuge in the hotel, not out of fear but foresight. The tempest might unleash its fury, and he wanted all hands safe and near should the storm turn vile.

At first, Gabrielle clung to stubborn resolve. She assured him she would brave the morrow and arrive as duty called. But in the quiet sanctuary of home, her husband's wise counsel swayed her. He painted a picture of roads turned rivers, where her beloved Mustang might falter against the relentless rain. So, with a bag hastily packed, he ferried her to the hotel for the days ahead.

There was Gabrielle, Charlie and his family, Todd, and the assistant housekeeper, Karen, who slipped in under the cloak of night. The rest of their colleagues chose to dance with uncertainty, waiting for the storm's hand to be revealed.

Duty beckoned at dawn's light, from 8:00 a.m. to 4:00 p.m. Gabrielle settled into her quarters, unpacked the essentials, and let the lull of television wash over her.

Outside, the rain began its tentative symphony: a whisper, not yet a roar.

Dawn crept through the curtains. Gabrielle awoke to the scent of rain, readied herself, and by 7:30 a.m., descended toward the hotel's public area. She expected breakfast and a phone call with her husband. But the elevator doors parted onto a scene of concern. Guests and staff huddled on the back steps, their gazes locked on the world beyond.

The breakfast attendant's voice was urgent. She painted a grim portrait: streets transformed into rivers, the city held in watery grasp. She recounted her own harrowing journey, a testament to the storm's might.

Then came Travis's tale, his car besieged by rising waters, windows barely holding. In a desperate bid, he braved the deluge, steered to higher ground, and used kitchen buckets to bail out the flood.

Elissa called from a block away, her voice strained. Her car was trapped, awaiting rescue from family.

Tammy appeared next, her vehicle abandoned at a car wash. She had braved the elements on foot, a testament to indomitable spirit.

Gabrielle peered out to see a transformed cityscape. Downtown lay dormant under a blanket of floodwater. Gratitude filled her; her Mustang would've stood no chance. She reached out to her husband. He, safe at home, spoke of rain but no floods. Gabrielle sent him visual echoes of the watery siege, promising to call later.

Replacing Travis, who wisely chose sanctuary, Gabrielle stepped into the fray. Todd arrived at 8:15 a.m. Gabrielle relayed Elissa's plight.

Tammy approached with news of her stranded team and her own trek through the storm.

A call to Elissa revealed she had retreated home. Gabrielle's frustration surged. Tammy had walked. Elissa was a block away. Gabrielle's words flowed, a torrent of disappointment, stemmed only by Todd's cautionary hand. He understood her ire. Elissa was one he hoped to keep against the lure of the new resort.

The hotel stood as an island amidst chaos. Tammy was a solitary soldier on the battlefield of bedspreads and bathrooms. None of her housekeepers made it in. Karen had disappeared during the night, retreating to her own home.

Tammy's distress was palpable, a storm within a storm. The skeleton crew: Gabrielle, Todd, Tammy, and a lone kitchen warrior.

Gabrielle stepped into the breach, trading her usual post for the frontlines of housekeeping. Todd manned the front desk. Charlie, though lodged within the hotel, embarked on a quest for McDonald's and vanished into the flood. Todd extended a plea for an early return. But fate had other plans. The clock ticked on without him.

The day unfolded, a comedy of errors. Gabrielle became an artisan of linen, a steward of the spotless, her hands moving with necessity's rhythm.

The kitchen lady declared her intent to flee once her shift ended. Guests fled the flood, vacancies soared, carving out pockets of respite. Yet some, trapped by nature's whim, extended their stays, unwitting allies in the quest for order.

By 4:00 p.m., exhaustion was Gabrielle's shadow. Todd deemed the remaining rooms off limits for the night. Relief washed over her. Charlie, true to his timetable, appeared at 2:00 p.m., not a moment sooner. Gabrielle's frustration simmered.

The day's end brought small comforts: a meal from Todd, words of gratitude that soothed the rough edges.

Yet as they dined, Gabrielle unleashed a torrent of words about the absentees, those who shunned the call to arms despite Todd's offer of shelter. Especially Karen, who had a room but vacated before the storm hit, leaving her post in housekeeping.

He spoke of new beginnings: a fresh face set to join the desk, and a pivotal offer to Elissa, assistant GM, a title dangled before her indecision.

But the day's events had cast doubt upon her worthiness, a sentiment Gabrielle echoed with fervor. Todd held onto hope. Gabrielle wondered if the trials of that day would finally tip the scales.

As twilight draped the day, the waters began their retreat, relinquishing their hold on the streets that cradled their hotel. The world outside, once a canvas of nature's fury, returned to its familiar form, a serene painting restored.

Within the hotel's walls, the echoes of the day's tumult still resonated in her bones. The role of housekeeper, an unexpected performance, had demanded every ounce of her vigor.

Gabrielle chose sanctuary over the journey home. The hotel offered quiet reprieve for another night. A call to her husband carried the promise of reunion. She assured him that after the next day's duties, she would return to the warmth of their hearth and home.

With the curtain falling, Gabrielle surrendered to slumber's embrace. Her room became a cocoon. In its solace, she found respite.

That night, the realm of dreams summoned the image of Jeffrey. An unexpected visitation within the sanctum of her slumber, to the very heart of her home.

There he was, seated across from her at the dining room table, an emblem of camaraderie and kinship. This table, a gathering place for friends and family, now hosted a man who had reserved no nook within his heart for her.

With the weight of unspoken words, Gabrielle mustered the courage. "Jeffrey," she began, her voice steady, laden with years of unshed emotion. "Why grace us with your presence now? What wind has carried you to this table of fellowship, to this circle of trust you've so long denied me?"

Her questions poured forth, testaments to the ache of exclusion. "Why have I not been a friend in your eyes? What lacking within me has rendered me unworthy to step into the tapestry of your life?"

His eyes met hers, a flicker of silent understanding. He stood on the precipice of revelation. But before words could traverse the chasm, reality intruded—a cacophony of hallway sounds jolted Gabrielle awake.

And just like the countless times in the waking world, she was left bereft of his response. The silence echoed louder than any spoken truth.

As September dawned, golden and humid, they welcomed a new face to the front desk. Leslie, expanding their team to a quartet of customer service maestros. Yet the wind of change stirred. One of their own was soon to embark on a new adventure at the resort. Their harmonious ensemble would soon be a trio once more.

The resort, a beacon of leisure, faced its own trials. Relentless rains delayed its grand unveiling. Amidst the turmoil, they found solace in the hope of one more month intact. Todd was poised to recruit before Elissa's departure, her final day still shrouded in mystery.

Leslie brought with her a treasure trove of hospitality experience. Her initiation was a breeze. Only the intricacies of their system remained to master. She was poised to welcome travelers from near and far.

During her tutelage, Travis expressed a yearning for daylight responsibilities. He aspired to ascend as Todd's right hand.

Gabrielle pondered his motives; he had been the guardian of their nights for many moons. Todd sought to test the water. A collaborative trial before any crowning. Travis traded midnight soliloquies for bustling afternoons, guiding Leslie through the 2:00 p.m. to 10:00 p.m. ballets of checkins and farewells.

But fate wove a tangled web. Travis's schedule faltered, tardiness, renewed pleas for advancement. Todd insisted on further collaboration. The decree stirred discontent.

Travis resigned, a chess move masked by an offer from the resort. In his final act, he donned a cloak of dissent, sowing seeds of discord and dreams of resort grandeur. His campaign was short lived.

Gabrielle's birthday journey with her beloved shielded her from the tempest. For her birthday, Gabrielle and her husband escaped the mundane: a casino adventure, a day of chance and anticipation. Slot machines jingled, cards shuffled, but fortune withheld its smile.

Seeking solace, they retreated to a quaint hotel. Dinner was a celebration. Tacos and Tequila, where flavors danced and laughter flowed as freely as the drinks.

Later, a rustic biker bar, a haven for dart enthusiasts. Gabrielle's competitive spirit soared. Victory after victory, her husband's pride lovingly bruised.

They returned to their hotel, hearts full, bodies weary. Gabrielle craved ice cream, a sweet companion to left over birthday cake. Together, they wandered the halls, a whimsical quest for dessert.

Then, the unexpected: his phone buzzed. A voicemail from Jeffrey. Her husband's casual interaction with the man who had once closed his heart to her stirred a tempest within.

As he dialed, Jeffrey's voice filled the room, easy conversation, mundane updates, a birthday wish relayed through her husband. Gabrielle sat silent, her cake and ice cream turning bittersweet.

She had sent Jeffrey a new friend request at 11:11 p.m. on September 1st: a prayer, a wish, that he would accept and send her a birthday message.

Now, on her birthday, he spoke to her husband instead. It wasn't the same. As sleep claimed her, tears carved silent rivers. She pondered the mysterious ways life unfolds.

Back at the hotel, Travis's departure had barely settled when the houseman erupted. At the 10:00 a.m. morning assembly, he declared the hotel toxic, a place of indifference, his efforts unnoticed. He called out the maintenance man, questioned his title, and with a final flourish, resigned on the spot.

Gabrielle, absent during the spectacle, arrived at 2:00 p.m. Surprise gripped her. His conduct was uncharacteristic, his disrespect unanticipated. Disappointment weighed heavy. Whispers revealed he had been in talks with Travis, an offer from the resort casting new light on his theatrical exit.

A calculated performance, emboldened by Travis's misleading narrative of dismissal rather than resignation. Gabrielle understood the context, but her respect for the houseman dimmed in the shadow of his final act.

In the days that followed, Todd welcomed a new face: Linda. A companion from the kitchen staff, recommended with confidence. After a thoughtful interview, Todd entrusted her with the 2:00 p.m. to 10:00 p.m. shift and night audit duties twice a week post training.

The ink had barely dried when another opportunity blossomed. Tina, a friend of Elissa's, was in search of employment. Motherhood dictated her hours; night audit was her only option.

Todd offered her the role, paired her with Charlie, the seasoned sentinel of the night. His mentorship would guide her through the quiet complexities of nocturnal hotel life.

Tina began her journey. Linda transitioned to daylight, training under the day shift's watchful eye. Leslie, freshly trained, was assigned the 2:00 p.m. to 10:00 p.m. shift, ready to spread her wings in the vibrant bustle of evening. The front desk, once a revolving door, now felt like a mosaic, new tiles settling into place.

Scarcely had the dust settled from the previous houseman's dramatic exit when, in a bold act of repetition, another seemed poised to follow suit. Inspired by his predecessor's brash departure, he attempted to orchestrate his own grand exit amidst the solemnity of the 10:00 a.m. meeting.

But Todd was swift. With a firm directive, he cut through the theatrics. "If resignation is your intent," he said, "then the stage is set for farewell today."

The houseman, undeterred, found solace and new prospects within the welcoming arms of the resort, joining forces with the one who had led the way. His absence was felt, not only in the rooms he tended but amidst the clatter of pots and pans where he had lent a hand.

Yet Todd, ever the conductor, filled the culinary void with a new hire who seamlessly stepped into the kitchen's rhythm.

The days marched on. Todd, in a flurry of recruitment, brought on board a houseman and a housekeeper. Their arrival heralded a return to equilibrium.

October became a symphony of training, a harmonious blend of instruction across the front desk, the kitchen, and the houseman corridors.

As the month waned, the promise of normalcy beckoned. Gabrielle found herself on the cusp of reclaiming her sales role, the Monday to Friday 8:00 a.m. to 4:00 p.m. schedule within tantalizing reach. The allure of weekends unfettered by work was a siren's call.

Yet fate, ever playful, turned the tides once more. Charlie, custodian of the night audit's secrets, cast his gaze toward the resort's distant shores. Lured by Travis's tales of camaraderie and the promise of becoming an indispensable ally in the nocturnal realm, he too contemplated departure.

But pragmatism anchored him. The resort's doors remained closed. His accrued vacation, a December promise, tethered him to his current post.

His proposal to Todd: part time allegiance to both hotel and resort, a dual existence to sustain financial necessity. Gabrielle, privy to the undercurrents, urged Todd to anticipate the inevitable, to seek a new guardian for the night audit. But Todd, swayed by immediate need, chose patience over action. Charlie remained, albeit, in a diminished position.

As November's autumnal leaves began their graceful descent, the hotel's staff found their rhythm. Each moved with confidence born of thorough training and newfound independence. Gabrielle reclaimed her niche within the sales domain. Her presence at the front desk became a rare cameo, reserved for days when the ranks thinned.

Leslie, the first of their recent hires, found her stride. She seamlessly wove between two morning shifts and three evenings from 2:00 p.m. to 10:00 p.m., her versatility a boon. Linda, her counterpart, dedicated her talents exclusively to the evening shift.

The night audit, once a duo, now saw Tina confidently holding the fort solo. Her training was complete, her rhythm steady. Charlie, her mentor, stepped in only on her days of rest, ensuring the night's watch remained unbroken.

In the kitchen, the plot took an unexpected turn. The young culinary artist, in a moment of impromptu decision, abandoned her post midshift. Her departure was swift, silent. Yet the impact was cushioned by their trio of breakfast attendants, their numbers sufficient to absorb the loss.

Fortune smiled again. The last of their new recruits revealed that providence had sent a friend her way, one in search of employment. With serendipity at play, this friend crossed the threshold the very same day.

Todd, sensing the alignment of fate and opportunity, extended an offer of immediate employment. Thus, the kitchen's brief interlude of want was resolved. Its hearth, once again, was fully staffed.

As the autumn leaves began to fall, the much anticipated resort opened its doors, making the hospitality scene abuzz. Farewells and new beginnings unfolded at the front desk.

Elissa handed in her notice, Todd clinging to a waning hope that she might stay. But the resort's allure proved stronger.

Charlie, once a fixture two days a week, sought to pare down his presence further, a single day at the hotel, the rest devoted to the resort's nocturnal realm. Todd accepted the compromise. Gabrielle, once more, became the guardian of the front desk as Todd searched for new anchors.

November's chill brought Tina's vacation, prompting a cascade of changes. Linda stepped into the night audit, a temporary arrangement that soon unraveled.

Tina returned, only to resign. Linda, too, found the night's solitude not suitable to her rhythm. The role was vacant again.

Todd's swift hiring of Denise, a seasoned hotelier, offered a glimmer of hope. But her preference for afternoons meant Gabrielle's nights were still spoken for.

Leslie, now the most tenured, requested day shifts, a request granted once Denise was ready.

Amidst these shifting sands, Gabrielle's own role felt adrift. The sales department, her intended harbor, seemed a world away.

Two years had woven her into the hotel's fabric, yet the front desk remained a puzzle incomplete. Todd's efforts, though well-intentioned, could not outpace the departures.

Revelation: A Prayer at Midnight

"Surely, I am coming soon. Amen. Come, Lord Jesus."

—Revelation 22:20

As the year closed, Gabrielle sat beneath the soft glow of the night audit screens. The promise of training a new auditor flickered faintly, a hope tempered by experience.

New Year's Eve found her alone, the lobby hushed, the revelry long faded. At midnight, she whispered a resolution: *No more nights. I need balance.* The hotel had been a chapter of growth, but the time had come to turn the page.

Her phone chimed with distant celebration. For the second year, she and her husband bridged the miles with a brief exchange of wishes. His voice was a balm; then silence reclaimed the night. Gabrielle returned to her vigil, solitude pressing in like a tide.

In the stillness, Gabrielle traced the arc of five years, a tapestry woven with joy and sorrow:

- A friendship severed, Jeffrey's absence echoing like a hymn unfinished.
- A career dissolved, a new life blooming in Florida's sunlit embrace.
- A hurricane's fury, a home reborn.

Through it all, three constants endured: God's presence, her husband's unwavering love, and Jeffrey's distant shadow.

Gabrielle felt God in sunrise hues and midnight whispers, in laughter shared and tears shed. Doors opened, paths converged, grace threaded through broken dreams. Community became a celestial tapestry, woven by divine hands.

In serving others, Gabrielle discovered purpose, her life a living prayer, ordinary moments transfigured into sacred offerings. She whispered gratitude into the quiet: *Thank You.*

Her husband was the heartbeat of her existence, a steady rhythm through tempests and triumphs. Their love was etched not in grand gestures but in quiet constancy: the way he tucked her hair behind her ear, the way his hand found hers in silence.

Together, they navigated storms, their roots intertwined, their laughter echoing in kitchens and across sunlit lanais. His eyes held eternity, the promise of countless sunsets and whispered secrets. He was her rock, her refuge, her guiding light.

Jeffrey lingered like a spectral guardian, his name a forbidden melody, his memory a fragile ache. Gabrielle yearned for reconciliation, for forgiveness to bridge the chasm. Was he more than a man? A messenger, perhaps, a whisper from the universe guiding her toward grace. She surrendered the ache into God's hands, trusting that if healing were meant to come, it would arrive on wings unseen.

As the clock ticked toward dawn, revelation unfurled. Gabrielle relinquished the quest for absolution, embracing the truth: grace was infinite, flowing beyond human comprehension. She forgave herself, letting imperfections dissolve into the grand design of mercy.

For half a decade, God had charted her course, a celestial navigator steering her toward shores unseen. She yielded to His current, whispering into the silence: *Lead me.*

Hymns resonated with the rhythm of her being, echoing the heartbeat of grace. Blessings poured forth, washing away the remnants of doubt and fear.

Gabrielle's narrative unfolded, a chronicle of resilience etched upon her soul. A poignant reminder that amidst life's tumult, God's hand penned a straight line with her crooked strokes, a masterpiece of grace and redemption.

About the Author

Jesse Rose is a spiritual seeker who stumbled into the Catholic Church the way some people stumble into thrift store treasures—by accident, during a crisis, and with a story to tell. After moving to Florida in 2020, the pandemic delayed her baptism and sent her into a season of unexpected grace, awkward holiness, and divine plot twists. Her debut memoir, *COVID Catholic*, invites readers to notice God hiding in the crooked lines of everyday life.

Final Reflection

If you've walked this crooked path with me, thank you. May the threads of your own journey, grief, grace, silence, and song, lead you home. May you find God not only in the sanctuary, but in the solitude, the struggle, and the strange beauty of becoming.

www.ingramcontent.com/pod-product-compliance
Lightning Source LLC
LaVergne TN
LVHW050616100826
845148LV00011B/1607

* 9 7 9 8 3 8 5 2 7 2 9 7 6 *